THE SECONDARY SCHOOL PRINCIPAL: MANAGER AND SUPERVISOR

THE SECONDARY SCHOOL PRINCIPAL: MANAGER AND SUPERVISOR

CHARLES L. WOOD

EVERETT W. NICHOLSON

DALE G. FINDLEY

Allyn and Bacon, Inc.
Boston, London, Sydney, Toronto

Library of Congress Cataloging in Publication Data

Wood, Charles L 1928–
    The secondary school principal.

    Includes bibliographical references and index.
    1. High school principals. 2. High schools—Administration. I. Nicholson, Everett W., joint author. II. Findley, Dale G., joint author.
III. Title.
LB2831.9.W66   373.1'2'012   78-12288
ISBN 0-205-06165-6

Printed in the United States of America.

Second printing . . . June, 1979

Contents

THE DEVELOPMENT AND OPERATION OF A STUDENT ACTIVITIES PROGRAM   201

10

DEVELOPING DESIRABLE STUDENT BEHAVIOR   221

11

GUIDANCE AND COUNSELING SERVICES FOR STUDENTS 247

12

EFFECTIVE SCHEDULING:
A KEY TO THE EFFICIENT OPERATION OF THE SECONDARY SCHOOL 277

CONTENTS

13

THE SECONDARY SCHOOL PRINCIPAL AND COLLECTIVE BARGAINING   303

14

THE PRINCIPAL AND THE MANAGEMENT OF SUPPORTING SCHOOL SERVICES   317

CONTENTS

Preface

The primary purpose of this book is the development and improvement of knowledge, understanding, and skill in the leadership and management of secondary schools. In regard to leadership, constant focus is directed to important elements of staff personnel administration, student personnel concerns, and program development. In each instance, conceptual frameworks undergirding these areas are presented and followed by reality-oriented guidelines and suggestions. Such an approach provides for educational leadership which is thoughtful, profound, and practical.

The management aspects of secondary school administration and supervision are also treated in some depth. The technical tasks associated with personnel and program maintenance and improvement are important ones. In addition, appropriate management of facilities, supplies, transportation, food, and other support services is imperative for the successful secondary school executive.

This book, then, is both conceptual and reality-oriented in nature. As such, it is well designed to serve as a textbook for students in college and university preparation programs as well as a valuable, readily usable inservice guide for secondary administrators and supervisors already in the field. The relationships between management and leadership are addressed in such areas as problem solving, decision making, evaluation of teachers and educational programs, development of secondary school schedules, improving instruction, innovations in secondary schools, student affairs including student government and athletic activities, and auxiliary school services. In essence, the comprehensiveness of this book allows the reader, whether it be a graduate student, a professor, or a principal, to select sections of greatest value and interest. The range of topics from the evolution of secondary education and the secondary school principalship to the management of the school office bears this out.

School administrators of today are finding forces with which they must deal to be increasing in intensity and complexity. These include student and teacher values, interests, and needs; shifting populations with enrollment changes; discrimination of many kinds; keener competition for the tax dollar; escalation of litigation and court mandates; increased beauracratic paper work; and, environmental and energy concerns to enumerate a few.

It is against this backdrop that the authors have written about leadership concepts and managerial skills which are needed for enlightened educational leaders who are also astute practitioners.

C. L. Wood
E. W. Nicholson
D. G. Findley

Acknowledgments

No endeavor of this kind is accomplished without the assistance, suggestions, and critical analysis of ideas by many people. Thus, to the several graduate students, practicing administrators, fellow teachers, and typists who have affected the outcome of this effort, the authors extend their heartfelt gratitude.

Special thanks is also extended to our families who provided moral support and patient encouragement which were constant sources of inspiration from the beginning to the completion of this project.

1

The Secondary School Principalship

In recent years the role of principals has become increasingly complex. Teacher negotiations, staff evaluation, student due process, student files, discipline, racial strife, sexual freedom, accountability, increasing school programs, fluctuating enrollments, and school budget funding problems have served to complicate the task of school principals. If principals are to develop an understanding of their appropriate role, they must consider how that role evolved from the past to the present. Further, if they are to prepare for future roles, they must consider the forces currently affecting their function and attempt to predict what forces will do so in the future.

Chapter 1 gives consideration to the evolution of the principalship and those forces which affect the role of the secondary principal. This chapter can serve as a base for gaining a better understanding of the function of the principal for those who do not have administrative experience. For the experienced principal, chapter 1 provides a pertinent review and may indeed contain additional factors not previously considered concerning the role of the secondary principal.

THE EVOLUTION OF THE PRINCIPALSHIP

The local school principal was the first educational administrative position to evolve in the United States. The Massachusetts law of 1647 required that secondary schools be provided in towns of one hundred families. While these schools were not staffed with a person called "principal," they did provide a base for public recognition of the need for secondary education and its management.

The early colonists gave lay people the responsiblity to establish and administer such tasks as providing supplies and employing teachers. But, as it became clear to the lay boards of education that these tasks were consuming too much of their time, the position of head teacher was established. Gradually, head teachers assumed more and more of the responsibilities of administration of local schools.

As the size of schools increased, the need for an administrative head became more apparent:

> Indeed, it appears that at the height of the development of the academy, about 1850, the average number of teachers per school was but two. So here again, as in the English schools and in our own Latin Grammar Schools, the relative need for administration was small, far overshadowed by the teaching function.
>
> In the academies that attained considerable size the school heads were known by varying titles, such as head master, rector, preceptor, provost, and occasionally principal. At Phillips Andover, one of the truly great academies of New England, the official title of Eliphalet Pearson, the first head was preceptor, but in the records he is frequently referred to as principal Pearson; and in 1786 the title was so designated in the contract of the new principal.[1]

As towns grew larger, local school committees found that one- and two-teacher schools were inefficient, so smaller schools were combined. And as the schools became larger, more and more authority was given to the head teachers. During the period of 1840–1870, school committees in the larger cities felt the need to delegate administrative responsibility. The first superintendents of schools were appointed in 1837 in Buffalo, New York, and in Louisville, Kentucky. Superintendents soon realized that the head teacher who also taught classes was not in a position to provide the administrative assistance that was needed.[2]

The school principalship developed into an official staff post as the head teacher assumed increasing responsibility for the administration of the local school. As these head teachers were relieved of their teaching responsibilites, the word *principal* came into common use. The school committees, or lay boards of education, relinquished their "administrative" responsibilities to the local schools only as it became quite clear they needed more professional assistance.

FORCES AFFECTING THE SECONDARY PRINCIPAL

The role of the principal has continually changed from closely resembling the role of a teacher to a role quite different from a teacher. There is no reason to suspect that this trend will be reversed. The major factors influencing this changing role of the principal are: (1) continuing evolution of secondary education, (2) urbanization, (3) population changes, (4) school district reorganization, (5) technological advances, (6) student and teacher action to gain increased voice in decision making, (7) changing societal values, and (8) teacher collective bargaining. Many of these factors are interrelated. Furthermore, changing political environments, both national and international, have had an impact on education and thus an impact on the role of the principal.

Continuing Evolution of Secondary Education

Development of the Secondary School

The early secondary schools of the colonists were primarily religion oriented. The function of these Latin Grammar Schools, as they were called, was to prepare boys for the ministry, develop the basic language skills that would enable students to read and understand the scriptures, and provide religious and moral training for young men who aspired to become leaders in the church and government of their colonies. Much of the prerevolutionary education for most boys and girls was "life adjustment" education. They learned from the elements; their fathers, mothers, and close associates.

The settlers of the Massachusetts colony were the leaders in establishing a system of education. In 1647, the first formal legislation providing for the establishment of public secondary schools in America was passed. This law, frequently referred to as the "Old Deluder Satan Act," provided for the establishment of elementary schools in towns of fifty householders, and secondary schools in towns of one hundred families. The purpose of the act involved the teaching of reading so that persons could read the scriptures in spite of attempts by Satan to keep them from doing so; thus, the name applied to the act.

The name given to the secondary schools was Latin Grammar Schools. Their purpose was to teach Latin grammar, the common grammar taught traditionally in British schools. The Boston Latin School was established in 1636, and the secondary schools established under the 1647 law were patterned after it. But the Latin Grammar Schools were destined for failure. They simply did not meet the needs and desires of the early colonists for whom survival and education for life were the greatest concerns.

The "academy," which replaced the Latin Grammar School, was a result of the dissatisfaction with the conventional model resulting from increased attention to the separation of church and state and from the gradual development of a middle class. Many Latin Grammar Schools did not go out of existence, but merely became academies. Benjamin Franklin's academy, which was chartered in 1751, and is generally designated as the first, offered a curriculum designed for the needs of youth. Such subjects as

writing, arithmetic, merchants' accounts, history, geography, natural history, logic, mechanics, farming, navigation, algebra, geometry, surveying,
astronomy, natural and mechanical philosophy, Greek, Latin, English,
French, and German were offered. Its founder, Franklin, recommended:

> That a house be provided for the academy, if not in town, not
> many miles from it; the situation high and dry and if it may be,
> not far from a river, having a garden, orchard, meadow and a
> field or two.
> That the house be furnished with a library, (if in the country,
> if in the town, the town library may serve) with maps of all
> countries, globes, some mathematical instruments, and appara-
> tus for experiments in Natural Philosophy and for mechanics;
> prints of all kinds, prospects, buildings and machines, etc.
> All should be taught to write a fair hand . . . to form their
> style, they [students] should be put on writing letters to each
> other, making abstracts of what they read; or writing the same
> things in their words; telling or writing stories lately read in
> their own expressions.[3]

Franklin's academy was composed of three schools—Latin, English, and
mathematics. Each school had a separate master.

The academies, while generally not under public control and not free,
continued to gain in popularity. However, in the nineteenth century, the
demand for free secondary education for all, as well as the desire to keep
students close to home rather than sending them away to boarding schools,
led to the development of the high school. The first free high school in the
United States, the English Classical School, opened in Boston in 1821. This
high school, not designed to provide classical preparation for college, later
took the name of English High School.

The first Commissioner of Education, Henry Barnard, supported the
creation of public high schools in 1848 for both boys and girls. The possibility of youth of all social and economic classes learning together in one
high school, according to Barnard, would open to all "the prizes of life, its
best fields of usefulness and sources of happiness." In addition, the education found by all in the public high school would:

> . . . add to the general wealth, multiply workshops, increase the
> value of farms and carry forward every *moral and religious*
> enterprise which aims to bless, purify and elevate society.[4]

President Charles Eliot of Harvard, concerned about the increasing age
of students admitted to Harvard and the lack of uniformity of high school
work, proposed that more be done in elementary and secondary schools to
lower this age and to provide a more uniform high school program. (The
average entry age to Harvard in 1888 was 18 years 10 months.) Eliot, who
chaired the National Education Association Committee of Ten in 1894, pro-

posed in 1898 that the secondary school period be made to begin two years earlier which would change the elementary school from the standard eight to six years.

Kindred, summarizing the impact of the recommendations issued by the Committee of Ten states:

> . . . It is rather clear in this report that the Committee believed the high school should remain a four year unit but that the two years below it should be placed in an intermediate unit. This recommendation suggested the organizational beginning of the junior high school.[5]

In 1874, with the rendering of the decision of the Supreme Court of Michigan, public tax support of the secondary school was insured. Prior to that time public support was limited to the elementary level.

Junior High School and Middle School Development

While there is some dispute as to the exact date and location of the first junior high school in America, Richmond, Indiana, is generally given this credit in 1895. Other claims on having the first junior high school include Providence, Rhode Island, in 1898; Baltimore, Maryland, in 1902; Kalamazoo, Michigan, in 1902; New York City during 1905–1907; and finally Berkeley, California, and Columbus, Ohio, in the school year 1909–1910.

Only fifty-five separate junior high schools had been established by 1920. By 1930, 1,842 had been established and by 1964, 7,143 were in operation. In 1920, there were 828 junior high schools that were part of a six-year junior-senior high school. This figure rose to 3,287 in 1930, and 6,042 in 1964.[6] During the 1967–68 school year there were 7,437 junior high schools. This figure increased to 7,750 by 1970–71.[7]

Kindred cites four major reasons for the growth of the junior high schools:

1. Lack of adequate housing and heavy enrollments in both elementary and secondary schools resulted in the construction of junior high schools.

2. The offering of a broad educational program on the junior high level. Departmentalized instruction, better teaching methods, enriched subject matter, introduction of foreign languages, lectures, shops, and laboratories were not usually found in traditional elementary programs but were present in the junior high school.

3. The improved holding power of the school for students beyond the fifth grade.

4. A realization that the junior high school offered a program better fitted to the nature and needs of young adolescents.[8]

Today, there is a growing belief that the junior high school is no longer serving its original purpose and is taking on more and more characteristics of a senior high school. Some also believe that American children today are reaching adolescence much earlier than children of many years ago. These factors have caused many educators to focus their attention on an organizational arrangment which includes a middle school concept.

Compton, citing United States middle school surveys by Alexander in 1968, Kealy in 1970, and herself in 1974, indicated that there were 1,101 middle schools in 1968, 2,298 in 1970, and 3,723 in 1974. Compton further indicated that by 1974 only the District of Columbia did not have any form of middle school organization.[9]

Lounsbury and Vars indicated that the growth in middle schools did not occur entirely at the expense of existing junior high schools. Concerning the history of the middle school movement, the authors stated:

> . . . Looking at the junior high and middle school movements with a historical perspective, one can see the cyclical nature of social change. The junior high school cycle could aptly be characterized as moving from one Harvard president to another: that is, from Charles W. Eliot's earliest advocacy of reorganization in 1888 through James B. Conant's junior high school report in 1960. In that first cycle, the school started with a college dominated concern for academic efficiency, with shortening the length of elementary education and introducing high school subjects earlier. Later, the junior high school became an instrument of the progressive era. Concern with individuality, creativity, student needs, and personal values was reflected in the widespread acceptance of the core curriculum, for example. In the late 1950's, the cycle shifted back toward academic emphasis as the post-sputnik obsession with intellectual development swept the land.

> The middle school cycle began in the 1960's as the discipline-centered national curriculum projects were bringing "new" English, and other programs into the schools. Intellectual concerns led some intermediate schools to cast off the ninth grade so that it could be reattached to the senior high, where, presumably, more effective sequences in the sciences, mathematics, and foreign languages might be developed. Adding fifth and sixth grades to the middle unit was advocated to bring students the benefits of instruction by more specialized teachers, a further downward extension of the secondary pattern of curriculum organization. . . .

> Only the passage of time will reveal how much further the middle school will retrace the junior high cycle. But it seems certain that it will be no less influenced by the varied realities

of school size, pupil population, and existing buildings than was the junior high school before it. The middle school is hardly immune to the same viruses that handicapped the full development of the junior high school. One need not be surprised, then, if a middle school somewhere organizes a marching band, fields a varsity football team, conducts formal graduation exercises, or otherwise follows the American secondary pattern, thus illustrating the well-known gap between theory and practice.[10]

Some research has shown that eighth graders seem to fit better socially with seventh graders than with ninth graders. The evidence, however, is not conclusive that the middle schools (grades six, seven, and eight, or in some cases, grades five to eight or grades seven and eight) are any better or any worse than the traditional junior high school of grades seven, eight, and nine.

Without question, the middle school is becoming vogue on the American scene. However, the question is whether or not it will develop into a school which fits the needs of its students. Stanavage believed that:

. . . (1) The values ardently purported for the middle school essentially are values that should accompany all education. (2) The values claimed for the middle school echo the plangent phrases of some sixty years back when the junior high school was in early bloom. (3) The curricular and programmatic goals of the middle school do not differ substantively from either that of the elementary school or the junior high school.[11]

Gatewood provides evidence that (1) the junior high school and the middle school are more similar than different, (2) grades five to eight consisting of 500 to 700 students develop most positive self concepts in students, (3) most middle schools have been established for reasons more administrative than educational, and (4) research gives no definite answer on the best organizational structure for physiological, psychological, and sociological arrangement of early adolescents, whether it be the junior high school or senior high school.[12]

Apparently it does not make much difference whether pupils are organized into a six-year high school, or a four-year high school, a junior high school or a grades 5–8 middle school. In fact, Stanavage suspected that our generation gap may be a result of our "walling children from children—young people from children, and young adults from early adolescents," and that this has been accomplished with frightening thoroughness.[13]

The Carnegie Unit

One significant event in the development of secondary education was the work of the Carnegie Foundation for the Advancement of Teaching in 1905.

This commission desired to create a logical method of recording earned credits, so that they could be compiled and transferred from the high school to college. A neat business-like system for recording credits would reduce the amount of time college admission officers would need to spend when reviewing records in order to determine admittance.[14]

The goal, although laudable on paper, saddled secondary schools with quantitative standards rather than qualitative standards that most educators deem desirable. The Carnegie unit (½ unit for each semester of work in most high school subjects meeting five 45-minute periods for eighteen weeks) provides a convenient method for bookkeepers and clerks to record credits and grades, but it has imprisoned the secondary schools by restricting the curriculum and limiting the use of variability in scheduling classes. Most classes in high schools today meet daily for 45-55 minutes to conform to the rigidity of the Carnegie unit. Some innovative high schools are moving away from this by offering classes two or three times a week with longer daily periods.

In a study of the Carnegie unit in 1954 by the U.S. Office of Education, criticism of the credit accounting procedure included: "(1) asks few questions about a pupil's ability to master the required body of knowledge, (2) pays too little attention to what he already knows, (3) forgets conveniently that some learn the same facts or skills in a fraction of the time required of others."[15]

While the Carnegie unit still persists as a method of accounting for student progress, other standards are being applied today such as narrative descriptions of student progress and the wide use of the American College Test as a basis for admission to a college or university in lieu of the high school diploma. Nevertheless, rules and regulations of state departments of education that have applied the Carnegie unit as a standard for accounting for student progress have continued to support the concept of the Carnegie unit.

National Statements of Purposes

The Commission on the Reorganization of Secondary Education developed the following Seven Cardinal Principles of Secondary Education in 1918: (1) health, (2) command of fundamental processes, (3) worthy home membership, (4) vocation, (5) citizenship, (6) worthy use of leisure time, and (7) ethical character.

Because of the economic depression that began with the crash of the stock market in 1929, attention was turned to the schools to see what could be done to make them more efficient. Several major studies concerning the role of the secondary schools were conducted during the 1930s. One such study was conducted by the American Youth Commission to determine what students thought of the education they were receiving. In general, many youths indicated the schools were not meeting their interests or their needs.

The National Education Association Educational Policies Commission in 1938 spelled out the following objectives of American Education: (1) self-realization, (2) human relationship, (3) economic efficiency, and (4) civic responsibility.

World War II caused Americans to again examine the purpose of secondary education. In 1944, the Educational Policies Commission published a list of "ten imperative needs of youth" which reflected their point of view concerning the purpose of secondary education. This point of view was similar to that expressed in the Seven Cardinal Principles of Secondary Education.

Major reexamination of the purpose of secondary education occurred during the White House Conference of 1955 and again after the October 4, 1957 launching of Sputnik by the Soviet Union. The National Defense Education Act of 1958 was enacted by Congress in response to public reaction to the launching of Sputnik.

James B. Conant, former president of Harvard University, provided the American public with several recommendations for improving public secondary education in 1959 with the publication of his book entitled, *The American High School Today*. These recommendations favored a comprehensive high school with an academically oriented curriculum.[16]

The purpose of the Elementary and Secondary Education Act of 1965 was to improve educational opportunity by (1) providing better educational programs to low income area children, (2) providing additional teaching resources, (3) providing funds for supplementary educational services, (4) encouraging educational research, and (5) strengthening state departments of education.

It was soon discovered that money for instructional materials and equipment was not enough. The equipment was often placed aside in some school closet to gather dust. To be effective, teachers had to be taught the value of using the equipment as well as how to use it. In essence, it became apparent that to improve education, one must improve the teacher. This encouraged the passage of the Educational Professional Development Act in 1967 which provided funds for the improvement of professional talent.

Also, several reports issued in the early 1970s have had an influence on secondary education. Among these are:

1. The Charles F. Kettering Foundation established the National Commission on *The Reform of Secondary Education* in 1972 with B. Frank Brown serving as chairman. A report was published in 1973 which listed thirty-two recommendations.[17]

2. *The Greening of the High School* (1973) by Ruth Weinstock, which reports on a conference co-sponsored by the Educational Facilities Laboratories and the Institute for Development of Educational Activities, Inc.[18]

3. *Youth: Transition to Adulthood* (1973), Panel on Youth of the President's Science Advisory Committee by James S. Coleman.[19]

4. *The Education of Adolescents: The Final Report and Recommendations of the National Panel on High School and Adolescent Education* (1976) by John Henry Martin, Panel Chairman.[20]

5. *Secondary Schools in a Changing Society: This We Believe,* A Statement on Secondary Education prepared by The Task Force on Secondary Schools in a Changing Society of the National Association of Secondary School Principals (Task Force appointed June, 1974 and report published 1975).[21]

The first four of these reports advocate a diverse educational program designed to meet the social, emotional, and vocational needs as well as the academic needs of youth. The reports stress a need for experience-oriented alternative schools in a variety of settings. The fifth report expresses a concern about gaining a public consensus on the purpose of secondary education and indicates that the experience-based education should be a complement to, and not a replacement for, the more traditional curriculum. This report further indicates that a diploma should signify that the holder is sufficiently prepared to assume the responsibilities of adulthood and should not represent a readiness for a job or college.

Urbanization and Suburbanization

According to Table 1.1, in 1970 approximately 75 percent of the American people lived in urban areas. The past decades have seen a rapid shifting of population from rural to urban areas. Recent years have witnessed population movement from urban areas to suburban areas. The social disorganization of this shifting population has created immense problems for the school principal. Many rural families came to the cities lacking urban cultural values and employable skills. The schools were expected to provide these cultural and employable skills necessary to adjust to urban living. At the same time, a move to suburban areas by wealthier families and by industry led to a decreasing tax base of the city. This movement resulted in a greater concentration of social and economic problems in the inner cities.

Westby-Gibson writes about the dramatic shift of the non-white. She reports:

> Whereas in 1900, three out of four of the nine million Negroes lived in the rural south, today only one in five remains there. Negroes now live predominately in urban settings. A large proportion of southern Negroes, furthermore, have moved to the North and West. These immigrants have tended to congregate in the central cities along with other non-white newcomers, such as the Puerto Ricans in New York City.[22]

The concentration of large numbers of people in small land areas created a whole realm of problems related to education. The nature of edu-

Table 1.1

United States Urban and Rural Population from 1900–1970*

	Old Definition**			New Definition†	
Year	Percent Urban Population	Percent Rural Population	Year	Percent Urban Population	Percent Rural Population
1900	39.6	60.4	1950	64.0	36.0
1910	45.6	54.4	1960	69.9	30.1
1920	51.2	48.8	1970	73.5	26.5
1930	56.1	43.9			
1940	56.5	43.5			
1950	59.6	40.4			
1960	63.0	37.0			

* U.S. Bureau of the Census, U.S. Census of Population: 1970, *Number of Inhabitants,* pp. 1–42.

** *Old Definition* (from 1900 to 1950): Urban population was defined as "all persons living in incorporated places of 2,500 or more and areas classified as urban under special rules. . . ." Many large and densely settled areas were excluded under this definition because they were not properly incorporated.

† *New Definition* (from 1950 to 1970): Urban population was defined as "all persons residing in urbanized areas and . . . in all places incorporated or unincorporated (of) 2,500 inhabitants or more." This definition includes most areas which were excluded under the earlier definition.

cation itself changed. Whereas those in rural areas could formerly get by with a general education and learn occupational skills from their fathers, urban youths found that the large city industry was in need of technically skilled employees.

Urbanization may not have created as many problems for education as suburbanization did. This process essentially created financial and social problems for the central city. All of a sudden, the realization of the hoped-for concentration of number of students, through school district reorganization and greater concentrations of population, to provide a base for curriculum improvement, resulted in a new problem. Larger student bodies meant different kinds of tasks for the secondary principal. The principal discovered he or she could no longer be all the things to all people. The result was specialization and a division of labor to handle problems related to discipline, supervision, curriculum development, support services, etc. Now the principal had the opportunity to do those tasks which he or she felt required personal attention, and let the assistants perform those tasks he or she was unable to do. Perhaps past experience did not prepare the individual well for this new role though. Perhaps teachers, who were now better trained and more specialized, did not allow the principal to perform the leadership role he or she desired to assume.

Table 1.2

United States Population from 1900 to 1970*

Year	Population	Percent Increase by Decade
1900	76,313,168	21.0
1910	92,228,496	21.0
1920	106,021,537	15.0
1930	123,202,624	16.2
1940	132,164,569	7.3
1950	151,325,798	14.5
1960	179,323,175	18.5
1970	203,211,926	13.3

* U.S. Bureau of the Census, U.S. Census of Population: 1970, *Number of Inhabitants,* pp. 1–42.

Population Change

The growth in population in the United States since 1900 can be seen in Table 1.2.

The influx of students during the 1950s resulting from increased births after World War II caused overcrowding problems because the new facilities were not financed at a pace rapid enough to meet the demand. In addition, a backlog of buildings that needed replacing also existed since little building occurred during the 1930s and 1940s because of the depression and wars. Reorganization also caused an increase in the number of new buildings needed during the 1950s and 1960s. The principal had to devote time to these new building programs, which meant spending less time on other assigned duties. One can only speculate as to the effect this had on the evolution of the role of the principal. Perhaps the reduction in enrollment that began taking place in the early 1970s will allow the principal to redirect his or her attention to duties other than those associated with an expanding enrollment.

However, some projections indicate that enrollment may again begin to increase within the next few years.

Based on Series II U.S. Bureau of Census population projections, elementary school enrollment will continue to fall on a national scale until 1982. The decrease in enrollments between 1975 and 1982 will be 3.4 million. This compares with the decline of 2.4 million already experienced between 1970 and 1974. Beyond 1982 and lasting until the end of the projection period in 1990, Series II projections indicate that elementary school enrollments will rise again, though slowly.

By 1990 an additional 4.4 million children will be enrolled in elementary schools over the enrollment level projected for 1982.

However, the total enrollment of 33.8 million would still fall short of the peak figure of 37.1 million established in 1969 . . . The population aged 14–17 years is expected to decline steadily until 1990, and from 1976 through 1990 secondary school enrollments will decline.[23]

Consolidation

Much of the reorganization effort in the past took the form of consolidation in the rural areas. Table 1.3 indicates the effect that reorganization has had on the number of school districts in the United States. As shown in Table 1.3, during the school year of 1973 there were 16,730 public school disricts in the United States, which represents a significant decrease from the 1931 figure of 127,531. The interesting thing to note is that the number of high schools has remained fairly constant over the years while the number of elementary schools has decreased. As noted, there has been a steady decrease in the number of school districts since 1931. This decrease has resulted from consolidation of small districts and the elimination of nonoperating districts.

Reorganization in Urban Centers

Many educators in the past were occupied with the task of establishing school districts which were large enough to offer a comprehensive educational program. They now find themselves trying to establish school districts which allow for some of the flexibility that is difficult in a large bureaucratic organization.

Table 1.3
Number of School Districts (Basic Local Administrative Units),
Elementary Schools, and Secondary Schools in the U.S.
from 1931–32 to 1973–74 *

School Year	Number of School Districts**	Number of Elem. Schools	Number of Sec. Schools
1931–32	127,531	232,750	26,409
1941–42	115,493	183,112	25,123
1949–50	83,718	128,225	24,542
1959–60	40,520	91,853	25,784
1967–68	20,010	70,879	27,011
1970–71	17,995	65,800	25,352
1973–74	16,730	65,070	25,906

* *Digest of Educational Statistics,* 1975 edition (Washington, D.C.: U.S. Government Printing Office, 1976), p. 57.
** Includes operating and nonoperating school districts.

Much of the school district reorganization in the past took place in the rural areas. Today reorganization is an urgent problem in the cities, concerned to a great extent with (1) decentralization of decision making, (2) financial aid for inner city areas, and (3) racial integration.

Table 1.4 illustrates the large size of some school districts in the United States. In 1969, one hundred and eighty school systems each enrolled over twenty-five thousand pupils. Together these systems enrolled over thirteen million pupils; more pupils than any other category of school systems based on enrollment size. The second largest total number of pupils is in the 300 to 2,499 category. In that category, over eight million pupils were enrolled in almost eight thousand school systems. Table 1.5 lists the ten largest school districts in the United States, with New York City leading with an enrollment of over one million.

Currently, blacks account for approximately 15 percent of the total public school enrollment. Table 1.6 gives the number of black students attending public elementary and secondary schools in the fifty largest school districts in the United States in 1972. Twenty-three of the fifty districts listed had black enrollments which exceeded 30 percent, while eleven districts had black enrollments which exceeded 50 percent.

It is evident by analyzing the data presented in Table 1.6 that if integrated schools are to be achieved, some dedicated planning must take place. The Bundy Plan, which includes the controversial Oceanhill-Brownville school district, is an example of a decentralization plan in New York City.

> The plan recommends the reorganization of the single New York City school system into a federation of 30 to 60 largely autonomous local community school districts—each run by its own board of education and superintendent. The centralized

Table 1.4
Selected Statistics on Public Elementary and Secondary Schools
According to the Enrollment Size of School Systems*

Enrollment Size of School System	1968		1969	
	No. of Operating School Systems	No. of Pupils Enrolled	No. of Operating School Systems	No. of Pupils Enrolled
25,000 and above	181	13,139,273	180	13,475,792
10,000–24,999	519	7,691,090	538	8,098,168
5,000– 9,999	1,099	7,758,403	1,097	7,643,252
2,500– 4,999	1,940	6,835,550	2,026	7,185,434
300– 2,499	8,199	8,623,559	7,924	8,509,353
300 and below	7,571	639,457	6,890	609,777

* *Digest of Educational Statistics* (Washington, D.C.: U.S. Government Printing Office), 1970, p. 30; 1971, p. 30.

Table 1.5
Enrollment of the Ten Largest School Districts in the U.S. from Fall 1968 to Fall 1974*

City	1968	1969	1970	1971	1972	1973	1974
New York	1,128,000	1,123,165	1,120,082	1,149,068	1,128,996	1,106,234	1,094,859
Los Angeles	656,101	654,201	648,986	637,188	622,633	612,638	607,206
Chicago	554,477	562,196	563,178	573,474	557,141	539,365	536,657
Philadelphia	295,224	294,381	295,888	291,151	282,981	267,902	266,044
Detroit	296,089	292,931	292,934	289,446	281,764	262,826	263,011
Houston	245,396	236,861	239,410	231,522	225,427	216,589	211,369
Baltimore	192,169	193,150	192,826	190,735	186,600	182,733	173,198
Dallas	157,272	159,820	160,224	156,313	154,112	148,605	151,215
Cleveland	153,043	150,734	150,818	147,367	144,520	138,454	134,997
Washington, D.C.	149,020	149,054	145,704	142,512	139,918	136,036	131,691

* *Digest of Educational Statistics* (Washington, D.C.: U.S. Government Printing Office), 1969, p. 24; 1970, p. 10; 1971, p. 31; 1972, p. 37; 1973, p. 37; 1974, p. 36; 1975, p. 40.

Table 1.6

Number and Percent of Black Students Attending Public Elementary and Secondary Schools by Level of Isolation; 50 Largest School Districts: Fall 1968, Fall 1970, and Fall 1972*

| Districts | Number of Pupils | | Percent Black in: | | | | | | | | |
| | Total, 1972 | Black, 1972 | Total | | | 0-49 Percent Minority Schools | | | 90-100 Percent Minority Schools | | |
			1968	1970	1972	1968	1970	1972	1968	1970	1972
New York, N.Y.	1,125,449	405,177	31.5	34.5	36.0	19.7	16.3	16.5	52.2	57.9	60.9
Los Angeles, Calif.	620,659	156,680	22.6	24.1	25.2	4.7	5.9	8.1	83.0	83.3	81.4
Chicago, Ill.	553,342	315,940	52.9	54.8	57.1	3.2	3.0	1.7	86.6	89.7	88.6
Philadelphia, Pa.	282,965	173,874	58.8	60.5	61.4	9.6	7.4	6.7	67.1	70.0	75.9
Detroit, Mich.	276,655	186,994	59.2	63.8	67.6	9.0	5.8	7.2	69.0	73.9	73.9
Dade County, Fla. (Miami)	241,809	63,826	24.3	25.4	26.4	12.4	21.7	23.6	80.7	41.9	41.6
Houston, Tex.	225,410	88,871	33.3	35.6	39.4	5.3	8.4	8.8	88.0	73.7	76.6
Baltimore City, Md.	186,600	129,250	65.1	67.1	69.3	7.7	9.4	7.8	78.6	79.2	80.9
Prince Georges County, Md. (D.C. area)	161,969	40,397	15.2	19.9	24.9	56.1	40.8	39.7	20.7	20.2	22.3
Dallas, Tex.	154,581	59,638	30.8	33.8	38.6	2.1	2.7	15.0	87.6	91.4	78.8
Cleveland, Ohio	145,196	83,596	55.9	57.6	57.6	4.8	4.2	4.8	86.0	89.2	90.3
Washington, D.C.	140,000	133,638	93.5	94.5	95.5	0.9	1.2	0.4	94.2	95.0	95.1
Memphis, Tenn.	138,714	80,158	53.6	51.5	57.8	2.6	6.5	7.3	92.7	89.5	81.6
Fairfax County, Va. (D.C. area)	135,780	4,509	2.7	3.2	3.3	100.	100.	100.	.0	.0	.0
Baltimore, Md.	131,987	5,604	3.5	3.8	4.2	100.	100.	94.4	.0	.0	.0
Broward County, Fla. (Ft. Lauderdale)	128,889	29,363	23.8	23.2	22.8	14.5	15.1	83.9	79.7	39.2	8.0
Milwaukee, Wis.	127,986	38,060	23.9	26.0	29.7	12.4	12.2	15.4	63.2	60.4	72.4
Montgomery County, Md.	126,707	8,131	4.0	5.1	6.4	100.	100.	96.3	.0	.0	.0
San Diego, Calif.	124,487	16,492	11.6	12.4	13.2	25.1	32.1	32.5	54.7	46.4	43.7
Duval County, Fla.	113,644	37,100	28.2	29.4	32.6	12.6	25.6	70.4	87.4	54.9	7.8
Columbus, Ohio	106,588	31,312	26.0	26.9	29.4	28.8	25.9	29.4	40.7	45.2	37.0
Hillsborough County, Fla. (Tampa)	107,540	20,367	19.0	19.4	18.9	18.3	23.4	95.9	73.3	49.4	.0
St. Louis, Mo.	105,617	72,629	63.5	65.6	68.8	7.1	2.5	2.5	87.6	82.7	88.8

Orleans Parish, La. (New Orleans)	103,839	77,504	67.1	69.5	74.6	8.8	7.8	4.9	81.2	78.6	75.8
Indianapolis, Ind.	98,076	38,522	33.7	35.8	39.3	22.4	20.5	25.1	57.6	55.6	46.2
Boston, Mass.	96,239	31,728	27.1	29.8	33.0	23.3	18.0	17.8	43.1	52.8	49.9
Atlanta, Ga.	96,006	73,915	61.7	68.7	77.1	5.4	6.6	6.2	90.0	77.9	81.0
Jefferson County, Ky. (Louisville area)	95,762	3,725	3.7	3.6	3.9	73.6	81.0	73.3	26.4	19.0	9.0
Denver, Colo.	91,616	15,729	14.1	14.7	17.2	20.0	44.6	45.5	56.1	37.5	36.0
Pinellas County, Fla. (Clearwater)	90,182	14,313	16.2	16.2	15.9	21.7	45.5	98.9	72.1	20.0	.0
De Kalb County, Ga. (Decatur)	86,963	8,412	5.3	6.3	9.7	44.6	70.5	51.2	47.0	14.7	18.7
Albuquerque, N. Mex.	86,658	2,221	2.4	2.4	2.6	27.6	36.2	41.0	31.4	27.1	18.1
Orange County, Fla. (Orlando)	86,407	16,060	17.2	18.1	18.6	20.1	40.7	43.5	77.1	33.3	22.3
Nashville-Davidson County, Tenn.	85,406	23,866	24.1	24.6	27.9	16.8	25.0	76.6	61.3	62.4	.0
Fort Worth, Tex.	82,268	24,416	24.7	26.7	29.7	9.7	9.8	20.8	85.4	75.3	61.6
San Francisco, Calif.	81,970	25,055	27.5	28.5	30.6	15.5	14.2	5.2	34.3	31.7	8.4
Charlotte-Mecklenburg County, N.C.	79,813	25,821	29.2	30.8	32.4	27.7	90.7	97.8	58.9	1.8	1.5
Newark, N.J.	78,492	56,736	72.5	72.2	72.3	2.1	2.9	2.3	85.6	86.4	87.0
Cincinnati, Ohio	77,878	36,808	42.9	45.0	47.3	21.9	16.9	11.6	43.9	39.5	39.1
Anne Arundel County, Md. (Annapolis)	77,083	9,713	13.6	13.0	12.6	80.3	78.7	88.7	.0	2.4	1.9
Seattle, Wash.	75,239	10,837	11.0	12.8	14.4	44.3	40.6	44.4	8.1	3.1	6.9
Clark County, Nev. (Las Vegas)	75,223	10,092	12.2	13.0	13.4	48.1	62.3	100.	51.9	30.0	.0
Jefferson County, Colo. (Lakewood)	74,185	144	.1	.1	.2	100.	100.	100.	.0	.0	.0
San Antonio, Tex.	72,305	11,443	14.7	15.3	15.8	10.6	9.3	8.1	85.3	60.1	56.3
Tulsa, Okla.	71,190	10,950	12.2	13.7	15.4	15.6	27.5	43.5	77.0	68.7	24.8
Pittsburgh, Pa.	70,080	29,274	39.2	40.3	41.8	21.3	23.3	22.7	52.5	56.5	50.7
Portland, Oreg.	68,632	7,307	8.1	9.2	10.6	57.4	62.1	67.5	20.5	17.4	8.7
East Baton Rouge Parish, La.	67,342	26,184	37.3	38.6	38.9	5.6	22.0	21.8	91.0	68.7	67.1
Palm Beach County, Fla.	67,030	19,172	27.8	27.8	28.6	18.6	25.1	65.7	76.2	29.4	2.7
Mobile County, Ala.	66,263	30,255	41.7	44.5	45.7	10.9	18.2	37.8	87.5	47.1	39.6

* "The Condition of Education," HEW, U.S. Government Printing Office, Washington, D.C.: 1975. Sources: U.S. Department of Health, Education, and Welfare, Office for Civil Rights, "Fall, 1972 Racial and Ethnic Enrollment in Public Elementary and Secondary Schools" and *Directory of Public Elementary and Secondary Schools in Selected Districts, Fall 1968.*

Note: Minute differences between sum of numbers and totals are due to computer rounding.

board of education would then become a coordinating agency, concentrating upon essential central functions such as long-range planning, integration, and labor relations.[24]

Decentralization raises questions such as: (1) Do teachers bargain with the centralized board or the local board? (2) Which board, the central or the local, can hire and fire teachers? (3) How should a conflict between the local board and the central board be resolved? Continued experimentation with decentralized plans may lead to more effective guidelines for implementation and the avoidance of many of the problems encountered in New York City.

City-county consolidation is one procedure used to help provide a financial base for the central cities which are suffering from the economic effects of ghetto areas. By extending city boundaries to county boundaries, people living in urban fringe areas are forced to give financial support to inner city schools as well as suburban schools.

Two states in which city-county consolidation has taken place are Indiana and Tennessee. The city of Indianapolis has extended its boundaries to coincide with those of Marion County, and the city of Nashville has extended its boundaries to coincide with those of Davidson County.

Busing is required in many situations to achieve racial balance because of housing patterns that separate whites and blacks. However, the issue of busing is a very sensitive one that has caused considerable disruption in many communities. The supreme court has, by its recent decisions, tended to reduce the "big push" to achieve racial balance in schools through massive busing.

Edwards emphasized the efforts to improve education for non-whites when he said:

Because of low average incomes and discriminatory housing, non-whites were heavily concentrated in densely settled portions of the inner city . . . The attempt to achieve racial balance in the schools in the face of the restrictive housing patterns has led to proposals for rezoning of school districts, transportation of children by buses from their neighborhood schools to schools in other areas, open enrollment plans, and a number of other devices, all of which have drawn community opposition . . .[25]

The secondary school principal needs to be aware of these problems and work toward their resolution.

Technological Advances

Automation and scientific discovery have made a tremendous impact upon the environment. While increasing the ease of living, they have also created problems for many Americans to gain economic means to enjoy this higher level of living. Automation simply reduces the need for human labor. Increasing technological advances makes finding a job difficult for youths. Automation then, forces the principal to change the curriculum to meet the needs of the students to train them to cope with automated technology.

The principal of today's school is interested in what living in tomorrow's world is going to be like. One aspect of this life will be increased emphasis on deriving benefits from space exploration and related research. Increased world-wide communication will tend to break down pockets of cultures which now exist in our world. Increasing environmental problems related to air and water pollution will need to be resolved, as well as problems associated with decreasing energy supplies.

Certainly the schools of the future will be utilizing the communication and technological aids to a much greater extent than today. Educational television and computerized learning will receive increased utilization. Teachers will be less of a dominant figure in the classroom of the future. Their primary role will be to assist and guide students in their learning—not to demonstrate and lecture as in the traditional teaching of today. Teachers may find themselves playing the role of team leaders in charge of teacher aides and teacher assistants.

A large part of the principal's role deals with the development of an educational program to meet the needs of students. Changes in job requirements will cause the principal to continuously reevaluate the educational program being offered. A further responsibility will be providing inservice programs for teachers to improve their ability to utilize education devices developed through increased technology. The ever increasing pace of changing technology in the world of work and within education itself will have an effect upon the role of the principal.

Student Action to Gain Increased Decision-Making Involvement

Much of the attention to student unrest during the middle and late 1960s was focused on the college level student. There was a gradual downward shift of this unrest to the high school level. Concerns ranged all the way from hair cuts and short skirts to a desire for more freedom of expression in the student newspaper. While alcohol and smoking were once major moral concerns of principals, problems of drug use now confronted them. Students were demanding more involvement in decisions that affected them. The courts handled cases ranging from the wearing of armbands by students who were protesting the Vietnam war to those involving the right of male students to wear long hair. Underground newspapers sprung up across the country on the high school level. Minority student groups complained of prejudiced faculty members and administrators.

According to a survey conducted by the Syracuse University Research Corporation in 1970, 85% of all responding schools said they had some form of student or teacher disruption within the past three years.

Education U.S.A. reports that a survey conducted by the House Subcommittee on General Education found that only 18% of the nation's high schools experienced "serious student protest" in 1968–69.

The findings of the congressional survey may seem to contradict the findings of the Syracuse survey. However, the discrepancies between the results of every survey can be accounted for by several factors. One, the congressional survey used a strict definition of "serious protest" while the Syracuse survey included teacher disruption. Two, the Syracuse survey included teacher disruption as well as student disruption. And three, the congressional survey accounts for protest during only the 1967–68, 1968–69, and 1969–70 school years . . .

Trenton, New Jersey was the scene of many disruptions in the fall of 1970. On October 30, all public schools in the city closed when fights between black and white students got out of control. "Police said 59 persons were arrested and 61 injured in clashes between blacks and whites . . . windows in downtown areas were smashed and police were pelted with rocks. Mayor Arthur J. Holland declared a 'local disaster emergency' providing a 9 P.M.-to-dawn curfew . . ."[26]

School violence and vandalism was of such concern that Dr. Owen B. Kiennan, Executive Secretary of the National Association of Secondary School Principals testified on April 16, 1975 before the Senate Subcommittee to Investigate Juvenile Delinquency to express the concerns of the association on the topic.

Principals, while recognizing the right of students to dissent, nevertheless, are concerned about maintaining control. The principal of the secondary school often faces a demanding and questioning adolescent society. The adolescent is groping for adult status and resists dependency status. This sometimes puts their collective values in conflict with adult values. Their idols are their peers and not necessarily adults. Hence, the secondary principal needs to be skillful in working with student and teacher groups to deal with these value conflicts.

Many principals in the past may have been preoccupied with tasks such as scheduling, attendance taking, grade reporting, and building maintenance. These tasks for the most part did not involve working with the human side of students. Principals were perhaps overly concerned with controlling student behavior and thus may not have dealt constructively with the student population. While it is easier to deal with nonhuman activities, this day is past for most high school principals, since students are demanding attention.

Courts have increasingly recognized the citizen rights of the American high school student. High school students who resist infringement upon their individual rights are supported by organizations such as the American Civil Liberties Union and others. The "in loco parentis" status of the teacher and the principal is being questioned. Recently, high school students placed increased reliance upon the courts to assist them in their efforts to attain due process rights in schools. Thus, these guidelines which are being established by the courts limit many actions principals once employed when dealing with students.

Teacher Action to Gain Increased Decision-Making Involvement

According to Table 1.7, the number of teacher strikes increased from 3 in 1960-1961 to 180 in 1969-1970, with the largest increase occuring after 1965-1966. *Education U.S.A.* reports, however, that teacher strikes in 1970-1971 decreased to 130, a 28 percent drop from the previous year.[27] Only 89 teacher strikes occurred during 1971-1972, while the number of teacher strikes rose to 145 during 1972-1973 according to *Education U.S.A.*[28] Cuts in schools' budgets and the over supply of teachers may account for this decrease.

Table 1.7
The Number of Teacher Strikes
in the U.S. from 1960-61 to 1972-73*

Year	Number of Teacher Strikes	Percent of Personnel Involved
1960–61	3	.6
1961–62	1	.2
1962–63	2	.4
1963–64	5	1.0
1964–65	12	2.4
1965–66	18	3.6
1966–67	34	6.8
1967–68	114	22.8
1968–69	131	26.2
1969–70	180	36.0
1970–71	130	
1971–72	89	
1972–73	145	

* National Educational Association Research Bulletin, Vol. 48, October, 1970, pp. 67–72.

Education U.S.A., September 27, 1971, p. 20; September 3, 1973, p. 2.

In 1971 opposition to Richard Nixon's freeze on teachers' salaries replaced teacher strikes as the major focus of teacher grievance throughout the nation. The National Education Association and the New Jersey Education Association filed a suit charging that the "capricious and arbitrary action of (Nixon's Cost of Living) council and the Office of Emergency Preparedness . . . on the teacher wage increases issue violates the due process and equal protection provisions concept of the U.S. constitution." Similar suits were filed in various states.[29]

Principals are in the middle between teachers and the central administrative staff, and the role of paternalistic leadership is vanishing. Therefore, greater skill is needed which will increase their working relationships with teachers. Principals more and more are found in an environment where they no longer hold the balance of power.

The Effect of Collective Bargaining on the Principal's Role

Principals face the problem of conflict when viewing their role as individual leaders and as administrators of school personnel policy. They need to work in an instructional leadership capacity with their faculty at the building level, yet the central office expectations visualize the principal as an extension of their office in a team management role. As a result, principals sometimes feel they are on neither side and organize their own principals' negotiation team.

The National Association of Secondary School Principals has given considerable space in their publications to the topic of negotiations. In general, most of the writing in this area supports the view that too much is being negotiated away from the principal. He or she is rapidly becoming the keeper of the keys and kids in trouble. They defend the right of the teacher to negotiate on welfare issues, but they deplore the negotiation on curriculum matters that should be made on the basis of professional skills and research.[30]

Epstein gives the position of NASSP as follows:

At the same time NASSP affirmed its full support of the right of teachers to negotiate with school boards on the subjects of "salaries, health and welfare benefits, hours and loads of work, grievance machinery, and physical working conditions." It went on to say, "There are many other problems in education, all of which are of great importance to teachers and administrators as part of their professional lives. Types of school organization, curriculum, textbook selection, extra-curricular activities, academic freedom, in-service training, auxiliary services, and the handling of discipline are but a partial listing of a considerable number of such items that might be enumerated." NASSP believes that teachers, through their representative organization, should be involved in formulating policy for dealing with these matters. On the other hand, NASSP emphasizes that discussions and decisions on purely professional problems cannot be considered in an atmosphere of colleagues working together as a professional team. It welcomes the establishment of formal councils made up of representatives chosen by teachers, principals, and supervisors.[31]

Concerning collective bargaining, Epstein later stated,

Few would deny that scope of everyday responsibilities has increased tremendously within the past few years. Although one might expect the necessary authority to have been maintained or extended to permit fulfillment of greater performance expectations, the very opposite has occurred. Written agreements negotiated by school boards with teachers and other employees contain a plethora of provisions that many times restrict and reduce the principal's prerogatives. This results from negotiations—in which principals neither participate nor are consulted—that are based on the expediencies of reaching settlements rather than the protection of educational effectiveness.[32]

Weldy, however, indicates there is no need to fear collective bargaining.

The principal's leadership has not diminished as a result of collective bargaining of master contracts. He need not be threatened or intimidated into submission or inactivity. His style must change because the role and the rules have changed. Weak administration under strong master contracts creates a power imbalance, causing confusion and inertia. Teachers, students, and community members still expect and respect good sound leadership. They will all be looking toward the principal to provide it.[33]

This section has presented only the basic issues surrounding the effect collective bargaining has had in shaping the role of the principal. Because the factor of negotiations will continue to play a major part in shaping this role, an entire chapter is presented later in this book.

Political Environment: National and International

Principals have a tremendous stake in national and international political environment. They are the protectors of the educational system which must transmit cultural heritage, develop democratic attitudes, and survive the hazards of the atomic and space age. Schools must serve as a model of democracy—a place where students may practice local, national, and international living.

Westby-Gibson writes:

Never before has man had to face the awesome potentiality that
he can totally destroy himself. If he is to survive, he must learn
to achieve peace, peace with honor for all men. Only in a world
made safe for man's existence can a given society perpetuate
itself. To achieve the goal of social survival, nations of vastly
different cultures must interact. To act intelligently in international relations requires knowledge and understanding of other
cultures, of mutual problems and concerns, and of the avenues
that can promote communication and cooperation.

What, then, is the role of the school in educating for social
survival? One approach provides opportunities for students to
gain information and understanding about diverse cultures and
to develop attitudes and skills that can contribute to relations,
of foreign languages, of creative arts, indeed of all that can aid
man's understanding man.[34]

The principal often works in an environment where the rich, poor,
unskilled, and professional persons of different religious groups are
together. However, unless there is a change in present attendance boundaries and the development of some plan to insure a heterogeneous student
body, the concept of the school as a melting pot is losing ground. The
present trend indicates that middle-class families are moving to suburbs and
forming schools of their own economic class, or sending their children to
private schools.

The most exciting, but demanding role of the principal is that of dealing
with the crisis of international relations. Increased capability for better and
faster transportation and communication will demand better ways to utilize
these avenues to reduce tensions. Cultural progress exchanges, foreign language, and international diplomacy will continue to receive emphasis in the
secondary school of the future.

THE PRINCIPAL'S ROLES: PRESENT AND FUTURE

Current Status

With the advent of community pressure groups using the schools as a plat-
form to give their point of view and the increasing demand by parents for a
larger share in decisions that affect them and their children, principals
indeed need expertise in community relations.

Principals must be able to utilize the community to provide support for
needed change. They should also be skilled in interpreting to the community
the policies prescribed by the board of education and the central administration. It is essential that they be able to mediate differences of opinion
concerning educational matters which exist among those in their district.

The increasing demand for accountability forces principals to provide to the community relevant information concerning educational progress being made by students.

It would appear that the principals of today, in order to remain informed of the desires of the school community, need to become involved in community activities outside the school building. Further, principals often need to assess the resources available in the community for use by the school to provide a more relevant education.

The emphasis today, and for many years prior to this time, has focused upon a leadership role for the principal. This role has not been universally assumed by secondary principals. One might argue whether this is because of inability on the part of the principal or because local school systems expect a different role to be performed by the principal.

Preparation of the Secondary Principal of the Future

The decade of the 1960s and the early 1970s revealed in the United States many exciting yet frightening situations. These years produced tremendous advancements in technology and provided a larger majority of our citizens with a decent standard of living. They also provided the most unpopular war of the country's history, anarchy in certain local areas, and increased tensions within our country in internal affairs and among minority and majority groups. Watergate and related matters created an environment which most certainly continues to have impact upon the United States. The task of the local educators is to promote an educational system which will help solve as well as cope with these many problems.

In order to cope with the changing secondary school and its myriad of problems, the student preparing for the secondary school principalship or related leadership positions in secondary schools should develop a dynamic set of usable skills. One group dedicated to developing the new educational leader of the secondary school is represented by Professors of Secondary School Administration and Supervision. This group, working closely with the National Association of Secondary School Principals, has sponsored studies and workshops to develop realistic preparation programs.

They have agreed that the continuous progress model should be utilized in designing individual preparation programs for leaders of secondary education. That is, determine the present state of development of each candidate and develop a program which could provide needed skills to bring the graduate student along the way toward effective leadership of the secondary school. Areas of preparation that they consider important for the secondary school principal are listed alphabetically. The list is illustrative rather than all inclusive.

1. Change, innovation, diffusion
2. Curriculum and instruction
3. Effective communication

4. Finance
5. Human relations
6. Learning environment
7. Negotiations
8. Organization and development
9. Political science
10. Problem solving
11. Research and evaluation
12. School law
13. Social awareness
14. Systems analysis for educational planning[35]

Nickerson conducted a survey of professors of secondary school administration and supervision and came to the following conclusions:*

1. The principal should spend the greatest part of his on-the-job time in the improvement of instruction.
2. The principal must work directly with teachers and students as resources for improvement ideas.
3. The principal must delegate routine matters plus supervisory activities to assistant principals, department chairmen, and administrative assistants.
4. The principal's preparation program must include human awareness training and be different from that of researchers and other administrators.
5. The principal's preparation program must be wide and varied. It should include work in industrial relations, the humanities, political science, and business administration. Foreign language requirements are not necessary.
6. The principal's preparation program must be made more flexible—tailored to the individual's unique strengths, weaknesses, and interests.
7. The principal's competencies rather than credit hours are the preferred measure of adequacy of preparation.
8. The administrative internship is a highly desirable part of the preparation program and should be required.
9. Clinical experiences other than the internship should be required at the M.A. level.

---

* From Neal C. Nickerson, "Status of Programs for Principals," *NASSP Bulletin* 56:352 (March, 1972), p. 20. Used by permission.

10. Simulation, small group projects, role playing, using re-
    source people from the field, and field trips should be
    used as instructional techniques.
11. In recruitment of students, for graduate education pro-
    grams, less importance should be put on standardized
    tests.
12. Colleges and universities must expand their in-service
    programs.
    Finally, college professors do see a need to change their
    efforts. Less rigid specific course requirements and
    expansion into other areas will improve the quality of
    secondary school principal pre-service and inservice
    programs in educational administration.[36]

Among trends which will affect the role of principals in the future are
the following:

1. Increased demands by students and teachers for a larger role in
   making decisions along a wide spectrum. These include salaries,
   supervision, and the content of the educational program.
2. Increased action by the superintendent to encourage team management.
3. Increasing world population, with the continued national and
   international tensions of living together in a changing world.
4. Increasing automation and improved technology which free
   workers for more leisure time activities.
5. Increasing public acceptance of the value of education as a means
   for fulfilling personal needs and demands.
6. Increasing participation by all people in governmental processes.
7. Pressures to move away from local control of the public schools to
   a more centralized control. There is also pressure in large districts
   to provide for more control at the subdistrict level.
8. Increasing median years of schooling for our population.

These trends will demand principals who are trained in the following
professional areas:

1. The principals of the future must be well versed in the area of the
   behavioral sciences including: psychology, sociology, history,
   government, and international relations. This training in the
   human behavioral sciences will enable them to understand the complexities brought about by increasing world population and instant
   communication with people all over the world.
2. The principals of the future will be trained so that they understand
   the value of educational technology such as the computer and other

electrical aids. They should be able to advise teachers on the use of these aids as providing a systems approach to their local school building. Simulated situations will be in common use for the principals of the future. Therefore, they must know the make-up of a good system design to utilize the educational technology within their school building.

3. Financial resources, buildings, materials, and spaces will continue to be scarce commodities for the principals of the future as the desire and time for education continue to expand. They will continue to be educated in the most efficient and desirable use of these scarce commodities. Principals will be responsible for increasing the curriculum available to their students in meeting the demand for longer years of education for all citizens.

4. Thus, the principals of the future will have increasing skill in the design and implementation of many types of curriculum. Education will continue to become more individualized, but this will largely be accomplished through the use of electrical and non-human teaching aids.

5. Tomorrow's principals will have wide demands placed upon them. In order to cope with these demands and understand the wide variety of feelings and cultures of their public, successful principals must have a liberal education as well as a broad interest in a variety of activities.

6. Their intensified role, as a coordinator of their increasingly diverse faculty and students, will make it necessary for principals to be well-trained in communication skills. Speaking, writing, and listening will become continually more important as criteria for the professional education of principals.

7. Collective bargaining will require that secondary principals become adept at assisting teachers to become better teachers and the emphasis will move away from evaluation toward an emphasis on supervision.

8. As more specialization occurs in the area of secondary administration resulting in more assistant principals, the secondary principals must develop skills to coordinate the activities of their assistants.

Increased emphasis is being placed on competency-based administrator preparation programs. Attention to this matter is being given by California and New York as well as other states and individual universities. The implementation of the competency-based approach involves the very difficult problem of defining roles, responsibilities, and competencies of the principal. The push for accountability may indeed force a rapid movement toward these types of programs.

If the principalship is to survive as a viable, dynamic position in education, then it is imperative that further research be conducted on how best to prepare and continually update the training of the secondary school leader. Many principals already in positions of leadership will need to reassess their skills in light of the challenge they are currently facing and will continue to face in the future.

SUMMARY

It is important to understand how both the secondary schools and the secondary school principalship developed and evolved in order to have a clearer perspective of how we have arrived at the current point in the development of secondary school administration.

It is also significant to realize the importance of the current forces at work in the secondary education milieu and their impact for the administration and supervision of schools devoted to meeting the challenges of these forces. In thinking about the background, training, and experience that is needed to successfully launch a career in administration, and ultimately move into a highly functional leadership role, the many essential areas of knowledge, understanding, and competencies involved not only in leadership, but also administration, have been advanced.

From this springboard, then, the remainder of this book is devoted to not only awareness of these areas, but also alternative courses of action which may prove fruitful in successful administrative endeavors in secondary school situations.

The day-to-day realities of what must be done, in a practical sense, often overshadow the long range goals upon which one must rely to feel comfortable to combat the frequency with which frustrating dilemmas beset the administrator. Thus, the next section is designed to provide basic leadership guidelines which can be utilized as one approaches the multiplicity of administrative task areas.

NOTES

1. Forest C. Ensign, "Evolution of the High School Principalship," *The School Review* 31 (March, 1923), p. 187.

2. Paul B. Jacobson, William C. Reavis, and James D. Logsdon, *The Effective School Principal in Elementary and Secondary Schools* (New York: Prentice-Hall, Inc., 1954), pp. 28–29.

3. T. H. Montgomery, "A History of the University of Pennsylvania, 1749–1770," taken from Nelson L. Bossing, *Principles of Secondary Education* (Prentice-Hall, 1955).

4. John S. Brubacker, ed., *Henry Barnard on Education* (New York: McGraw-Hill, 1931), pp. 96–103.

5. Leslie W. Kindred and associates, *The Intermediate Schools* (Englewood Cliffs, N. J.: Prentice-Hall, Inc., 1968), p. 19.

6. Ibid., p. 25.

7. Statistics of Public Elementary and Secondary Day Schools (Washington, D.C.: U.S. Government Printing Office, 1971).

8. Kindred, *The Intermediate Schools,* p. 26.

9. Mary F. Compton, "The Middle School: A Status Report," *Middle School Journal* (June, 1976), pp. 3–5.

10. John H. Lounsbury and Gordon F. Vars, "The Middle School: Fresh Start or New Delusion?" *The National Elementary Principal* 51 (November, 1971), pp. 12–19.

11. John Stanavage, "Beyond the Middle School: A Review and a Prospect," *American Secondary Education* (March, 1972), p. 1.

12. Thomas E. Gatewood, "What Research Says About the Junior High School vs. the Middle School," *North Central Association Quarterly* 46:52 (Fall, 1971), pp. 264–276.

13. Stanavage, "Beyond the Middle School," p. 8.

14. Ellsworth Thompkins and Walter Gaummitz, "The Carnegie Unit: Its Origin, Status and Trends," *NASSP Bulletin* 48:1 (January, 1964).

15. Ibid., p. 2.

16. James B. Conant, *The American High School Today* (New York: McGraw-Hill, 1959).

17. B. Frank Brown, Chairman, National Commission on the Reform of Secondary Education, *The Reform of Secondary Education* (New York: McGraw-Hill, 1973).

18. Ruth Weinstock, *The Greening of the High School* (New York: Educational Facilities Laboratories, 1973).

19. James S. Coleman, Chairman, Report of the Panel on Youth, President's Science Advisory Committee, *Youth: Transition to Adulthood* (Washington, D.C.: U.S. Government Printing Office, 1973).

20. John Henry Martin, Chairman, The National Panel on High School and Adolescent Education, *The Education of Adolescents: The Final Report and Recommendations of the National Panel on High School and Adolescent Education* (Washington, D.C.: U.S. Government Printing Office, 1976).

21. Scott D. Thomson, Chairman, *Secondary Schools in a Changing Society. This We Believe.* A statement on secondary education prepared by the Task Force on Secondary Schools in a Changing Society of the National Association of Secondary School Principals (Reston, Va.: The National Association of Secondary School Principals, 1975).

22. Dorothy Westby-Gibson, *Social Perspectives on Education: The Society, The Student, The School* (New York: John Wiley & Sons, Inc., 1966), pp. 26–29.

23. Russell G. Davis and Gary M. Lewis, "What Are the Consequences? Coping with Declining Enrollments," *The National Association of Secondary School Principals Bulletin* 61:407 (March, 1977), pp. 2–3.

24. "Is Decentralization the Answer?" *Education Summary* (December 15, 1968), p. 4.

25. G. Franklin Edwards, "Contemporary School Problems and Public Policy," in *Schools in a Changing Society,* ed. Albert J. Reiss (New York: The Free Press, 1965), pp. 192–193.

26. "As Violence Spreads in High Schools," *U.S. News and World Report* (November 30, 1970), pp. 18–20.

27. *Education U.S.A.* (September 27, 1971), p. 20.

28. *Education U.S.A.* (September 3, 1973), p. 2.

29. *Education U.S.A.* (December 20, 1971), p. 92.

30. Robert L. Ackerley and W. Stanfield Johnson, *Critical Issues in Negotiations Legislation* (Washington, D.C.: The National Association of Secondary Principals, 1969), pp. 9–10.

31. Benjamin Epstein, *What is Negotiable?* (Washington, D.C.: The National Association of Secondary School Principals, 1969), p. 20.

32. Benjamin Epstein, *Principals: An Organized Force for Leadership* (Reston, Va.: National Association of Secondary School Principals, 1974), pp. 3–4.

33. Gilbert R. Weldy, *Administering A Negotiated Contract* (Reston, Va.: National Association of Secondary School Principals, 1973), p. 46.

34. Westby-Gibson, *Social Perspectives on Education,* pp. 375–377.

35. Donald Brandewie, Thomas Johnson, and J. Lloyd Trump, "The Preparation and Development of Secondary School Administrators: A Summary," *NASSP Bulletin* 56:352 (March, 1972), p. 32.

36. Neal C. Nickerson, "Status of Programs for Principals," *NASSP Bulletin* 56:352 (March, 1972), p. 20.

2
The Principal as a Leader and Manager

Few would question that school principals exercise more influence upon the learning which takes place in their school than any other individual. In a sense, they are a middle manager between the teachers and the chief executive officer of the school district, the school superintendent. But their responsibilities and opportunities are much greater than middle managers in other fields of work, since they must shape as well as transmit educational policies and procedures.

Since principals are dealing with students who are in a developmental stage of life, it is essential that leadership skills be developed which are humanistic in nature. Principals must be dynamic and perceptive individuals, as they deal with the complexities of the human mind, the personalities of many individuals, and the multifaceted organizational structures in educational systems.

Collective bargaining for teachers has led to much more input into the decision making process by teachers. This process has had an influence on the ability of principals to carry out their decision making function, which in turn, has influenced their style of leadership.

Leadership skills can probably be best developed through actual experience—administrative internship experiences, and/or simulated situations. However, it is important to acquire a basic understanding of what leadership is and how it is related to management. This chapter contains information which assists those who have little or no leadership experience to gain insight into the nature of leadership. Additionally, the chapter can be useful in analyzing and improving the leadership skill of those who have experience in this area.

THE MEANING OF LEADERSHIP

From the dawn of history, the experience of humans has been replete with the phenomenon commonly referred to as leadership. Our written record of experiences, from the caveman's simple drawing to the latest account of interpersonal relationships, includes some designation of group behavior and leadership.

Knezevich indicates leadership can be thought of in one of three ways: (1) symbolic leadership (primarily an attribute of personality); (2) formal leadership (status, title, or position recognized in a formal organization); and (3) functional leadership (role performed in an organized group). He begins by suggesting that symbolic leadership views the leader as having well-developed personality traits and gives rise to the remark, "Leaders are born and not made." Either a person has these traits at birth or he or she is not capable of being a leader. This approach to leadership resembles trait psychology and prevails despite the large volume of research during the last twenty-five years which has consistently concluded that leadership is not an attribute of personality.

Formal leadership positions grant special authority to those who occupy the position. Those who hold formal leadership positions have the power, because of their position, to execute certain actions. A person may be designated as a formal leader and yet not be a functional leader. Functional leadership is best understood from situations where the individual and group are in interaction. Recent research has viewed leadership as a product of interpersonal interaction and as a function or role within a specific social system, such as an organized group. Thus, to understand this concept of leadership, one must understand the nature of groups. As a leader is involved in a network of relationships with other members of the group, leadership is not an abstract phenomenon, but is related to some purpose or goal of a group.[1]

According to Knezevich, leadership and human behavior in organizations are two sides of the same coin. He describes leadership as being "concerned with human energy in organized groups. It is a force that can initiate action among people, guide activities in a given direction, maintain such activities, and unify efforts toward common goals."[2]

Styles of Leadership

Leadership style has been classified into autocratic, laissez faire, and democratic. As one reviews these three concepts, it becomes apparent that most leaders have characteristics of all three types. In fact, under certain conditions, each of these styles seems to be effective. Autocratic leadership, for example, may be effective when a student is about to strike a teacher. The decision of what the teacher should do cannot, in this instance, involve reason with the student; therefore, leadership of the class may be very autocratic.

Autocratic leadership centers authority with the status leader, who in turn passes orders down the line for subordinates to follow. In autocratic leadership, communication flows from the top down, and there is little feed-back communication from subordinates. In a school with an autocratic principal or supervisor, there is little or no provision for the organization of committees to improve or evaluate the school. The principal is the evaluator of the school, the students, the curriculum, and the teachers; and as an autocratic leader, is considered an expert in all fields of learning as well as an expert in administrative detail. Autocratic leadership works against our society's concept of the importance of the individual.

The second style of leadership has been identified as laissez faire. "Riding the fence," as well as "hands off" policy would be two characteristics of this leadership. While generally more acceptable in our society than autocratic leadership, it is inconceivable that worthwhile progress or change would be accomplished in a school in which the principal stood for neither this nor that. The principal under laissez faire leadership would provide no guidelines for such established committees as curriculum and advisory.

The democratic leader is not one who counts hands every time a decision must be made, but rather one who arrives at a decision by utilizing his or her own competencies as an educational leader as well as the opinions of the well-informed. However, the principal must always avoid viewing himself or herself as a superior individual. While certain line responsibilities do exist (that is, the supervising of teachers and students), the relationship with teachers is that of a friendly advisor and consultant, rather than as an "overseer" or boss.

It should be emphasized that the principals who practice a democratic leadership style may not be immediately and continually successful. It may be that they have assumed a school in which the teachers have been brought up under autocratic leadership. While the faculty may at first welcome a new approach to leadership in their school, if too much confusion develops, many may actually desire to return to a more authoritarian type of leadership. Therefore, successful principals train their faculty to accept and successfully cope with democracy in the operation of the school. It takes time to develop maturity and skills which are necessary to participate effectively in group activities. Hence, those principals who use the democratic model must be students of interpersonal relations.

Other problems of democratic leadership include that of groups actually compounding ignorance, and the failure to differentiate between policy formulation and policy execution. The group deliberates and makes decisions on policy, but it does not execute policy. Democratic leadership does not imply execution of adopted policies by members of the group.

In spite of its shortcomings, the most promising leadership style for effective school principals or supervisors is the democratic style. Teachers expect to work in an atmosphere of democracy. Under democractic leadership, teachers may be asked to serve on a curriculum revision committee, an activities advisory committee, or in some other capacity to assist in developing policy for the school. In democratic leadership, teachers would also be involved in the selection of teacher candidates for vacancies within a certain department. While this is not practiced in all schools, if one expects democratic attitudes among the teaching staff, and true cooperation to exist within each department of the school, this selection process would seem to be fundamental for all schools.

The leadership function of secondary school principals or supervisors is a known and important part of the overall role-expectation of secondary school supervision. However, the question of how best to perform the leadership function is not easily answered. By virtue of their position as the head of the school, principals have authority as the designated "leader" of the school. When educators are trained specifically for the principalship, an important part of their training should be designed to produce a "leader." The probability of successfully developing effective principals may be directly proportional to the ability of a program of training to instill leadership behavior in principals.

Humanistic Leadership and the Principal

The fundamental purposes of education and current social climates influence the behavior of principals and supervisors. The process of education seeks a way to secure for each student the full development of mind and body, to make maximum use of his abilities, and to increase personal responsibility for his own learning. Other goals are to help the student develop his inquiry and creativity, his effectiveness in critical thinking, his problem-solving ability, and his effectiveness in group cooperation while working with other people who are also trying to use their abilities and to develop their potential. In all these things, the principal has a high degree of responsibility.

Trump provides the following description of a humane school:*

1. Focuses on options rather than on uniformity in developing and administering policies and practices. In other words, it does not subject every individual to group standards even though it informs him about model behaviors and procedures.

2. Devises a program for each pupil in which he can move forward with success in terms of his own talents and interests no matter how diverse they may be.

3. Makes sure that every pupil is known as a total human being—educationally by a teacher-adviser who helps

---

* From J. Lloyd Trump, "On Humanizing Schools," *The Bulletin of the National Association of Secondary School Principals* 56:361 (February, 1972), p. 9. Used by permission.

him personally to diagnose his needs, plan his program, make and change his schedule, evaluate his results and plan accordingly for the future. (This procedure goes far beyond the typical homeroom or the programing by school counselors or assistant principals.)

4. Creates an environment in which each teacher may make maximum utilization of his professional talents and interests, one that recognizes individual differences among teachers and provides differentiated staffing to identify better the role of the professional teacher.

5. Separates curriculum content so that each learner knows what is *essential* for everyone as distinct from the cognitive, skill, and affective behaviors that are important for those learners with special goals in the area of hobbies and careers. The goal here is to reduce greatly the *required* learning so that each pupil at all ages has more time to develop and follow his special interests.

6. Systematically tries to interest each pupil and teacher to learn more than he thinks he wants to learn. The technique is through motivational presentations and discussions.

7. Practices accountability for pupils and teachers, realizing that such procedures show that the school *cares* as opposed to permissiveness or vagueness that indicates that it does not worry about what happens to individuals.

8. Provides a variety of places in the school and in the community where pupils may study and work with supervision so that each pupil may find learning strategies that suit him best instead of being required to learn in one classroom from one teacher.

9. Has continuous progress arrangements so that each pupil may proceed at his own pace under competent supervision with a variety of self-directing, self-motivating, and self-evaluating materials and locations.

10. Evaluates pupil progress and teacher performance on the basis of the individual's own past record rather than on a comparison with others in the same group, while at the same time provides data that will help each person know what others are accomplishing.

11. Substitutes constructive reports of achievements for the threat of failure as the prime motivational device of

the school. The school records the special projects that
each pupil completes, no matter how small, that go
beyond what the school requires of everyone.

12. Recognizes that the principal more than any one other
person creates a humane environment in the school;
and, therefore, frees him from routine managerial
tasks to permit him to get out of the office to work
with pupils and teachers to develop more humane programs and procedures for everyone.[3]

Principals are the key facilitators of high quality education. The educational process is at their fingertips and they help provide the proper setting
which maximizes opportunities for learning. Their role as humane leaders is
vital for the development of a school environment which creates a sense of
self worth in each individual.

LEADERSHIP AND THE TEAM MANAGEMENT CONCEPT

Collective bargaining for teachers has led to much more input into the decision-making process by teachers. This process has had an influence on the
ability of principals to carry out their decision-making function and thus
their style of leadership.

The National Association of Secondary School Principals (NASSP) has
identified the following list of issues which teachers have sought as rights,
but which the NASSP feels is an infringement upon necessary administrative
authority.

Clauses which call for the election of principals by teachers and
their recall if teachers disapprove of the principal's work

Specifications for procedures and conduct of employment interviews, notice to candidates, or prohibitions for the administrator in selecting teachers for employment

Provisions or clauses that are demeaning to administrators,
such as the requirement that they be courteous and respectful to
teachers, that they not discriminate because of race or religion,
or that they not ask embarrassing questions in employment
interviews (All practices avoided by good administrators or
those covered by law are not needed in teacher contracts.)

Clauses requiring administrators to report to teachers concerning actions or decisions that do not directly concern them

Clauses that unreasonably complicate the administrator's routine for carrying out supervisory duties

Clauses that allow teacher organization representatives to sit in
on supervisory conferences or to receive summary reports of

conferences, when the individual teacher has not requested such
representation

Clauses that give teachers the right to grieve over the content
and substance of their evaluations

Clauses that allow teachers to use the content of supervisory
evaluations in the school or in the news media to attempt to
embarrass or discredit administrators and supervisors

Clauses that require "concurrence" of the teacher bargaining
unit before policies can be made or changed or before educational decisions can be made

Clauses requiring the assignment or promotion of a teacher
according to seniority, with no regard for qualifications or
talent

Clauses calling for teachers to "concur" in their teaching
assignment or schedule, or clauses allowing teachers to ask for
changes in their assignment if they consider their assignment a
"hardship"

Clauses placing unworkable restrictions on teacher assignments,
such as arbitrary limits on the number of different classrooms,
arbitrary limits on the number of preparations, and unreasonably limited class sizes

Clauses giving teachers the right to veto their own transfers between departments or buildings

Clauses requiring laborious procedures for curriculum development or innovation

Clauses limiting the principal's discretion to adjust the daily
schedule for special purposes or programs

Clauses that in any way interfere with the board of education's
responsibility to adhere to the law or to respond to community
expectations in their schools.[4]

As a result of the feeling of infringement by teachers upon the building
level principal's decision-making role, many principals have responded by
requesting bargaining rights of their own. The response by superintendents
to this push and the collective bargaining push by teachers has been to call
for implementation of a team management or administrative team
approach.

The National Association of Secondary School Principals defined the
administrative team as follows:

An administrative team represents a means of establishing
smooth lines of organization and communication, common
agreements, and definite patterns of mutuality among administrators and the board of education as they unite to provide

effective educational programs for the community. There are two primary parties involved in the leadership of a school district, namely, the board of education, whose responsibility is policy-making, and the administrative team (including all administrators), whose major responsibilities include first advising the board in establishing district policies and then guaranteeing their effective implementation. A close, harmonious working relationship between these two parties is obviously vital to the successful operation of a school district.

It should also be clear that an effective administrative team has, in addition to its assigned legalistic and primary role of policy implementation, a vital leadership function to perform. Never before has more interest and concern been voiced about the need for strong and united educational leadership. An effective administrative team provides a collective means of strengthening school district leadership giving individual administrators needed assistance, opportunities, and job satisfaction.[5]

A publication published jointly by the American Association of School Administrators, the National Association of Elementary School Principals, the National Association of Secondary School Principals, and the National School Public Relations Association gave the following definition of the administrative team:

> The administrative team is a formally constituted, de jure body of administrators who exercise collaboratively all the administrative processes: goal setting, planning, organizing, coordinating, communicating, decision-making, and evaluating. However, with rare exceptions, it does not direct programs within specific administrative jurisdictions.[6]

The management team most often is composed of a variety of central office and building level administrative and supervisory personnel. Depending upon the role and function of department or grade level chairpersons, they may be involved in a management team.

Although most often board members are thought of as policy development personnel rather than someone who executes policies, it may be possible to have a team arrangement which includes board members. Likewise, although teachers are most often seen as other than management and thus, are excluded from the team, it is possible to find teachers involved to some extent in providing input into the management team. Teachers and board members would not be likely to be involved in actual administrative decision making.

Depending on the number of administrators found in a school system, it may be necessary to utilize representatives from groups such as building level principals in order to facilitate group work. Smaller systems may find that all administrative personnel can be included on the team.

Some teams are arranged as one single body headed by the superintendent, while others may be arranged in such a way that assistant superintendents are in charge of a cabinet or some major aspect of the organization such as curriculum, business, or school plant. The assistant superintendents as a group may then act as another cabinet to assist the superintendent in his or her decision-making role. The superintendent could very well be a member of each cabinet and use the assistance of each cabinet in his or her decision-making role.

The complaint is sometimes voiced that while the team management arrangement permits more input from more sources than the traditional line and staff arrangement, it still does not permit decision making to be done by anyone other than the superintendent. The superintendent's level of trust in his or her subordinates probably dictates the extent to which he or she feels comfortable in permitting decision making to be a team function.

Many building principals would prefer to have much more decision making delegated to the building level. In other words, many principals would prefer decentralized decision making rather than centralized decision making. Quite often the central office retains controls over the budgeting process and thus controls the extent to which building level principals can make independent decisions about budget priorities and/or expenditures.

MANAGEMENT BY OBJECTIVES

The advent of collective bargaining for teachers and an emphasis on accountability resulting in a renewed interest in teacher evaluation has resulted in a push for evaluation of building level administrators. Teachers are asking that the evaluators be evaluated. Even many principals asked for a clearer definition of their roles. All of this has led to a push for job descriptions for administrative positions as well as a search for techniques such as management by objectives. This would insure that administrators know what it is they should be doing and how well they are doing it.

Management by objectives (MBO) is a process which is designed to break down the administrative tasks into a series of objectives. Administrators are then evaluated on the basis of how well they achieve the objectives they set out to attain. Carried to its ultimate, MBO would call for instructional or learning objectives for each classroom and students would be evaluated on how well they were able to achieve these objectives.

COLLECTIVE BARGAINING AND LEADERSHIP
STYLE OF THE PRINCIPAL

The bargained agreement is a document which must be implemented by the building level principal. The contents of that document can indeed affect the style of leadership of the principal. The fact that most teacher agreements which have grievance procedures also designate the building principal as the person to handle the first level of the grievance has an effect on the principal's leadership style. Principals need to guard against situations which would limit their behavior primarily to following designated guidelines and would restrict them from initiating actions expected of a leader.

Principals also need to guard against permitting an environment to develop in which teachers meet only minimal expectations spelled out in a bargained contract. It indeed requires great leadership ability to inspire, guide, and coordinate a staff in a climate where all are only interested in meeting minimal requirements and are determined to pressure the principal into initiating little action on his or her own for fear a grievance will be filed.

The bargained contract can become a very helpful instrument in the day to day operation of a building. It can take care of routine matters which otherwise would require needless time of the principal. The contract can make provision for developmental activities by staff members which will enhance the learning environment for students. In short, the bargained contract is a document which can either enhance or restrict the leadership ability of the principal.

SUMMARY

Administration of the secondary school demands the best leadership skills that the principal can muster. While authoritarian leadership style may be necessary in emergency situations, the authors support the democratic style of leadership as being most effective. However, democratic leadership requires instruction and guidance for the faculty in developing a successful educational program. The faculty may assist in developing policy, but the execution of policy is the overall responsibility of the principal or supervisor. Means must be taken to utilize the best thinking of the group based upon a clear understanding.

Leadership may also be thought of as symbolic, formal, or functional. It is a social process which involves working with groups of people. No one type of personality or trait can be related to success in leadership; rather the situation and the ability of the person to lead in that situation seem to be most important. Teachers perform best under leaders who are creative and imaginative. The administrator who *leads* with vision, humility, and concern is a vital need in secondary education today.

Because schools are a service agency which deal with humans, it is extremely important for the principal to be able to establish a humane environment in the school which permits each individual to have a sense of self worth.

Collective bargaining for teachers and the resultant feeling of loss of power by principals, influenced superintendents to call for the implementation of a team management approach. Some management teams do not

SUMMARY

involve the members in directive action as a result of group discussion, but do rely heavily upon input from group members as a base for implementation of decisions. A variety of personnel can make up team membership, but normally membership is limited to central office and building level administrative and supervisory persons.

Management by objectives provides a more systematic approach to management and improvement of that process through a planned evaluation of objectives an administrator is expected to perform.

Principals need to be skilled leaders in assisting in the development and implementation of a bargained agreement for teachers if they are to retain flexibility to initiate needed actions and to insure that teacher performance exceeds minimal requirements.

NOTES

1. Stephen J. Knezevich, *Administration of Public Education* (New York: Harper and Row, Publishers, 1975), pp. 81–85.

2. Ibid., p. 81.

3. J. Lloyd Trump, "On Humanizing Schools," *The Bulletin of the National Association of Secondary School Principals* 56:361 (February, 1972), p. 9.

4. Gilbert Weldy, *Administering a Negotiated Contract* (Reston, Va.: National Association of Secondary School Principals, 1973), pp. 11–12.

5. National Association of Secondary School Principals. "Management Crises: A Solution" (Washington, D.C.: NASSP, 1971), p. 3.

6. Richard Wynn, *Theory and Practice of the Administrative Team* (Arlington, Va.: National Association of Elementary School Principals, 1973), p. 36.

3

The Principal as a Problem Solver, Decision Maker, Change Agent

In addition to attaining competence in learning theory and curriculum, principals must be able to interact with their staff to solve problems, make decisions, and assist them to make needed changes in the school. Skillful application of these processes will enable principals to fit the human and material resources together in an optimum manner so that the most efficient use of these resources will be realized.

A sincere effort has been made in this chapter to blend the discussion of the nature of the processes of problem solving, decision making, and change with the practical application of each of these processes. This enables the reader to gain knowledge about how to implement each skill and to improve existing skills while gaining a basic understanding of each process.

PROBLEM SOLVING AND THE PRINCIPAL

A *problem* is defined by John K. Hemphill as "a state of affairs that is perceived with dissatisfaction."[1] Therefore, ordinarily if a person views his environment with dissatisfaction, he has a problem; if he views his environment with satisfaction, he has no problem. This can be represented as a continuum. The line between the two extremes—the problem and the solution—can be viewed as the process by which the problem is solved.

In general, problem situations can be distinguished into two classes. The first refers to the type of problem with which only one person is involved and which is internalized by that one person. For example, a person has an itch. His solution is to scratch it. The second problem situation deals with problems that involve two or more people. This is a general class of social problems. A major subdivision of these is mutual problems. A mutual problem is a situation in which two or more people perceive the same problem and the solution that is required. A good example is a team of football players highly desirous of winning (solution) the game. They all perceive the same goal (winning) and work for the solution (the process).[2]

In the larger sense, not all social problems are mutual. The majority of them require greater difficulty in reaching a satisfactory solution. Two or more people may operate in an environment and only one may view it with dissatisfaction. Halpin explains it this way:

> A salesman approaches a stranger who he hopes may become his customer. The salesman's problem involves the behavior of the stranger (i.e., to satisfy the salesman, the stranger must buy the salesman's product), but at the time of the approach the stranger may not be dissatisfied in not having in his possession the salesman's product. (Later the sales)—situation may become a mutual problem in which both the salesman and the potential customer are definitely involved.[3]

Although the distinctions above are graphic, in practice they may not be as clearly defined. Most problems dealt with by administrators will be a mixture. Even so, administrators must be sure they have distinguished clearly between the social problem and its subclass, the mutual problem.[4] A social problem may not be a mutual problem, but a mutual problem is a social problem. Of course, not all social problems are perceived by their participants as having the same solution. The result is that the satisfaction for all participants becomes more complex as the divergence of solutions (desired by each participant) increases. What is needed by principals who are working with their staff (participants), is the coordination of all participants' efforts in order to reach a desired solution.[5]

Problem solving is a complex process due to the fact that every time two members of a group interact, their intentions may be changed. This must continue until the intentions of the group coincide with the environment; the result will be a solution to the problem.

In the final analysis, two main conditions determine a solution to a problem. First, if the environment changes to suit the group's perceptions, a solution will be found. Second, if the group's perceptions change and become congruent with the environment, a solution will be found. If neither of the above facilitates a solution, the principal should begin to look for other reasons.

One of the most common reasons for the failure of a group to reach a successful solution is organizational rules and regulations. Rules and regulations tend to limit the possibilities for developing alternatives that would result in a solution. This will be further discussed later in this chapter.

DECISION MAKING AND THE PRINCIPAL

A major proponent of administration as decision making is Daniel E. Griffiths. In the development of his theory, Griffiths begins with a set of assumptions (theory):

1. Administration is a generalized type of behavior to be found in all human organizations.

2. Administration is the process of directing and controlling life in a social organization.

3. The specific function of administration is to develop and regulate the decision-making process in the most effective manner possible.

4. The administrator works with groups or with individuals with a group referent, not with individuals as such.[6]

After making his assumptions, Griffiths begins to develop his concepts. They are: (1) decision making, (2) organization, (3) perception, (4) communication, and (5) power and authority.

Decision making is not an act; it is a process—a process of directing and controlling decisions. Since the making of decisions is considered the major aspect of an organization, an analysis of decision making will give keen insight into the way administrators operate.[7] Obviously, if administrators operate with decision making as their major task, there must be some guiding principles that ensure effectiveness. Decision making is an action that proceeds along a continuum. The continuum constitutes the recognition of the need for a decision to the eventual completion of all acts that are a result of the decision and that make the decision operational.[8] This particular concept is, therefore, construed to mean not only the decision, but also the acts necessary to put the decision into operation.[9]

As administration takes place within an organization, the nature of the organization is going to influence the outcome of a decision. Three types of organizations are detectable: (1) formal, (2) informal, and (3) neutral. The formal organization can be characterized as the traditional hierarchical approach whereby power and authority flow downward. The power and authority are directly aimed at goal attainment. This is true of all organizations. Inherent in the idea of attaining goals is the decision-making process which directs and controls the utilization of the resources of the system. Thus, in understanding the decision-making process in an organization, one must understand the organization's basic structure.[10]

Informal organization is composed of a system of interpersonal relations that exist between members of every group. These interpersonal relationships are in constant flux due to numerous formal and informal pressures. Informal organization can also be characterized by the groups that make and implement decisions. In fact, all groups within an organization inject impinging factors that alter any decision-making process. This can be supported by the fact that unintended or unanticipated consequences may overshadow the importance of predicted events. A situation such as this can either be detrimental or advantageous.[11]

The last group found within an enterprise is neutral. These are characterized as coffee groups, social groups, or bowling groups—all of which are disinterested.[12]

The concept of perception can be defined as a person's interaction with his environment and the fact that this interaction influences both the environment and the person. As both undergo alteration, each individual acquires a unique background. With this background, he begins to perceive his own psychological environment by identifying certain aspects of it to his outside environment. This process is called *externalization*.[13] Therefore, each person within an organization operates from a different frame of reference. This has a definite bearing on the decision-making process.

If based on the preceding explanation, each of us perceives and builds our own environment within which we operate, it seems logical that we really are limiting ourselves. Thus, in a sense, we are limiting our capability to communicate. Two people would have to have an identical psychological environment if they were to communicate with one hundred percent accuracy. Communication within an organization is obviously not that effective.[14]

Power is thought of as what is needed to attain the goals of the organization. The concept of power explains the amount of control an organization holds over its members. Griffiths states that power can be defined as follows:

> . . . power is a function of decision made and can be operationally defined as: $P = f(D)$. The person has power to the extent that he makes decisions which: (1) effect the course of action of an enterprise to a greater degree than do decisions made by others in the enterprise, (2) influence other decisions.[15]

Authority can be attributed to a person who is capable of persuading others to accept his or her power.[16]

Once the reader is familiar with the aforementioned concepts, then one can investigate how the concepts interact to provide the administrator with the knowledge of how to make effective decisions. According to Griffiths, the process of decision making follows these six steps:

1. Recognize, define and limit the problem.
2. Analyze and evaluate the problem.
3. Establish criteria or standards by which solutions will be evaluated or judged as acceptable and adequate to the need.
4. Collect data.
5. Formulate and select the preferred solution or solutions.
6. Put into effect the preferred solution.
   a. Program the solution.

    b. Control the activities in the program.
    c. Evaluate the results and the process.[17]

Before analyzing and evaluating a problem, administrators should be sure they understand the nature of the problem, how the problem is related to the organization, and what they want to do about it. Once this is accomplished, the administrators must decide whether or not the decision is theirs to make. If it is, there are three types they can identify: intermediary, appellate, and creative. Each has its own characteristics.

1. An intermediary decision is identified as that type that flows from the top of the hierarchical structure downward. This includes commands, orders, and policies. These decisions are implemental in nature.

2. An appellate decision originates from a person's subordinates within the organization. A typical decision would involve a subordinate who was proven incapable of making the decision; therefore, his superior must.

3. Creative decisions originate, not outside of the person as those enumerated above, but from within. A creative decision usually identifies a need for a decision and the administrator, recognizing this need, breaks policy and acts on the idea. Thus, a change in policy or even a new policy comes into being.[18]

At this point, the decision maker establishes his or her criteria, collects data, and begins the selection of preferred solutions.

In implementing a decision, the administrator must perform three functions: (1) programming, (2) controlling, and (3) evaluating. Programming is the process by which the necessary structure is built in order that the decision be properly initiated.[19] This decision creates a change in the environment for the individual members of the organization, which in turn causes them to begin the process outlined in administration as problem solving. The reader should note that decision making and problem solving are interrelated in that whenever a decision is made in an organization, it changes the individual's environment. This change, in turn, causes the individual to progress through a decision-making process himself. He compares his intentions with his environment.

The process of control can be described as assuring that performance corresponds with plans. To do so, the administrator sets limits in which the plans operate. The limits are, for many administrators, nothing more than the setting of policy.[20]

The last phase of decision making is evaluation. Evaluation determines whether or not the decision has solved the problem and has produced the desired changes.[21]

Decision Making Guidelines for Principals

If educators on every level are constantly making choices between alternatives, it is imperative that administrators attempt to maximize the possibilities of rational decision making. In doing so, principals will be able to guide the total program with more effectiveness. Second, by viewing administration and its core—decision making—principals will obtain a better concept of the function and responsibilities as they exist within the organization and groups that make up the organization. And last, if principals understand that decision making within the individual is a function of that individual's psychological environment, they will as administrators be better able to select the proper course of action.

Decision making is not necessarily restricted to administrators, but involves all types of individuals. For school principals, the ability to be decisive is critical for success. Some have said that administration is decision making; however, others would say that principals who regard themselves as decision makers per se, are likely to experience failure in their position.

Many decisions involving the implementation of policy within the local school are made by school principals. Principals who ask for a show of hands before making every decision are not likely to experience confidence from their faculty. Henry, in his study of characteristics of successful business executives, reports that:

> Decisiveness is the ability to come to a decision among several
> alternative courses of action—the breakdown of this trait
> (usually found in cases where some profound personality
> change has also occurred) is one of the most disastrous for the
> executive.[22]

According to Barnard, occasions for decisions originate from three fields—superiors, subordinates, and the executive concerned. He further states:

> The fine art of executive decision making consists in not decid-
> ing questions that are not now pertinent, in not deciding pre-
> maturely, in not making decisions that cannot be made effective
> and in not making decisions that others should make.[23]

Typically, executives make decisions more rapidly when initiated by superiors than when initiated by subordinates. It is much easier to delay decision making on questions raised by subordinates since they have less influence upon career success than superiors.

Principals should avoid the reputation of never acting upon problems initiated by teachers. It does not take long for subordinates to become discouraged when approaching the procrastinating principal with requests for materials or in making other decisions. Nondecisive behavior on the part of the principal "is a serious barrier to the continued initiation of problem proposing communication from teachers."[24] This does not mean that successful principals "shoot from the hip," but that through careful study and/or sharing with the faculty, they make or guide decisions.

The principal's ability to make or guide decision making is crucial to success as an administrator. It is a group process that may be accomplished by steps similar to those used in problem solving. The principal does not make all the decisions, but assumes a responsibility to see that they are made.

ADMINISTRATION AS A SOCIAL PROCESS

In the foregoing sections, administration as problem solving and decision making have been discussed. What is now proposed is a middle range theory that overlaps the two. Administration as a social process is basically derived from two dimensions of an organization—hierarchical structure and the individual. As decision making and problem solving operate within these dimensions, they are directly influenced by them. Consequently, administration as a social process is important not only in its own right, but also in terms of its interaction with other theories.

If one surveys the theories prevailing in the area of administration as a social process, Getzels and Guba's theory is the most notable. In order to explain their theory, they have devised a model (Figure 3.1). They start with the basic assumption that the process of administration deals essentially with social behavior in a hierarchical setting.[25] Within this setting, there exists a number of superior-subordinate relationships formed in a hierarchy. These relationships exist as laws from which integrated roles and facilities are allocated in order to achieve the goals of the social system. At this point, they distinguish between two dimensions that are independent yet interactive.[26] The interaction is perceived as social behavior.

Figure 3.1
Getzels-Guba Model of Social Behavior*

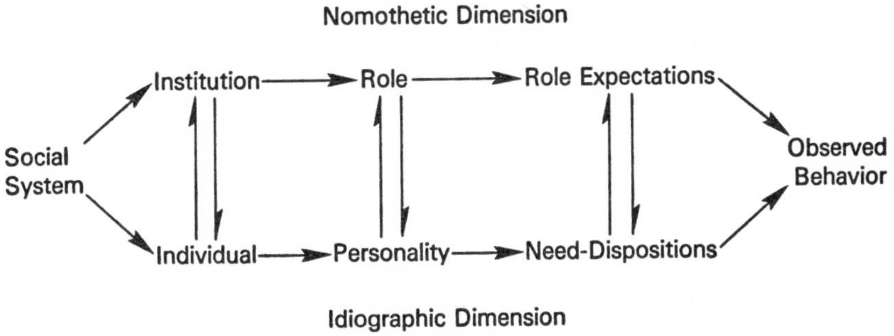

Nomothetic Dimension

Idiographic Dimension

*J. W. Getzels and E. G. Guba, "Social Behavior and the Administrative Process," *The School Review* Vol. LXV, Winter, 1957, p. 429.

The two dimensions are the nomothetic and idiographic. The nomothetic dimension can be characterized as requiring the members of the organization (teachers) to display a certain role in order that the goals and objectives (expectations) of the organization (school) are met. The idiographic dimension can be viewed as the individual's personality combined with his need-dispositions—what he desires to do or be. The idiographic and nomothetic dimensions interact and result in observed behavior. Ideally, the principal should strive for every member of his or her staff to meet their need-dispositions and still perform to the role expectations of the school.

WORKING WITH INDIVIDUALS WITHIN THE ORGANIZATION

Since administration is working with human beings who are complex organisms, part of the professional education of administrators and supervisors should be a study of interpersonal relations which may be found among teachers, students, and others in given school situations. The social relations among several hundred individuals create a variety of problem-laden situations. This alone is difficult for any person charged with the responsibility of bringing these human resources together for the ultimate purpose of meaningful educational experiences. Add to this the difficulty of organizing the material and physical resources of the school, and one readily sees the complexity of school situations.

Principals must have an understanding of their role in this complex social system and be competent in describing teachers' and students' roles as well. Teachers often have specialized interests in one grade or in one or two subject areas and tend to concentrate on these areas. Even principals are specialized in their role as chief administrator of the school system, and may become so deeply involved in administrating that they are unable to see the purpose of the educational program. This specialization is even more pronounced in the behavior of teachers. There is often conflict and competition within and between departments and subject areas. The athletic coach is in competition for talent with such faculty members as the dramatics coach, the band instructor, and special interest club advisors. Often, students are caught in the middle and are confused as to which organizations they should join.

Over-specialization of persons within an organization may lead to certain limitations concerning how "specialists" perceive the broad picture or the purpose of the organization. Laski identified this characteristic as the trained incapacity of the expert.[27] He identified four ways that the expert is limited as a contributor of the organization:

1. The expert sacrifices common sense insights to the intensity of his experience in his special field.

2. The second typical feature of the expert's trained incapacity
   is a marked aversion to new ideas. Experts in a field
   are usually first to take up arms against an innovation.
3. Experts seldom see things in their entirety. They take the
   subject of their specialty necessarily as the center of
   importance and relate everything to that.
4. The fourth aspect of the expert's trained incapacity is the
   feeling of superiority that is likely to be associated
   with his position. The lack of humility often makes experts fail to see the obvious when it is in front of their
   noses.[28]

Specialization often contributes to the success of an organization, but it should be clear to the principal that specialization also contributes to disunity within a school. Part of the inservice education of teachers should be in developing a wider view of the total educational program. Unless the principal recognizes the problems inherent with "trained incapacity" or over-specialization of teachers, the school will have little interest in the total education of pupils. "Trained incapacity" may, indeed, seriously hamper the development of a broad comprehensive educational program.

The relationship between the principal and the teacher should be one of mutual confidence. Each has certain responsibilities, the acomplishment of which would fail without cooperation. Oftentimes, the teacher's concept of the principal's role is confused. A discussion by the principal with the faculty concerning his or her responsibilities will often pay handsome dividends.

What promotes wholesome interaction with a faculty? Once again we may turn to human behaviorists to help us answer this question. Maslow provides a model of the theory of human motivation which is appropriate for a clearer understanding of humans in an organization. According to Maslow, there are five basic human needs: physiological, safety, love, esteem, and self-actualization, which are related to each other by hierarchy of prepotency.[29]

In our society, the physiological needs of sex, hunger, and thirst are for the most part satisfied, as are the safety needs. Love, esteem, and self-actualization needs become extremely important to the teacher in understanding human behavior in organization. Principals who make serious attempts to satisfy these higher level needs of teachers are well on the road to becoming successful administrators. While recognizing their own need for self-actualization, principals should organize a school so that teachers may gain esteem and self-actualization.

Argyris has developed a model which helps one understand the frustrations of individuals who fail to achieve self-actualization within an organization. According to this model, human beings in our culture:

1. Tend to develop from a state of passivity as infants to a state of increasing activity as adults.
2. Tend to develop from a state of dependence upon others as infants to a state of relative independence as adults.
3. Tend to develop from being capable of behaving only in a few ways as an infant to being capable of behaving in many different ways as an adult.
4. Tend to develop from having erratic, casual, shallow, quickly dropped interests as an infant to having deeper interests as an adult.
5. Tend to develop from a short time perspective as an infant to much longer time perspective as an adult.
6. Tend to develop from being in a subordinate position in the family and society as an infant to aspiring to occupy an equal and/or superordinate position relative to their peers.
7. Tend to develop from a lack of awareness of self as an infant to an awareness of and control over self as an adult.[30]

Many problems of conflict, according to Argyris, occur when individuals are put in situations in which they are dependent, submissive, and use few of their creative abilities. When they are in dependent and submissive situations, they tend to be frustrated and will form such informal activities as:

1. Leave the situation (absenteeism and turnover).
2. Climb the organizational ladder.
3. Become defensive (daydream, become aggressive, nurture grievance, project and feel a low sense of self-worth).
4. Become apathetic, disinterested, non-ego involved in the organization and its formal goals.
5. De-emphasize in their own minds the importance of self-growth and creativity and emphasize the importance of money and other material rewards.
6. Accept the above described ways of behaving as being proper for their lives outside the organization.[31]

Principals should recognize that individuals strive for independence of action and strive to be active and worthy members of an organization. Absenteeism, defensiveness, disinterest, and apathy on the part of teachers are clues that tell administrators that something is wrong with the esteem and self-actualization needs of their teachers. How may principals, who recognize that their teachers are excessively absent and showing disinterest in the school, help their teachers achieve self-actualization?

Involvement becomes a key word for any administrator in a dynamic organization. This involvement can occur in the decision-making process concerning curriculum revision, activity organization, and the general organizational structure of the school. A word of caution about involvement: committees should not be established without guidance and genuine purpose. The principal must be willing to live with the decision of the group. If, for example, a principal has assigned an athletic committee to determine schedules and practice times, he or she must accept the decision of the committee. This does not mean that the principal remains aloof and does not participate in their decision making, but the consensus of the group must be accepted after the principal has had an opportunity to voice his or her opinion.

The purpose of an established group must be genuine as well as clear. In addition, the members of the group must have an interest in the purpose of the group. Seldom do "status leader imposed goals" become accepted as the real goals of the group. The faculty must have a felt need for solving or discussing a problem.

WORKING WITH GROUPS WITHIN THE SCHOOL ORGANIZATION

The administration and supervision of a secondary school is primarily a group process. Principals will work with groups such as policy, advisory, curriculum, personnel, subject area, specialized services, activities, and athletic committees. Their purpose is to further the coordination and success of these groups in attaining the goals of the organization.

It is impossible for a school to function without a group organizational structure. The administration of a local school may be autocratic in that the principal tells the faculty what to teach, how to teach, and devises the organizational structure to meet his or her own aims. Even if the principal uses the autocratic method of administration, he or she must meet with the faculty as a group to communicate orders.

The autocratic principal will utilize groups infrequently in administering the school. However, the principal who is aware that individuals have personal needs, will utilize the group process to mediate differences between individual expectations and institutional expectations. Self-esteem and self-actualization may be realized by teachers through group interaction. The group provides the principal with an opportunity to receive feedback from the faculty and to coordinate school activities; as well as provides opportunities for teachers to share their ideas.

Principals will want to be sure that their appointees to the various groups within their building will be representative as well as inclusive of persons having different abilities and interests. An advisory committee on faculty-principal relations which is composed of departmental heads would be less effective than one composed of appropriate representation from departmental heads, classroom teachers, athletic coaches, drama coaches, and other such groups representing all the various endeavors.

One of the most perplexing problems that a principal will face in the establishment of groups is whether they should be appointed by the principal, or elected by the faculty. While no clearcut statement can be made either way, committees for planning the faculty meetings, the principal's advisory committee, and social committees will probably be more effective if they are elected by the faculty. On the other hand, some short term ad hoc committees, such as text book adoption committees, could very well be composed of knowledgeable persons as determined by the principal. In the latter case, the task force notion may be the best way to accomplish certain short-range objectives.

Achievement of group tasks may be low if there is antagonism between members of the group. The principal who is aware of the dislike of one teacher for another should avoid assigning them to the same committee. This is not an easy practice to comply with, since the principal is often the last to know of friction between faculty members. Clues may be obtained, however, by observing faculty room cliques and by noticing who sits by whom at faculty conferences.

Shepherd lists the following features of a successful group:

1. Generally a successful group has clear objectives, not vague ones and the members of the group have personal objectives which are identical or compatible with the group's objectives.

2. A successful group is one in which each member's role is clear and known to himself and to others in the group.

3. A group in which members do not share at least some relevant values is likely to be successful only for limited and short-run objectives.

4. Communication in a successful group is open and full. No one withholds relevant information, whether it be ideas or feelings and each member provides that information when appropriate.

5. Membership in a successful group is clearcut and members are heterogeneous.[32]

In many instances, a group may be composed of a task leader and a social-emotional leader. The task leader has the skills that are needed for the accomplishment of goals of the group, but maintains a greater social distance with group members than the social-emotional leader. The social-emotional leader is easily approached and serves the group as one with whom they can candidly discuss their problems. In school settings, the principal often serves as the task leader, whereas the social-emotional leader often is a member of the faculty. Since the social-emotional leader of a group receives complaints from faculty members and is usually aware of most personal problems of faculty members, it would be wise for the principal to have this person on his or her advisory committee.[33]

Principals who are students of individual behavior within groups are likely to be more successful as administrators than those who are students of mechanical detail. The peer relationship which occurs within all human groups has many implications for school principals. They would expect, for example, that teachers would not identify as readily with them, but rather tend to identify more with teachers of their own peer group. Group pressures, while often subtle, often determine the behavior of individuals within a group. Principals who recognize the effect of group pressure and peer influence upon teachers may use this to better understand their faculty and to promote desirable educational change.

Wise principals recognize the great value of utilizing the group process in obtaining feedback from their faculty, in promoting change, and in initiating the goals of the school. They recognize the individual differences within a group and encourage leadership to emerge from within the group. They encourage the members of the group to better understand each other. Communication is structured to be multi-directional rather than to be in a single line up or down the hierarchy. They recognize the value of social-emotional leaders in groups and encourage their freedom of action, since these leaders contribute to the morale of groups and serve as sounding boards for feedback.

THE PRINCIPAL AND THE CHANGE PROCESS

Change has been defined as a planned, systematic, controlled effort to alter more than one of the following aspects of the organization: (1) its tasks, (2) its structure, (3) its technology, or (4) its participants in ways thought to be more effective in achieving the organization's goals.[34]

There can be little doubt that principals and supervisors are deeply immersed in the change process of our society. In recent years, schools have been given increased responsibility for:

1. Preparing citizens for fluctuating economic conditions.
2. Preparing technicians for automation and new skills.
3. Preparing a host of persons to work in foreign service positions.
4. Meeting the science and technology needs of the space age.
5. Coping with the problems of the social revolution of minority groups.
6. Coping with the explosion of knowledge, and teaching children the ability to think rather than merely to accumulate facts.
7. Educating citizens for a society with changing population, decaying cities, and tensions in international relations.

These responsibilities have forced schools to reexamine their organization, and experiment with new methods of teaching. As a result of these increased pressures and our constantly advancing technology, many changes are being made in the schools. Some of these changes are new ideas and some are merely a redressing of the old. Team teaching, closed circuit television, programmed learning, flexible scheduling, learning resource centers, computerized library references, national programs such as PSSC physics, para-professionals, continuous progress, computerized instruction, and language laboratories are some of the changes which have appeared in schools in recent years.

It has been said that change should not be made for the sake of change itself. However, change which gives new perspectives to faculty groups or individual members may indeed be worthwhile. It is extremely easy for teachers to feel a sense of monotony in their position, which may result in great frustration. Involving these teachers in team teaching, sending them to a summer institute, or encouraging them to experiment in using new media in their instruction, may bring back their enthusiasm for teaching. In such cases, the values occurring from the change process itself may be beneficial.

While it is often difficult for secondary school leaders to initiate change without the encouragement of their superintendent and the board of education, it is possible for them to be prime influences in creating a belief in their superordinates that change will bring about an improved educational program. However, principals who work under an administration that is reluctant to allow freedom to experiment within the local schools, may be severely handicapped in their efforts to promote a more challenging school environment. It is equally true that superintendents having a principal who is reluctant to change are also severely handicapped. Freedom to innovate is dependent upon the appropriate attitude of the board of education as well as the superintendents and the principals.

If principals have all the necessary components for change, such as the financial resources, proper support, and a climate for change, one further reference will be helpful in their effort to get the faculty to accept the change. Schein proposed a model of influence and change which has valuable implications for administrators who feel that certain behavioral changes of personnel within the organization are desirable. According to this model, change in behavior " . . . does not occur unless the individual is motivated and ready to change." The following is Schein's description of this model:

> Given these general assumptions about the integration of attitudes in the person, it is appropriate to consider influence as a process which occurs over time and which includes these phases:
>
> 1. *Unfreezing:* an alternation of the forces acting on the individual, such that his stable equilibrium is disturbed

sufficiently to motivate him to make him ready to change; this can be accomplished either by increasing the pressure to change or by reducing some of the threats or resistances to change.

2. *Changing:* the presentation of a direction of change and the actual process of learning new attitudes. This process occurs basically by one or two mechanisms:

   a. *Identification:* the person learns new attitudes by identifying with and emulating some other person who holds these attitudes or

   b. *Internalization:* the person learns new attitudes by being placed in a situation in which new attitudes are demanded of him as a way of solving problems which confront him and which he cannot avoid, he discovers the new attitudes essentially for himself, though the situation may guide him or make it probable that he will discover only those attitudes which the influencing agent wishes him to discover.

3. *Refreezing:* the integration of the changed attitudes into the rest of the personality and/or into ongoing significant emotional relationships."

The principal who desires change on the part of personnel, according to the Schein model, would provide opportunity for communication to take place with those who have the desirable behavior and those whose behavior is to be influenced and changed. The refreezing of the desired behavioral change requires much interaction of the individual with his associates.

An interesting question is why some school organizations seem to change and adapt to more relevant learning environments with ease, while others do not. This is a phenomenon which is extremely difficult to understand and explain. What effect does the nature of the school organization have upon the individual? What effect does the individual have upon the school? What causes innovative individuals to be attracted to some school organizations and not to others? What causes some school organizations to change rapidly and others to resist change and, in some cases, to decline? What does the principal or the supervisor do to effect change?

Orlosky and Smith studied educational changes attempted during the past seventy-five years and reached the following conclusions:*

---

* From Daniel Orlosky and B. Othanel Smith, "Educational Change: Its Origins and Characteristics," *Phi Delta Kappan* 53:7 (1972), pp. 413–414. Used by permission.

1. Changes in methods of instruction are apparently more difficult to make successfully than changes in curriculum or administration.

2. Changes in instruction are most likely to originate within the education profession. In no case in the past did a successful change in instruction come from outside of education. Changes in ways of teaching and organizing instruction are neither the result of legislation nor of social pressure, but rather are the outcome of professional wisdom and research . . .

3. A change that requires the teacher to abandon an existing practice and to displace it with a new practice risks defeat. If teachers must be retrained in order for a change to be made, as in team teaching, the chances for success are reduced unless strong incentives to be retrained are provided.

4. Specific curricular changes such as the establishment of the elective system are often initiated from within the field of education. Successful changes in curriculum can originate either within the profession or from the outside. Neither point or origin monopolizes ideas for curricular change.

5. Curricular changes involving the addition of subjects or the updating of content are more permanent than changes in the organization and structure of the curriculum. Efforts to change the curriculum by integrating or correlating the content, or by creating new category systems into which to organize the content, are made at great risk. Complete or considerable displacement of an existing curriculum pattern is not likely to be permanent even if the faculty initially supports the change . . .

6. Changes in the curriculum that represent additions such as new subjects or changes in the substance of subjects can be made most securely with support from legislation or organized interest groups . . . On the other hand, if social opposition is pronounced, the probability of the change not being made is very high, or if it is made it is likely not to persist.

7. Efforts to alter the total administrative structure, or any considerable part of it, are likely to be unsuccessful.

8. Changes that represent additions or extensions of the educational ladder, such as junior college, are more likely

to be lasting than changes that entail general modifications of the administrative organization, such as flexible scheduling.

9. The lack of a diffusion system will lead to abortive change.
A change initiated in a particular school, in the
absence of a plan for diffusion, no matter how loudly
it may be acclaimed, is not likely to become widespread or to be permanently entrenched.

10. Changes that have the support of more than one critical
element are more likely to succeed. Compulsory education, with legal, social, and educational support, did
not have to overcome as much resistance as it would
have if only educators had supported it.

11. Changes will be resisted if they require educational personnel to relinquish power or if they cast doubt on educa-
tor roles. Accompanying legislative, legal, and financial impetus increases the probability of success in
such changes.

12. The weight of the cognitive burden is one of the significant
factors that determines the permanence of a change. If
the cognitive load is light, i.e., if not many people are
required to learn many new facts and procedures, a
change is more likely to persist than if the burden is
heavy. . .

13. . . .The source of the change appears to have far less to do
with its staying power than the support the change
receives and the strain it places upon the school personnel. . .[36]

The following eight generalizations by Owens and Steinhoff tend to
facilitate rapid diffusion and adoption of change:*

1. Relatively little new behavior is required as most of the
existing behavior may be retained.

2. The change is directed toward meeting needs that the participants in the organization already recognize and,
preferably, have already tried to meet.

3. The change promises practical payoff in terms that are
meaningful to the participants. This could be money,
prestige, recognition, or satisfaction from achievement.

---

* From Robert G. Owens and Carl R. Steinhoff, *Administering Change in Schools* ©
1976. Reprinted by permission of Prentice-Hall, Inc., Englewood Cliffs, New Jersey.

4. The change is introduced within the existing local power structure, utilizing local leadership, and respecting important local customs and traditions.

5. Those who are expected to implement the change are involved from beginning to the end, from planning through to evaluation: the participants have meaningful influence over important decisions in the process and are not merely engaged in peripheral matters.

6. Provision is made for a free flow of two-way communication between those responsible for managing the change and those expected to implement the change so that problems may be detected and considered quickly.

7. The managers of the change effort are flexible so that their tactics may be changed as needed to meet local conditions and unforeseen circumstances.

8. Provision is made for maintaining and supporting the change in the organization over time as it passes from the experimental stage to becoming part of regular operations. For example, it is difficult to prevent the washout of a change if the trial adoption was financed by external funding and final adoption of the change will require significant new outlays in the local expense budget in order to maintain it.[37]

The educational leader of the secondary school recognizes the school as a system in which any one change can effect all parts of the system. A simple schedule change such as dropping a class causes students to be scheduled in other classes, activities, or studies; gives the teacher another free period; requires reassignment; and on and on, until a large number of faculty is involved.

Change is a social process as well as a system process which involves forces for the change as well as forces against the change. The social processes demand that the educational leader provide opportunity for such interaction among the faculty, students, and in many instances, parents as well. Of course, some changes may be made unilaterally, and in some cases, they *must* be made unilaterally. Success of the change depends upon its magnitude and its acceptability to the school organization.

The school administrator usually has a choice between developing desirable change, or allowing it to occur without direction. The very nature of human organizations with changing personnel, students, and pressures from the outside will make change a constant variable within the local school.

Conner and Gingrich see the principal as unable to be a change agent if he or she is considered an administrator who is primarily "maintaining a smooth operation, status quo in procedures and successful goal achievement." According to them, principals have been found to be submissive, avoiding conflict, and resistant to change—the change agent role for principals is difficult to attain because of the layers of hierarchy which are part of the school organization.[38]

Conner and Gingrich believe "the main role of the change manager in public education is to provoke, facilitate and support the efforts of the school to understand itself." They list the following as essential areas of competence necessary for the change manager.

1. The ability to utilize appropriate findings from behavioral sciences.
2. An understanding of organizational dynamics and growth.
3. A working knowledge of informational and structural systems.
4. A working knowledge of personality growth and development.
5. The development of a philosophy of organizational change and growth related to our present knowledge of the individual, the group, the organization and the community in which we live.
6. A good working knowledge of accepted methods and techniques and the ability to utilize them effectively in the design of an organization renewal process.
7. The ability to plan and work with people in the organization on effective, immediate and long-range organization renewal efforts.[39]

The management of change is a necessary administrative function in a secondary school. There are tools, skills, and knowledge that can be attained by principals, to assist them in the direction of successful change. Skillful principals will find ways to overcome barriers. Development of a dynamic school organization that is able to cope with a changing society and provide leadership to society rather than follow it, is a desirable goal for educational leaders.

The authors suggest the following guidelines as helpful in developing a plan for change in the secondary school.

1. Learn to know and understand your community—communities have limits to the amount and kind of change they can bear.
2. Learn to know and understand your school, your faculty, and your students so that you can anticipate and cope with problems that arise with change.
3. Study and analyze carefully the possible effects that a change may have in the future. It may look good today, or next year, but what about five years from now?

4. Involvement of the faculty, students, and the community is essential in developing change that may affect them.

5. Your faculty and students must be convinced that a proposed change will enhance them before it will be accepted.

6. A gradual change is likely to be more successful than a sudden change. Use of the pilot approach should enhance the chance of success.

SUMMARY

Understanding the administration as problem solving, as decision making, as a social process, as working with groups, and as the process of change helps secondary leaders more fully comprehend the magnitude of their position.

The supervisor or principal of secondary schools should be knowledgeable in group theory as well as individual behavioral study. An understanding of group theory helps the educational leader receive feedback and promote improved education programs. Democratic administration demands much interaction with the faculty through various kinds and sizes of groups. Successful groups have common objectives, differentiation of roles, and shared values and norms.

Change can take place which affects various aspects of an organization including its (1) tasks, (2) structure, (3) technology, or (4) participants. Change is a social process which involves the interaction of people. It is also a systems process where a change in one subsystem may affect several other subsystems. Change has been studied to the extent that several guiding principles are available to assist in implementation.

NOTES

1. Andrew W. Halpin, ed., *Administrative Theory in Education,* cited by John K. Hemphill (Belmont, Calif.: Wadsworth Publishing Company, 1966), p. 89.

2. Ibid., p. 90.

3. Ibid., p. 91.

4. Ibid.

5. Ibid., p. 92.

6. Daniel E. Griffiths, *Administrative Theory*, copyright © 1959. Reprinted by permission of Appleton-Century-Crofts, Educational Division, Meredith Corporation.

7. Sherman Prey and Keith R. Getschman, eds., *School Administration: Selected Readings* (New York: Thomas Y. Crowell Co., 1968), p. 220.

8. Donald R. Cruickshank, "The Use of Theory in Educational Administration," *The National Elementary Principal* 44 (May, 1965), p. 17.

9. Griffiths, *Administrative Theory*, p. 76.

10. Ibid., pp. 77-80.

11. Harry J. Hartley, "Administrative Theory for the Practitioner," *The Bulletin of the National Association of Secondary School Principals* 59 (October, 1965), p. 276.

12. Griffiths, *Administrative Theory*, p. 82.

13. Ibid., pp. 82-83.

14. Ibid., pp. 84-85.

15. Ibid., p. 87.

16. Ibid., p. 88.

17. Ibid., p. 94.

18. Ibid., pp. 98-102.

19. Ronald F. Campbell and William W. Wayson, "Decision Making in the Elementary Principalship," *The Elementary Principal* 41 (January, 1962), p. 21.

20. Griffiths, *Administrative Theory*, pp. 108-112.

21. Campbell, "Decision Making," p. 72.

22. William E. Henry, "The Business Executive: Psychodynamics of a Social Role," *Human Relations in Administration*, ed. Robert Dubin (Englewood Cliffs, N.J.: Prentice-Hall, Inc., 1961), p. 169.

23. Chester Barnard, "Decision Making in Organization," *Human Relations in Administration*, ed. Robert Dubin (Englewood Cliffs, N.J.: Prentice-Hall, Inc., 1961), p. 322.

24. Jack Arthur Culbertson, "An Evaluation of Techniques for Studying Communication in School Organizations" (Ph.D. diss., University of California, 1955), p. 8.

25. R. J. Hills, "A New Concept of Staff Relations," *An Introduction to School Administration: Selected Readings*, ed. M. Chester Nolte (New York: Macmillian, 1966), p. 373.

26. Ibid., pp. 374-375.

27. Harold J. Laski, "The Limitations of the Expert," *Harper's Magazine* (December, 1930), pp. 102-106.

28. Ibid.

29. A. H. Maslow, "A Theory of Human Motivation," *Readings in Managerial Psychology*, ed. Harold J. Leavitt and Louis R. Pondy (Chicago: The University of Chicago Press, 1964), pp. 6-31.

30. Chris Argyris, "Individual Actualization in Complex Organizations," *Organizations and Human Behavior, A Book of Readings*, ed. Gerald Bell (Englewood Cliffs, N.J.: Prentice-Hall, Inc.), pp. 209-210.

31. Ibid.

32. Clovis R. Shepherd, *Small Groups, Some Sociological Perspectives* (San Francisco: Chandler Publishing Company, 1964), p. 69.

33. Ibid.

34. Robert G. Owens and Carl R. Steinhoff, *Administering Change in Schools* (Englewood Cliffs, N.J.: Prentice-Hall Inc., 1976), p. 52.

35. Edgar H. Schein, "Management Development as a Process of Influence," *Readings in Managerial Psychology*, ed. Harold J. Leavitt and Louis R. Pondy (Chicago: The University of Chicago Press, 1964), p. 335.

36. Daniel Orlosky and B. Othanel Smith, "Educational Change: Its Origins and Characteristics," *Phi Delta Kappan* 53:7 (1972), pp. 413–414.

37. Owens and Steinhoff, *Administering Change,* p. 32.

38. Daryl R. Conner and Newt Gingrich, "The Principal as a Change Manager," *American Secondary Education* 5:4 (September 1975), pp. 5–9.

39. Ibid.

4

Communication Between School Leaders and Their World

The school principal, as the center of the communication network within a school, is in a position to facilitate communication which leads to understanding and concerted effort on the part of members of the organization. Communication is considered by many writers to be the essence of the administrative process. Some would describe the school system as an elaborate communication network which permits coordination of the diversified function of the educational program.[1]

Communication, according to Van Miller et al., as an activity and as an instrument, is a pervasive concern of administration. They indicate that administration occupies the central position in both external and internal communication systems.[2]

Most writers differentiate between two kinds of communication systems or networks: formal and informal. The formal comes from official sources through channels consciously and deliberately established by the institution. Informal communications are transmitted in friendship groups or by the grapevine, and are based on social and personal relationships rather than on authority and positions.

Student and faculty size, complexity of educational programs, and specialization are making word-of-mouth and the informal communicative structure no longer sufficient. Hence, formal communication programs and procedures will have to take over where they have not been in use.

What guidelines should the educational leader follow in organizing the school for effective communication? While the literature does not reveal any concrete answers to this question, the increased emphasis on the study of communication and other aspects of administrative behavior in recent years is providing important clues for the administrator in designing an effective communication system. The educational leader who is successful should have knowledge of what constitutes good communication practices. Communication promotes success in cooperating with one another and determines, to a large extent, the efficiency and cohesiveness of an organization.

Communication practices of the educational leader play a vital role in faculty morale. Since it has been shown that student achievement is highest in schools with high faculty morale, it is essential that the school principal use effective communication practices.

Effective communication is not a one-way process from the principal to the faculty, but it is two-way as well as multi-directional. In democratic school organizations, principals facilitate communication, but do not attempt to channel all communication through their office. Principals must encourage dialogue among faculty members as well as with the faculty and themselves. Under autocratic administrations, communication is often from the top down; but in democratic organizations, communication is circular and originates from several sources.

The line and staff concept can be used to describe the basic organization of a school system. In the line, the authority and communication flow from the board of education through the superintendent and through the principal to the teacher. The staff personnel of this organizational concept have no line authority, except with their secretaries and assistants. The responsibility of staff personnel is to advise line personnel. Examples of line personnel would be the superintendent, the principal, and the teacher. Examples of staff personnel would include curriculum coordinators, secondary school coordinators, and elementary school coordinators.

In democratic school organizations, communication does not always follow the line or staff channel, but is often multi-directional. Administrators encourage horizontal as well as vertical communication. Certain policies in the use of communication channels are desirable, but they are designed to facilitate rather than to limit contacts.

THE MESSAGE, THE GATEKEEPERS, AND THE RECEIVERS

A two-step flow of communication from the originator of the communication, through another person, to the receiver of the message, is an important concept for the educational leader. Schramm's description of this concept, which he describes as gatekeeper, has bearing on school-community communications:

> Gatekeepers are placed throughout the information network.
> They include the reporter deciding which facts to put
> down . . . , the editor deciding what to print . . . , the librarian
> deciding what books to purchase, the teacher deciding what
> textbooks to use, the briefing officer deciding what facts to tell

his superiors and even the husband at the dinner table deciding what to tell his wife about the day's events at the office.[3]

Opinion leaders act as judges who interpret the message as they pass it on, so that the effectiveness of the communication is largely dependent on whether the gatekeepers are favorably or unfavorably disposed toward it. Administrators should realize that directly reaching all the citizens of a community is not necessary to be influential. Key leaders of opinion exist which have a strong influence on others. These opinion leaders are not necessarily members of the community power structure or those who are usually thought of as power leaders. Opinion leaders are distributed among all social and economic strata and all occupational groups.

Regardless of how much opinion and information may be passed on by opinion leaders within their own interest groups, they seldom pass information or opinion on to interest groups other than their own. Hence, the need exists for a school-community communications system in which one of the chief targets is groups.

Another facet of communication is the receiver of the message, which is the pivotal point in the communication process. The "basic challenge" of school-community communication is to communicate at the most effective level to the intended audience. Communications to the public may be wasted effort unless the community is analyzed and the message structured so that it will have maximum impact. A good communications system and the choice of appropriate communication media demand an understanding of the persons to whom communications are to be sent.

Communication of the Principal With Faculty

The communications of school principals with teachers can be divided into at least seven areas: (1) written, principal-initiated memos to faculty members, (2) written, principal-initiated bulletins to faculty members, (3) written, teacher-initiated memos to the principal, (4) oral, principal-initiated communication to faculty groups, (5) oral, principal-initiated communication through individual conferences with the principal, (6) oral, teacher-initiated group conferences with the principal, and (7) communications through the use of the intercom system.

Much of the principal's communication efforts will be spent in communicating with his or her faculty. Klahn, in his study of communication, found that "principals communicate most frequently with subordinates—38.5 percent of their communication was with teachers."[4] Administrators normally find that they are more successful with internal communications than with external communications with parents and community leaders. Homogeneous grouping, team teaching, nongraded schools, flexible scheduling, curriculum, and independent learning have common meanings for educators, but may mean something entirely different for the lay public. Principals who desire to communicate with the lay public must use words and symbols which transmit their messages so that they are accurately interpreted.

People often listen, but do not hear; they look, but do not see. If principals want to insure that a message they have sent has been received and interpreted in the intended way, they should question and receive feedback to determine the accuracy of perception. Principals who use the group process and allow for much dialog within the group is assuring that group members understand one another. While the school bulletin may appear to be a safe and convenient method of communication with the faculty, principals can never be sure that what is written has been read, or if it has been read, what the reader's interpretation will be.

Developing a more effective communication system can be accomplished if one is aware of barriers which must be overcome. Wiles and Lovell include the following as barriers to communication.

1. People use symbols or words that have different meanings.
2. Members of the group have different values.
3. Different perceptions of the problem.
4. Emphasis on status.
5. Conflict in interest.
6. Making decisions by majority vote rather than seeking consensus.
7. Attempts to keep feelings out of the discussion.
8. Use of words to prevent thinking.
9. Lack of desire to understand the other person's point of view or his feelings or his values or his purposes.
10. Lack of acceptance of diversity.
11. A one-way concept of cooperation.
12. Feelings of superiority.
13. Vested interests.
14. Feelings of personal insecurity.
15. An obvious attempt to sell.
16. The concepts that the sender and receiver have of their roles.
17. Negative feelings about the situation.[5]

These barriers will tend to cause both the sender and the receiver to distort the intended communication. Vested interests and conflicts of interest can be eliminated as communication barriers if both the communicator and the communicatee are assured that the sharing of ideas and thoughts will not deteriorate one's position, but actually enhance each other. Mutual respect, shared goals, and trust are essential ingredients of a successful communication system. While it is undesirable for all members of an organization to have similar shared values, improved communication can be a result if different value systems are understood and appreciated by the group.

The communication practices of a school principal can be improved in quality, channel utilization, and media. The quality of the principal's communication involves his or her speaking ability as well as writing style. A tape recorder would be a valuable aid for the principal preparing a talk for the faculty, students, or lay public. Effective speech habits can be attained and will insure a greater degree of accuracy in communication.

The principal's bulletin is more likely to be read if it is attractive as well as carefully written. Important announcements may be included in the bulletin, but the principal should determine if the bulletin has been read, and if so, how the message has been interpreted. This can be done best through informal questioning of the faculty.

The school intercom system is rapidly becoming a standard form of communication within a school. In some schools, the principal monopolizes this system, which results in many uninterested listeners. More effective utilization of the intercom system will occur through the use of a variety of persons making announcements or presenting programs. Regular periods for making announcements and the use of student announcers are two practices that are effective as well as being more popular with students and teachers. Announcements such as: "Will the student who is driving a blue Ford with license number 77-11578 please turn out his lights?" or "Please send Johnny Jones to the office," in the middle of the class period contribute to the ineffectiveness of the intercom system.

Principal's Communication With Students

The principal's communication with students should be more than through the intercom. Regular meetings with a student advisory committee can improve the understanding between students and the principal. Nicholson and Vanderbush conducted a study of communication between high school students and principals. They found that:

1. Principals communicate better with girls than boys.

2. Upperclassmen perceived themselves as being better informed than underclassmen. However, underclassmen were less cynical about their opportunity for input in the decision making process. Juniors and seniors tended to become disillusioned about the principal's desire to listen to them and consider their ideas.

3. Students in larger schools were more satisfied with communications with their principals than were students in small
schools. Communications reached their lowest point in middle
sized schools with 500 to 1,400 students. Large schools tended
to have more avenues of communication than did small
schools. Faculty-student committees, student representation on
school boards, representative student governments were more
common in larger schools than small schools. Large schools
have more administrative personnel than do small schools.
Almost all large schools have intercom systems, closed circuit
television, and school newspapers.

They recommend that open forum type communications with the
principal can improve upward communication, since this eliminated the
discomfort caused by students when they sit across the desk from an
authority figure.[6]

The principal's communication with students should be a regular
planned program. Assemblies, informal "coke" sessions, eating lunch
with students, the school newspaper, and visiting classes are some ways
that this "planned program" of communication can be accomplished.

Communications With the Lay Public

While change cannot always be regarded as good, suffice it to say that it
does and will occur. Since change can bring with it confusion as a result
of incomplete understanding, it is imperative that the secondary school
communicate with its public to attain the parental financial and moral
support that can strengthen the educational program. Support from
patrons is directly proportionate to the truthfulness, accuracy, and timeli-
ness of the public relations program. Public relations must be filled with
truth and facts. If the financial support offered by the community is
minimal, the public must share the responsibility of accepting the equa-
tion that they are getting what they are paying for. Secondary school personnel cannot embellish the facts to make them appear that more can be
purchased or serviced than money will allow. The glamour of such a
public relations program will not be so exciting, but it will administer to
the satisfaction of a properly informed community, the reward of which
will be continual respect and possibly more support. The basic concept of
school-community relations must involve two way communication and
not be based on a "selling approach" by the school.

Whereas the job of public relations may someday be assigned to a
specially trained person, today's principal is still held accountable for it
in his or her school. The principal is the major source of information
regarding school programs and activities.

There is no single approach to an effective community relations program, however, the following elements have been proposed as basic to a sound community relations program.

1. Community relations involves a planned effort.
2. Community relations involves everyone in the educational system.
3. Community relations includes involvement as well as information.
4. The community relations program must support innovation and creativity.
5. The community relations program must be accompanied by a commitment of time, resources and personnel.
6. The community relations program must provide for appropriate evaluation procedures.
7. The community relations program must reach the community power structure.[7]

One extremely important phase of a school-community relations program is determining the effectiveness of the program. Evaluation should be a continuous, planned effort. Included among those aspects to be evaluated are the following:

1. Analyze the effectiveness of the various types of media being utilized.
2. Insure steps are taken to remedy problems discovered in the school-community relations program.
3. Determine if appropriate messages are being received by intended receivers.
4. Analyze community feedback channels to see if they are effective.
5. Determine if the lay public and the school personnel are clear on the goals of the school.
6. Determine to what extent the school personnel is involved in community activities.
7. How effective is the use of available community resources?

An analysis of the community is vital if one is to achieve maximum effectiveness of the school-community relations program. The following activities have been suggested as contributing to a more effective community analysis.

1. Determine the organizational structures within the community and outside state and national agencies that affect it.

2. Identify individuals who have decision-making roles.
3. Review available statistics, records, and documents related to the local community.
4. Study the media and press treatment of the schools.
5. Study the community norms and values.
6. Maintain visibility in the political arena in order to understand how to be functional within the political community.[8]

It is readily apparent that the principal alone is not able to conduct an effective school-community relations program, but must enlist the assistance of others such as faculty, students, employees, and patrons. It is vitally important that the involvement and support of faculty, students, and employees be secured through an effective internal communications program in order that they can be effectively utilized in the school-community relations program with the lay public.

SUMMARY

The best communication provides for a two-way flow of information. If principals are to improve their schools, or even maintain status quo, they must have a clear understanding of the goals of the educational program. These goals may come from state legislation, local school board policy, community interests, and objectives developed by members of the local school staff, or pressures from any of these groups. Those goals that the principals feel are inappropriate should be reviewed with their staff, the community, and state officials in order that they may be modified or deleted altogether.

The task is not completed with a mere understanding of the goals; principals must interact with the faculty and community members to insure all these groups have adequate understanding, and then provide avenues to receive feedback for possible change that may be desirable.

NOTES

1. Stephen J. Knezevich, *Administration of Public Education* (New York: Harper and Row, Publishers, 1975), p. 66.

2. Van Miller, George R. Madden, and James B. Kincheloe, *Public Administration of American School Systems* (New York: The Macmillan Company, 1972), p. 372.

3. Wilbur Schramm, *Men, Messages and Media, A Look at Human Communication* (New York: Harper and Row, Publishers, 1973), pp. 138-139.

SUMMARY

4. Richard P. Klahn, "An Analysis of Patterns of Communication of High School Principals in Selected School Systems," (Ph.D. diss., University of Iowa, 1962).

5. Kimball Wiles and John T. Lovell, *Supervision for Better Schools,* 4th ed., (Englewood Cliffs, N.J.: Prentice-Hall, Inc., 1975), pp. 91–93.

6. Everett W. Nicholson and Walter A. Vanderbush, "Communications Between High School Students and Principals: Problems and Promises," *American Secondary Education* (Akron, Ohio, Ohio Association of Secondary Administrators) 6:3 (June, 1976), pp. 7–8.

7. Robert Byrne and Edward Powell, *Strengthening School Community Relations* (Reston, Va.: National Association of Secondary School Principals, 1976), pp. 2–4.

8. Ibid., pp. 14–16.

5

Recruitment, Selection, and Orientation of Professional Staff

Of all the tasks faced by the secondary school administrator, none is more important than the acquisition and maintenance of a highly qualified and productive teaching staff. The opportunity to perform this task in an exemplary manner has been enhanced recently as the teacher supply and demand picture has changed markedly. Projections of teacher supply and demand indicate beginning teachers will be in excess supply ranging from 80 to 150 thousand through the 1980–81 school year.[1]

It is well known how administrators for too long had to be greatly concerned with making sure each vacancy on the teaching staff was filled prior to the opening of school in September. Now, however, in many subject fields the number of available teachers exceeds the number of positions open. This is almost unprecedented in the history of American education. Exceptions to this, of course, include the depression period of the thirties and the war years. Of course, geography plays an important role and some areas of the United States will always find they have a short supply of teachers. Overall, however, the opportunities for administrators to be more selective in filling teaching vacancies have never been better.

Many reasons may be suggested for this reversal of the job market in teaching. Two of the more prevalent ones are: (1) the increased number of college graduates generally, which provides more trained people in all fields including teaching, and (2) the sincere desire of young people to enter fields where they can serve humanity, with teaching offering a very accessible entry to this type of concerned service.

Thus, the school administrator has the opportunity to approach the important task of securing teachers with substantial discernment. While more teachers are currently available for openings on faculties, it should be remembered that high caliber teachers probably will remain in short supply. Therefore, teacher recruitment and selection must be well planned in order to obtain the better teachers, and yet hold down the costs of recruiting.

This chapter is broken into three major areas. The first relates to recruitment, which is the process of providing the efforts to increase the number of professional personnel who are available to accept teaching positions. The second aspect is selection, which deals with the process of determining the professional staff from the available pool of applicants. A third section relates to the appropriate induction and orientation of new staff members.

RECRUITMENT

As indicated earlier, the next few years suggest a healthy surplus of candidates for teaching positions in the public schools. However, Gorton[2] says the primary objective of a district's recruiting should be to attract the *most* qualified and outstanding individuals. A commentary on teacher recruitment was offered by Lindley J. Stiles:

> . . . Teacher recruitment policies over the years echo the familiar refrain of cheering sections at high school football games. "Hit 'em again, hit 'em again—harder! harder!" The results achieved tend to prove that trying harder isn't enough—particularly when the trying is motivated more by fantasy than by reality.[3]

Stiles goes on to say that it is too often assumed that certain improvements will produce an adequate supply of high quality teachers. He lists these improvements as: (1) class size reduced, (2) certification based more on academic courses, (3) teachers given the security of tenure, (4) uniform pay increases and retirement annuities, (5) a respect by the general public for teaching is increased, and (6) more diligent recruitment campaigns. Rather than doubt the validity of such approaches when they fail, the response is only to try harder.[4] The suggestion for improved recruiting practices utilizing new approaches could well be heeded by teacher recruiters.

At the federal level the need for improved recruiting practices was recognized several years ago, when in June, 1967, President Johnson signed the Educational Professions Development Act into law. Recruitment of teachers was one of the provisions of the act. At that time, teachers in mathematics, physical sciences, English, and foreign languages were in short supply as were those trained in such special fields as remedial reading, speech correction, and early childhood development. This act provided recruitment energies be directed toward supplying teachers in these special areas of need. Also, money was provided for recruitment among talented high school students, homemakers, and others to engage them in these needed occupations.

As the provisions of this act were put into full operation, it did help a great deal in the recruitment of teachers in those fields where teachers were in short supply. However, it does not alter the fact that present recruitment methods are archaic and need to be overhauled. Every school district has its own method of recruiting teachers. Large cities sometimes rely heavily on formal civil-service types of tests while smaller districts tend to do very little formal testing. Most administrators try to culminate the search process with the personal interview. Of course, credentials and other written personal descriptive data are also necessary.

The Recruitment Program

Principals have a duty to identify and describe positions to be filled. Kimbrough and Nunnery[5] feel these needs should be communicated widely in order to comply with federal laws on affirmative action in recruitment, employment, and other aspects of personnel activities.

A total recruitment program does not begin with seeking prospective teachers after they have graduated from college. Too often this may be the case. The recruitment process should begin much earlier—at least during the secondary school years of the prospective teacher. Here, principals can initiate an activity for their faculty to obtain their combined judgments on the way prospects appear as future teachers. Principals will want their teachers to call attention to boys and girls with whom their contacts may be limited. In larger schools, some kind of committee may need to be formed to carry on this work.

Principals will also want to use their "good" teachers in another way that many times may be overlooked. The typical high school boy or girl probably has no notion that there is such a body of knowledge as that produced about learning in the past twenty to thirty years. Through proper utilization of their teaching staff, principals should be able to transmit some elements of pedagogy to worthy candidates through demonstrations and cadet experience programs. The idea here is to offer interested students an opportunity to explore teaching as a profession at an earlier age, while they are searching for possible professional careers. It may even be advantageous to do this at an earlier level than the high school.

Providing good public relations is another vital area in which principals must work. If principals want to encourage the young to enter the teaching profession, they, along with their guidance workers, must be able to show progressively improved conditions as to salaries, buildings, teaching loads, respectability of teaching, and personal prestige. In this same relationship, principals will want to enlist the assistance of parents and interested persons in the community to help students realize that the education of children is among the more desirable occupations of the community. It should be mentioned that there is more than the provision of salaries to be considered. Principals should direct their efforts to enlightening members of the community of the good work that teachers do in an attempt to bring about their worthy appreciation. Recognition of a job well done goes beyond the boundaries of monetary rewards. In the long run, this recognition will do much to add to the enthusiasm of the present group of teachers which will increase the attractiveness of the profession for the teachers of the future.

Another functional area in which principals should operate is the development of student teaching programs in their schools. Through professional guidance in the student teaching program, principals have one of the best opportunities to improve the teaching profession. It is they who will determine to a large extent whether the beginning teacher is to receive guided experiences or haphazard utilization of time. Principals should set the pattern of thinking in their schools which will determine whether a student teaching program will transmit some of the professional know-how that the experienced teacher has, or whether it is a questionable way of getting some of the routine aspects of teaching achieved. Principals should encourage their teachers to learn to withdraw from direct contact in teaching so that the beginner may receive the experiences that provide the opportunity to grow professionally.

The inservice program also can be a valuable recruitment tool. The kind of activity going on among teachers in the improvement of learning will have an effect upon the trainee in the kind of attitude he or she develops toward inservice growth. Just what is going on in the inservice program at a given time will depend greatly upon the skill of principals. They not only play an important part in developing the inservice program and providing it with proper direction, but in many instances, they are instrumental in procuring the amount of time that is allocated for the program.

Above all, as potential new recruits enter the schools for cadet or student teaching experiences, it must be remembered that their impression of teaching, and that which they will articulate to others, depends in many instances upon their first experiences. Principals must recognize this and insure that such people are provided with every condition for success. This does not mean they need to be coddled, but they should be given a chance to get their feet on the ground. For if they fail in teaching through no fault of their own, the teaching profession will ultimately be the prime loser. Such experience will have a ripple effect in providing the necessary stimulus to sound positive or negative notes to other prospective teachers contemplating entering the educational field.

It has been well established through the literature on recruitment and the analysis of the problems involved that a good recruitment program should be based upon research which has accrued. Considerable data on teacher supply and demand are available from the National Education Association, state teachers associations, State Departments of Public Instruction, college placement offices, and other similar agencies.

College and university placement bureaus are the usual source of supply of teachers. Here, a listing of new teachers as well as those with experience who are seeking new positions can be found. Most schools rely heavily upon the placement bureaus of institutions located within their own state. Others are also aware of the possibilities of recruiting in neighboring states, and contact the colleges and universities there.

It is good practice to establish good rapport with these placement bureaus. A negative attitude on the part of college placement bureau officials toward a school district could possibly affect its supply of new staff members. Personal visits plus frequent communications would assist in establishing and maintaining good rapport.

College and university placement services are not to be considered the only source of applicants. A few of the other sources include:

1. Private placement offices.
2. Professional organizations.
3. Association of School, College and University Staffing Computer Service.
4. National Education Association Search.
5. Teacher Recruitment Office, State Employment Security Division.[6,7]

Suggested information to accompany the announcement of vacancies might include: (1) previously prepared position descriptions, (2) information on the school and the community, and (3) application blanks.

Up to this point, we have considered how the administrator recruits teachers, but we have only considered the qualifications desired by the school system—not what characteristics of the school interest candidates. A study on the problem of how to attract first-year teachers was made by Robert J. Babcock. The survey reveals what 491 college seniors (all teacher education majors) considered most important in making decisions about their first teaching positions.[8]

Of course, the views varied widely and there were differences of opinions between groups of young men and women, between married and unmarried women, and between bachelors and benedicts. However, Babcock found that a broad picture does emerge from the survey results:

1. All respondents agree that geographic location is the prime consideration—though for different reasons.
2. The philosophy of a district means a lot to these young teachers—but not as much as the size of the paycheck.
3. If you are looking for young women to teach in elementary schools, be specific about grade-level openings.
4. It's not too important whether your principal is a great guy or a grouch.
5. The likelihood of romance apparently influences many neophyte teachers in deciding where they will start their careers.[9]

After considering the results of the study, Babcock lists six important points to be considered if one is going to effectively relate his or her school district to first-year teachers' employment wants:

1. Emphasize your district's geographic location.
2. Make information available on both the cost of living and the housing situation in your area.
3. Level with married men about salary potential.
4. Expand on your district's "educational philosophy."
5. Stress the freedom to teach that professionals enjoy in your school system.
6. Take a tip from the Madison Avenue ad pushers: Bait your hook with essence of orange blossom.[10]

A survey similar to Babcock's could be taken within any given school system or district to determine just why the teachers presently employed chose that particular school district. The data could well yield insight into promising recruitment practices for each individual school or school district.

THE SELECTION PROCESS

Once the applications are filed, secondary school principals, because they are expected to lead their staff, must be influential in the teacher selection process. However, Sergiovanni[11] indicates that the selection process should be developed as a team effort involving those at all levels of administration in the schools. This selection process takes on even more importance when one examines the current rate of teacher turnover. It is much lower than in past years, which means that once a selection is made, teachers are inclined to stay in the same school position for a considerable length of time.

The selection process can be a vehicle whereby principals can hire a diverse faculty—a faculty that reflects many beliefs, attitudes, and backgrounds. Robert Presthus[12] in his analysis of complex hierarchical organizations has theorized that such organizations contain three types of individuals or actors. These actors are referred to by Presthus as upward mobiles, indifferents, and ambivalents. The upward mobile actor is an "organization man." He is able to synthesize his personal goals with the goals of the organization. The indifferent actor is one who adapts to the organization by withdrawing from it. He has succeeded, in other words, in living a life apart from the organization without being insubordinate. The ambivalents have values that might be in conflict with organizational values and "are a source of conflict, but they provide the insight, motivation, and the dialect that inspire change."

Principals, as well as other school officials, have been prone to hire the upward mobile and indifferent actors. This is a natural result of an understandable aversion to conflict. But modern experts in the area of school administration suggest that conflict, provided it does not completely threaten to shatter the organization's equilibrium, is, in fact, a sign of organizational health. Therefore, the hiring of ambivalent actors is desirable.

What has not been determined yet is the degree of ambivalency or conflict a school system can withstand. Obviously, upward mobiles are useful in the school setting. The indifferent actor can also make a valuable contribution provided he is dedicated and knowledgeable. But neither of these types are capable of thinking about change—a task too important to be thrust solely upon the principal. The teachers must do some of it.

In addition to actually selecting teachers, principals can engage in other activities that will influence the selection process. They may become involved in setting up the general policy of the district pertaining to this area. They can help prepare job analyses and the standards the candidates must meet in order to obtain teaching positions. They can advise committees who are preparing applications and brochures. They can help determine specific procedures. Indeed, they can at least act in an advisory capacity in all the various functions directly connected with employment of professional staff personnel.

Teacher selection can be thought of as a process in which a professional judgment is made, both objectively and subjectively, in order to determine if a candidate will be hired for a particular position. Historically, in many instances, the major responsibility for choosing staff personnel singularly resided with the superintendent. As suggested before, this has changed rapidly in recent years. More and more teacher selection has become identified as an administrative function shared by secondary school principals, department heads, and in some cases, teachers representing both the subject area concerned and other subject areas. Functionally, representation from all of these should form a selection committee that could operate in a most optimum manner.

Of course, situations still vary from where the school superintendent has the major responsibility for screening teaching candidates (usually in small school systems), to systems where a centralized personnel department performs this function. In any case, consultation with secondary school principals has generally been increased. This trend is most commendable as it is the principal who will supervise and work most closely with the teacher.

Interview

The interview is a form of contact between the employer and the prospective employee which should receive the most careful consideration. Most employers regard it as the determining factor in the selection of beginning teachers. Most candidates regard it as an important element in their choice of corporations.

Thomas F. Koerner feels that the individual's personality has a way of permeating everything he or she does, and that the investigation of the applicant's personality should take priority in the interview. He feels that everyone who is to teach must have a personality that is conducive to working with youngsters. Koerner says that the skilled questions of an interviewer can determine an individual's basic notions about anything and everything. The job of the interviewer is to get the candidate to talk easily and freely in an uninhibited manner. Koerner believes that in order to accomplish this feat, the interviewer must be an effective questioner.[13]

The following twenty-five questions are ones which Koerner feels penetrate the superficial and uncover an individual's personality indirectly because they require the person to think while talking, and they require on-the-spot decisions as well as explanations and reexplanations. The questions are:

1. Where do you want to be ten years from now?
2. In your opinion, what are your strengths?
3. What weaknesses do you perceive in yourself?
4. How do you compensate for these weaknesses?
5. If you had to describe your personality, how important would a characteristic like sense of humor be?
6. What are your cultural interests?
7. How do you spend your weekends and holidays?
8. What kinds of vacations do you enjoy the most?
9. What importance do you place on communication skills?
10. What methods of communication would you say you are skilled in?
11. How do you react to persons with whom you have personality conflicts?
12. What kinds of community projects appeal to you?
13. What has been a recent activity which gave you satisfaction?
14. What has been a recent failure of yours?
15. How do you describe your physical and emotional reactions to failure?
16. What kind of project makes you most proud of your work?
17. What kinds of activities depress you the most?
18. What kinds of books and magazines do you find most rewarding?
19. What is your perception of the role of the student in his current school environment?

20. How would you describe the basic responsibilities of students, teachers, counselors, administrators?
21. What role do you perceive for yourself in the total environment of the school?
22. How would you describe your relation to your immediate supervisor?
23. How do you rid yourself of the traditional solution in order to approach the imaginative and creative solution?
24. What past experience do you value the most?
25. When you want something badly, how do you get it?[14]

This list of questions points out the many ways in which the interview process may be used to look into the personality of the prospective teacher. Thus, the interview can be utilized to determine information and observations which other methods cannot supply.

It is interesting to note some of the important considerations in the interview process which have recently been suggested by Castetter.[15] A preliminary interview is normally utilized for screening purposes, and the number and length of interviews with a candidate increases with the importance of the position to be filled. A structured interview is one which utilizes a set of questions as listed earlier in this section, and is used to compare candidates on a systematic basis. While there are many limitations and weaknesses to the interview as a selection tool, it still remains the most widely used technique. This plea is for a certain amount of training for the interviewers to become skilled in the utilization of the process.

ORIENTATION OF BEGINNING TEACHERS

Relatively few professions are quite as demanding of their beginners as is the teaching profession. And these demands have historically taken their toll in the rate of withdrawals from the profession. All too often bewildered novice teachers, fresh out of college, are tossed a schedule of classes and activities; weighted down with unexplained syllabi, handbooks, and sheets of directions and regulations; and then ushered into their classroom and career. Here, they are to prove their proficiency to their students, fellow faculty members, administrators, parents, and school boards. They are expected to measure up in just a matter of months to the teaching performance of experienced teachers firmly entrenched in the system. And they are often expected to take on without complaint the extra burdens of school activities and difficult classes which the elders on the staff no longer care to accept.

Thus, it could be a great waste of time, effort, and money to go to a great deal of trouble to select the right personnel only to lose much of the investment through failure to orient the new teacher properly. Far too often a prospective teacher is put through a thorough screening process when being hired for a position only to be poorly oriented to the school. A teacher is an important investment to the school and community, and proper orientation is one of the most important aspects of producing a successful and well-adjusted teacher. The number of first-rate teachers who leave the profession is not only higher than it should be, but a loss the teaching profession cannot afford.

New teachers may be in possession of a college degree, state certification credentials, and sufficient knowledge of their academic field, but they are still novices when it comes to teaching; and they, as well as everyone else about them, are fully aware of this fact. For them the experience will be a totally new one, more challenging than any other professional experience previously encountered. For one thing, they will have a wide audience of observers (delegated or otherwise) who will consciously or unconsciously rate their performance. As a result, they will often feel insecure, sometimes to a disconcerting degree. It is a vital task of principals and experienced staff members in the school to help the young teachers gain security and contentment with their chosen vocation. Failure to provide this systematic understanding and assistance is to take a real chance at losing potentially good or exceptional teachers.

Human relations in the teaching profession are no different than human relations in business, industry, or the world at large. Teachers seek the satisfaction of needs common to all humanity. The fulfillment of these basic aspirations is vitally important if teachers are to make the contribution for which they have been educated, and if their students are to attain the purpose for which they have enrolled in the institution. If a teacher is dissatisfied, is forced into a narrowness of outlook and professional practice, does not experience a bond of unity with the principal and faculty at large, the potentials of his or her students may also be stifled to a large extent.

In regard to their initial induction into the system, first-year teachers consider the following experiences as most significant in adjusting themselves to their new position: friendly fellow workers; conferences with the principal or supervisor; pre-school faculty meetings; faculty social gatherings; guided tour of the school plant; written statement of school policies; conferences with other school officials; school handbook; pre-school workshops; and participation in making school policies for the year.

What beginning teachers value as important to them must be made the core of such a program in the school. Beginning teachers as well as the veterans seek security, pleasant working conditions, a sense of belonging, fair treatment, a sense of achievement and growth, recognition of contribution, participation in deciding and carrying out school policies, and opportunities to maintain self-respect. A program built around these teacher needs is a far cry from the former programs of supervision, confined to classroom observation and inspection.

The beginning teachers are often faced with problems not of their own making. The school often expects the beginning teacher to be a finished product. A surgeon just out of medical school is not expected to go right into private practice. A newly graduated lawyer does not immediately begin arguing cases in court. An engineer fresh out of college often has an orientation ranging from three months to two and sometimes three years.[16] Why then does the school expect the beginning teacher to be a finished product ready to be in complete charge of numerous students plus assume the extra duties required of experienced teachers?

A Detailed Orientation Program

There are many sound ways of inducting and orienting new teachers. The principal plays a critical role in this stage of a new teacher's training but all staff members have important roles to play. The total staff should develop the kind of program best for their particular situation. However, the National Association of Secondary School Principals has been involved with one such program which utilizes the concept of a "buddy system" or pairing of new teachers with experienced teachers. The planning and allocating of the activities of the induction-orientation program remain prime functions of the principal. If success is truly desired, certain recommendations need to be carefully considered and implemented. The details of the program follow:

1. Take into account the individual differences in new personnel.
2. Give limited teaching responsibility to the new teacher.
3. Aid in gathering instructional materials.
4. Assign cooperative teachers whose own loads are reduced so that they can work with the new teachers in their own classrooms.
5. Shift to more experienced teachers those students who create problems beyond the ability of the novice to handle effectively.
6. Offer specialized instruction concerning the character of the community, the neighborhood, and the students he is likely to encounter.[17]

Activities in the induction-orientation program can be conveniently put into a time sequence that has four phases according to Hunt and his associates.*

---

* From Douglas W. Hunt, "Teacher Induction: An Opportunity and a Responsibility," *The Bulletin of the National Association of Secondary School Principals* 330 (October, 1968), pp. 132–134. Used by permission.

Phase I. Time Before School Starts

Emphasis during the summer should be on helping the beginning teacher feel at home. The principal and the cooperating teacher, who has already been assigned, might share the following:

1. Greet the beginner after the employment interview.
2. Introduce him to his department head and other administrative personnel.
3. Take him on a tour of the school.
4. Carefully explain his assignment.
5. Review texts and syllabi to be used.
6. Review the teacher's manual.
7. Discuss the nature of the community.

Phase II. Special Beginning Teacher Orientation

Emphasis during this period should be placed on helping the new teacher understand his assignment and prepare for the first week of school. This is not the time for speeches on theory but rather lots of practical assistance and advice. Some suggested activities are:

1. Familiarization with the building and special teaching resources.
2. Explanation of school schedule.
3. Explanation of attendance procedures and record-keeping system.
4. Identify supporting personnel and their functions.
5. Set up classrooms.
6. Review opening-of-school procedures.

It is particularly advantageous for the cooperating teacher or teachers to attend all orientation meetings so that they can review the more important points with the beginners.

Phase III. First Semester

At this time the regular daily group meetings begin with emphasis on the *practical* arts of teaching. Groups and individuals, led by the cooperating teachers, should concentrate on such things as lesson planning, organization of materials and methods, ability grouping, testing, grading, supplementary material, homework, disciplinary techniques and policy, guidance services, specialist services and parent-community relations.

In addition, activities during this period could also include observation of experienced teachers, visits to a materials or curriculum center, a tour of the community and training in use of audio-visual materials.

During the first semester, the first concern should be with survival and then getting on top of the job.

Phase IV. Starting About January

At this time, there should be a gradual shift from the practical daily concerns to a longer range, sometimes more theoretical, approach. Activities designed to help the beginners articulate and analyze their philosophy of education, their performance in the classroom, and their understanding of their students might include the following: case studies, observation of their students in other classrooms, demonstrations of various teaching techniques, increased cooperative teaching, and techniques in class participation.

As many beginning teachers have said and as the administrators now recognize, more constructive teacher *learning* can take place the first year on the job than in four years of teacher training, but for this to *happen* there must be a structure and direction.[18]

This format or modifications of it might indeed prove to be valuable to school administrators as they develop their own orientation and induction programs for beginning teachers or even new teachers to their particular school system.

SUMMARY

No task faced by the secondary school administrator is more important than securing high quality, productive teaching staff members. The current supply and demand picture is most favorable to securing a great number of applicants for any given teaching position in the school. Thus, the principal is in an excellent position to recruit top talent. Recruiting efforts should not diminish, however, even with the favorable supply and demand market, for the demand for the "best" teachers is always fraught with keen competition.

A second major phase of the staffing process is that of selection. This requires a team effort from all levels of the school staff. Teacher selection can be thought of as a process in which professional judgments are made, both objectively and subjectively in an optimum manner.

The third facet, and certainly as important as the first two, is the orientation programs for the new staff members. The teaching profession has historically been known as quite demanding on its beginners. It behooves the principal to develop a systematic, effective, and efficient way in which the new teacher is acclimated to the school environment with minimal chances of failure. One excellent orientation program is known as the buddy-system and has been developed to a most viable level by the National Association of Secondary School Principals.

NOTES

1. From Commissioners Report on the Education Professions, HEW, *Projections of Teacher Supply and Demand to 1980–81,* 1975, p. 10.

2. Richard A. Gorton, *School Administration: Challenge and Opportunity for Leadership* (Dubuque, Iowa: Wm. C. Brown Company, 1976), p. 149.

3. Lindley J. Stiles, "Policy and Perspective," *The Journal of Educational Research* 61 (July–August, 1968), p. 1.

4. Ibid.

5. R. B. Kimbrough, and M. Y. Nunnery, *Educational Administration, An Introduction* (New York: Macmillan Publishing Company, Inc., 1976), pp. 178–179.

6. Carroll L. Lang, and Emery Stoops, *Teacher Recruitment—Problems, Promises and Proven Methods* (Englewood Cliffs, N.J.: Prentice-Hall, Inc., 1968), p. 29.

7. G. E. Arnstein, "The American Education Placement Service," *School and Society* (Summer, 1967), p. 299.

8. Robert J. Babcock, "How to Hook Those First-Year Teachers," *School Management* 12 (March, 1968), p. 60.

9. Ibid.

10. Ibid., p. 62.

11. Thomas J. Sergiovanni, *Handbook for Effective Department Leadership* (Boston: Allyn and Bacon, Inc., 1977), p. 188.

12. Robert Presthus, *The Organizational Society* (New York: Alfred A. Knopf, Inc., 1962).

13. Thomas F. Koerner, "Interviewing: Ask the Right Questions," *The Clearing House* 44 (October, 1969), pp. 102–103.

14. Ibid., pp. 103–104.

15. William B. Castetter, *The Personnel Function in Educational Administration* (New York: Macmillan Publishing Co., 1976), p. 189.

16. Douglas Hunt and Associates, "Teacher Induction—A Key to Excellence," *The Bulletin of the National Association of Secondary School Principals* (May, 1968), p. 68.

17. Douglas W. Hunt, "Teacher Induction: An Opportunity and a Responsibility," *The Bulletin of the National Association of Secondary School Principals* 330 (October, 1968), pp. 132–134.

18. Ibid.

6

Improving Instruction

Improvement of instruction should be concerned not only with increasing students' academic achievement but must also involve development of better student attitudes and self-concepts.

The techniques and procedures involved in the improvement of instruction are many and varied. Three primary procedures are inservice education, teacher evaluation, and teacher supervision. As will become evident in this chapter, these concepts cannot be considered as separate entities, however, as they are highly related. The relationship between the terms *evaluation* and *supervision* is very strong. Evaluation will be considered as a part of a supervision program. Inservice education can occur in various ways such as at faculty meetings, workshops, school visitations, conferences, and university courses.

With the appearance of behavioral objectives, the open space concept, and the growing concern for the development of humane schools, the techniques utilized in measuring and fostering the improvement of instruction are changing. This chapter recognizes that not all schools are at the same stage of development as they relate to the concepts of behavioral objectives, open space schools, and humane schools. Therefore, some techniques will be presented for those at various levels of development.

With the continuing development of behavioral objectives, open space concept schools, and humane schools, the teacher will become less and less the center of attention and will function more and more as a consultant in the student learning process. The teacher will need to be skilled in (1) the development of learning activity packets, (2) the proper sequencing of learning, (3) remedial procedures to assist those who need individual assistance, (4) working with students at all levels on an individual basis, (5) working with small groups of students to clarify points and to motivate them toward increasing their knowledge, (6) developing techniques by which achievement of behavioral objectives can be measured, (7) cooperating with other teachers in the development of units of learning, and (8) assisting students to take responsibility for their own self-discipline.

The continuing development of behavioral objectives, open space concept schools, and humane schools will mean that teachers will be less concerned about (1) measuring group achievement through the use of group tests, (2) instructional techniques such as lecturing, (3) preparing detailed lesson plans, (4) dealing with discipline techniques to control groups of students, and (5) textbook assignments.

The improving of instruction is focused upon developing a meaningful and humane educational program. Trump describes some features of a humane school as follows:

1. Focuses on options rather than on uniformity in developing and administering policies and practices.
2. Devises a program for each pupil in which he can move forward with success in terms of his own talents and interests no matter how diverse they may be.
3. Has continuous progress arrangements so that each pupil may proceed at his own pace under competent supervision with a variety of self directing, self-motivating and self-evaluating materials and locations.
4. Recognizes that the principal more than any other person creates a humane environment in the school, and, therefore, frees him from routine managerial tasks to permit him to get out of the office to work with pupils and teachers to develop more humane programs and procedures for everyone.[1]

As stated, the instructional leader must be free of administrative details if he or she is to properly function in developing a program which has options rather than uniformity, and provides for individual needs rather than attempting to mold each student into the same pattern. Continuous progress programs form the basis for the building of the curriculum in secondary schools.

Improving instruction involves changing people. Therefore, the principal or the supervisor of secondary education must be aware of techniques to use in assisting people to accept and practice new ideas. There is no question that schools are lagging in developing more effective instructional techniques. The following illustrates the serious lag that schools currently exhibit:

An educational consultant likes to speculate on the probable reactions of Thomas Jefferson to the 20th century if Jefferson were to arise from the grave and accompany the consultant on a trip. Jefferson would surely find most of the experiences totally incomprehensible—airports, jet travels, cars and car rentals, credit card purchases, and so forth. The consultant is convinced that Jefferson would be in danger of losing his sanity, until they arrived at a school and entered a school room. Only then would Jefferson be able to breathe a sign of relief and say, "Ah, just as I remembered it."[2]

Glines suggests the following guidelines for planning and effecting improvements in individual schools:

1. Developing committed leadership.
2. Review the literature on the change process.
3. Evolve a philosophy for the school.
4. Create a dissatisfaction within the school. (Create dissatisfaction with the status quo.)
5. Overcome the barriers. (Some of these barriers can be attributed to school superintendents, some to college professors, to state departments, to boards of education, to parents, to teachers and to students.)
6. After identifying the barriers to change, one way of overcoming these impediments is to arrange for models.
7. Consider the budget.
8. Select an alternative—will all the teachers and all the students be placed in the new program or would it be better to start with a third of the students and staff?
9. Provide for ongoing evaluation.
10. Sell-implement sell. (For example, if the staff wants to begin flexible scheduling, they must be sure that enough of the school board and central office and parents and students are convinced that this would be a worthy endeavor if the project is to be a success.)[3]

There is no question but that the principal or the supervisor of the secondary school must provide the impetus and planning for improvement of instruction. The educational program of any school should be based upon clear objectives that can be measured.

The authors recommend that the educational leader use the "spin-out" approach in changing people and schools. That is, try an innovation on a pilot or experimental basis to determine its worth and acceptance. If deemed to be successful, expand to other parts of the school as it is approved by the majority of the faculty and students. Certainly, no educational program, no matter how worthwhile, can be forced on the faculty or students.

INSERVICE EDUCATION

There is no need for inservice education in the American school system if the system is currently accomplishing all of its purposes at the 100 percent level. That is, if the schools are perfect. Obviously, all schools and faculties can be improved, since perfection in American education is far from being attained. The principal must have a comprehensive knowledge of programs available for use in improving instruction.

The term *inservice education* refers to professional learning experiences of people who are employed as teachers. The primary characteristic of this type of teacher education is that it takes place after the completion of some program of teacher preparation, known as preservice education.

Today, a wide variety of sources provide inservice education for teachers. Institutions of higher education continue to offer a variety of evening, summer, and intensive courses in education. Although an individual's time and money are usually required to participate in this training, graduate credit is often awarded upon successful completion.

In addition to graduate courses, study councils are occasionally formed. These study councils are voluntarily formed by educators who have exceptional concern and/or knowledge about a specific educational topic. Their indepth deliberations often establish foundations for more refined experimentation and subsequent operational recommendations.

The numerous educational associations and societies have also afforded their members opportunities to learn about new ideas and practices. Within their particular areas of educational interest, these groups not only conduct workshops and presentations at conventions, but they also publish journals and occasionally provide consultative services.

State departments of education often provide curricular consultants and materials in the various subject areas. The states' involvement in vocational education requires the dispensing of certain knowledge, and the exchange of professional information should not be overlooked.

Private foundations and governmental agencies occasionally provide funds and/or facilities for special institutes. These sessions usually deal with very specific problem areas and may last from a few days to a few months.

Although these sources provide a very significant portion of inservice activities, commercial interests may account for a large part of the local inservice programs. These companies include textbook and other educational media publishers, audio-visual equipment manufacturers, data processors, and many other school suppliers. The demand for training in these areas accents even more the need for American education to provide teachers with continuous opportunities to become well informed of the many changing areas that affect their teaching.

Of all the possibilities for teachers to gain inservice education, the local school program of coordinated educational opportunities is often the most beneficial to the teacher and the school. This coordinated program is initiated by the supervisory or administrative staff, in an attempt to provide learning opportunities for the staff in many of the schools' problem areas. Because of unique characteristics of school resources and needs, a well-planned inservice program may be very satisfactory for one school and totally amiss for another. As noted by Zeralsky and Schester, "Diversity of action toward in-service programs geared to specific school needs cannot result in a tidy stereotyped package."[4] A cursory review of the professional periodical literature will disclose a bewildering variety of specific inservice education designs. This variety emphasizes the point that no one program may effectively serve as a model.

Guidelines for Developing Inservice Education Programs

The weakness, if not failure, of many programs is often attributable to a program structure that has not attempted to involve the teacher emotionally or intellectually in the educational activity. Problems to be solved through inservice education must be viewed as "real" to the teachers involved. The problems that appear to be unrealistic or overwhelmingly difficult will be met by participants with great indifference. Therefore, it may be advisable to select several areas that could be improved, then request the teachers to select the area of most interest in which to work. As they work in these areas, special emphasis should be placed on developing real encounter activities. Without these specific goals the participants may develop the attitude of "That's nice, but it's just talk."

Teachers are quick to realize that many problems require the cooperation and commitment of a group of their fellow teachers. Therefore, group activities are essential to most successful programs. The psychological reinforcements of group membership help teachers to modify their behavior in an atmosphere of confidence. The consensus decisions of the group, based on their expanded field of resources, are viewed by the members of the group as being more stable and acceptable than their individual opinion. The problems to be undertaken should be important enough to a group of teachers to warrant their continuing effort to solve them.

The motivation for professional advancement found in selection of a suitable study topic may be quickly lost if the study group is not allowed to develop their own method of solving the problem. That is, people in status positions should avoid dictating procedure to the group. Possible solutions should be enlisted from all members of the group. Provisions for this self-direction will instill confidence in the group's ability to formulate and execute its own plan of action. Administrators should be prepared to tolerate unusual requests by the well-motivated inservice groups. To capriciously veto their requests, because of their novelty, has the effect of dictating policy and procedure. The stifling effect of such authoritarian activity may serve to disrupt group unity and desire to participate.

Since not all people function well in larger groups, it may be advisable to establish provisions for the development of smaller units. This is especially important when the groups are dealing in the development of abstractions. Many people find it difficult to express themselves to large numbers of other teachers. To insure that these people will engage in the necessary informal interchange of opinion, these smaller groups should be formed. The reinforcement of the successful small group will tend to enhance the development of free interchange of ideas among its members. Much progress toward the solution of the problem may result when the teachers are allowed to relate to each other in this fashion.

Group leadership should continuously reinforce or run interference for individual and group problem solving. This may require special training for some members or the acquisition of outside consultants. The duty of these people is mainly one of group maintenance. They must be able to diagnose and avoid direct interpersonal confrontations among members. This may be accomplished by focusing attention on the problem at hand and by discouraging idle speculation. Encouraging the continual reassessment of goals, resources, cooperative efforts, and group process will tend to minimize intra-group conflict, and reinforce the progress of the attainment of the goals.

The administrator's success at providing a conducive atmosphere will depend largely on his or her pre-planning activities. The administrator attempting to develop inservice programs should also enhance the conducive atmosphere by withholding criticism, encouraging participants, and expediting the implementation of group recommendations. By stressing the acceptance of individual worth of each member, those in status positions may maximize the potential for the building of mutual respect within the group.

Red tape is responsible for the demise of more than an occasional inservice program. By allowing administrative process to bog down the implementation of inservice recommendations for change, the administrative staff stifles further professional growth. The administration must be willing to alter administrative procedure to accomodate the proposals of inservice groups. Minimizing the number of written reports and establishing implementation procedures prior to beginning the inservice program may also serve to expedite the realization of the group's goals.

As the preceding paragraph indicates, provisions for action are necessary. However, the suggestions of inservice study groups need not be automatically and universally implemented throughout the system. Pilot projects and other experimental procedures may be employed to test the appropriateness of the group's recommendation. Teachers are eager to avoid talking and put their plans into action. By ensuring them of an opportunity to test their hypotheses, the schools will help maintain the staff's professional quest for better solutions to educational problems.

Evaluating the results of the inservice effort is often a haphazard and meaningless affair. The administrator declaring "his" or "her" program a "success" will not afford much study for the improvement of future programs. By including the participants of the program in its appraisal, more meaningful data may be accumulated. Care should be taken to attempt to objectively measure the degree to which the program has achieved its goals. When this descriptive data is collected, all parties involved should share in the final value judgment.

With the diversity of problems that are subject to inservice study, it is easily conceivable that overlapping of activities may exist between groups. Every effort must be made to minimize the opportunity for conflict to arise. This coordination should attempt to plan system-wide activities to support and to supplement those in the individual schools.

Perhaps the last guideline is nothing more than the popular cry for relevance. Yet, this aspect has proven to be paramount in significance in the operation of successful inservice programs. Even if the topics for inservice are important to the teachers, it is the responsibility of the leaders to be sure that the teachers perceive the topic as important. The failure of the teachers to accept the significance of the topic may cause the program to result in failure, regardless of all the good intentions and planning of the school leaders.

Promising Practices for Inservice Education

Assuming that the guidelines for the structure of the inservice program have been considered, one might ask, "What activities are actually performed by teachers in inservice programs?" These activities vary widely according to the objectives of the session. The inservice design grid of Figure 6.1 is an attempt to graphically relate desired behavioral changes to promising inservice activities.

As the chart suggests, for objectives that are primarily concerned with the learning of factual material at the level of recognition and comprehension, an activity in the Design I area may prove appropriate. In like manner, objectives concerned with values and attitudes would more satisfactorily be met by role-playing or guided practice. The grid simply serves as a ready reference, and the activities suggested may be modified greatly to accommodate the specific needs of the program designer. The following activities are explained in the typical situation to which they are employed.

When the production of a multitude of divergent ideas concerning a given topic is desired, the brainstorming technique is often employed. Participants are urged to express their ideas, and these ideas are recorded. Spontaneous informal expression is the ground rule. Provisions are made to avoid discussion and debate. The production of alternative ideas is the main participant objective. When ideas are no longer expressed, the session is

Figure 6.1
Inservice Design Grid＊

ACTIVITIES	OBJECTIVES					
	Knowl-edge	Compre-hension	Appli-cation	Syn-thesis	Values & Attitudes	Adjust-ment
Lecture						
Illustrated lecture	Design I Cognitive Objectives		Design III			
Demonstration		Broad-Spectrum Objectives				
Observation						
Interviewing						
Brainstorming						
Group Discussion						
Buzz Sessions						
Role-Playing						
Guided Practice				Design II Affective Objectives		

＊ Ben M. Harris and Waitland Bessent, *In-Service Education: A Guide to Better Practice* (Englewood Cliffs, N.J.: Prentice-Hall, Inc., 1969), p. 37.

completed, and the recorded ideas may be discussed in a later session. Groups of up to seventy seem to work well, if provisions are made for sound amplification and idea recording.

With the variety of ideas expressed in the brainstorming session, the designer may desire to stimulate verbal interaction among the participants to arrive at consensus on some issues or to identify possible areas of controversy. Buzz sessions may be employed for this purpose. Groups of about fifteen participants gather around a table for a given time and discuss one particular issue. A group leader is appointed to coordinate the conversation; a recorder takes notes on the proceedings. The result of the proceedings may lead to further indepth studies or specific recommendations. A brief training session for the leader and recorder would prove invaluable, but no other special personnel considerations would be required.

The demonstration requires the participant primarily to watch the exhibition. The purposes of the demonstration would include informing, developing an understanding, and stimulating interest. The demonstrator should be very competent in preparing and executing his or her performance. Similarly, the audience should be able to benefit from the experience. They should have enough background experience to understand the demonstrator. Provisions should also be made for good audio-visual display. When such provisions are made, the size of the participant gathering may be unlimited. At the conclusion of a stimulating demonstration, follow-up activities are usually employed to direct the motivated participants in a more tangibly productive exercise.

Role-playing is a spontaneous dramatization in which participants are assigned particular roles to perform. The purpose of this type of activity is to develop understanding of feelings and attitudes of other people.

Concomitant outcomes such as developing verbal interaction skill and providing concrete examples of behavior are also attributed to the role-playing technique. Although the role-playing must be limited to very specific topics, the participant becomes emotionally involved in the activity. This involvement creates much interest, and the experience usually has a lasting effect on the participant's attitudes. No particular training is required, but an informal atmosphere will assist the role-players in gaining the necessary confidence to perform effectively. Some form of follow-up is necessary to help the participants interpret and apply the results of their session.

Practical Considerations for Inservice Education

Although the design for inservice education may have a sound theoretical and pedagogical foundation, practical consideration of the participants must be made. Time to engage in the training activities is essential. Many school systems require teachers to attend sessions after the normal school day. This practice produces rather good attendance in some districts, but tired, hungry, ready-to-leave teachers do not make very good students. One solution to the problem is to provide released time for the training sessions. This may be accomplished by devoting an afternoon of a given day in each month to the inservice program. Another option is to extend the school year by reducing vacations or by simply adding more days to the school calendar.

In order to maintain good interpersonal relations, any change in the calendar should be accompanied with an appropriate change in salary. Any extra time required for the staff to prepare for or participate in the learning activities, should result in proper remuneration. The money that is budgeted for inservice programs is often based on a percentage of the total budget. The optimum percentage may be more easily arrived at in successive installments over several years. An example of another method of budgeting for inservice education is to allot two weeks' salary of each professional for that purpose. Whatever method is employed for budgeting purposes, it must be recognized that appropriations are required.

Faculty Meetings

The faculty meeting can be an excellent tool for the improvement of instruction or it may turn out to be a dismal failure. Weaknesses of the faculty meeting which may exist include:

1. They are often held at the end of a long school day.
2. The meetings are much too long.
3. They are used primarily for the principal to make administrative announcements.
4. All teachers are not required to attend.
5. There is little opportunity for teacher discussion.
6. They are held too often.
7. They have no value in the estimation of many teachers.
8. They are held in too formal surroundings—hard chairs, no refreshments, etc.

With these common weaknesses, it is little wonder that the faculty meeting has such a low reputation. The principal may be in excellent shape at the end of the school day, as he or she has not been responsible for teaching any classes. Conducting the faculty meeting may be his or her major responsibility and interest for that day. However, for the teacher, the faculty meeting is merely an added burden to an otherwise very busy and tiring school day. The principal, refreshed and enthused over the prospect that the faculty meeting may introduce a new program or correct inadequacies of the present program, may indeed talk too long.

Teachers are resentful of the faculty meeting being added to a regular working day and may become irritable when the coaches or other activity leaders are not required to attend. The football coach does need the daily after school practice and cannot be expected to give this up for the faculty meeting. A solution to this problem is to hold the faculty meeting in the morning during part of the regular school session or prior to the time students arrive. The values obtained in meeting with an alert faculty will far outweigh the loss of school time by students.

A faculty meeting should be held only when there is a valid reason or need for such a large group meeting. The regular weekly or monthly faculty meeting is dated as an effective way to improve instruction. A better procedure would be to hold more frequent departmental or small group meetings to deal with specific tasks which concern group members. An agenda developed jointly by faculty and the principal is a must for conducting a well organized meeting. The principal must find a room that provides comfort and informality for the faculty meeting. Many principals have arranged for a light breakfast of rolls and coffee to be served in the early morning faculty meeting, or if later in the day, light refreshments are served. These special efforts cost little, but pay handsome rewards.

The all-inclusive faculty meeting is a necessary part of the secondary school. This type of faculty meeting probably should not exceed two per semester. It provides the opportunity for the principal to promote esprit de corps by keeping teachers informed and made to feel a part of the overall school effort. It makes it possible for the principal to coordinate school activities and keep teachers current of other activities in the school. Innovations may be introduced through the faculty meeting. It provides a clearing house for the exchange of ideas and gives the faculty an opportunity to participate in curriculum and policy matters of the school. It aids in the promotion of faculty professional growth and is an extremely important tool which the principal or supervisor can use to improve instruction within the school. It must be used wisely. The authors recommend that the following considerations be made for the faculty meeting:

1. It should be arranged so that all may attend.
2. It should not be tacked on at the end of the school day.
3. Light refreshments should be provided.
4. The agenda should be planned by a faculty committee except in purely administrative-type faculty meetings, such as when a schedule is being explained, etc.
5. Ideas and policy may be communicated more efficiently to the faculty members in other ways such as the faculty bulletin.
6. Meetings which include all members should be planned and announced well in advance. Teachers should not be expected to cancel their hair appointments or after-school social and recreational activities.
7. A definite starting and ending time should be followed. As a rule of thumb, one hour is the limit.
8. The faculty meeting should be held in comfortable surroundings.
9. The principal need not always chair the faculty meeting.
10. Frequent talks by the principal cause teachers to develop defensive and even antagonistic reactions and accomplish little, if any, real good.
11. Speakers should be used very rarely—discussion is much more effective. Panels are sometimes helpful.
12. Utilize departmental and small group meetings to carry out the necessary task-oriented activities which faculty must engage in to foster program improvement.

SUPERVISION AND EVALUATION OF TEACHERS

The effective teacher must be identified. If effective teachers cannot be identified how then can teaching be established as a profession? Without adequate evaluation, effective teachers are equated with the mediocre or inferior, and the concept of individual differences among teachers is denied.

Teacher Evaluation by Teachers

Teachers could be forced to effect an evaluation program quickly if suggestions by Engel were followed.[5] He notes that teachers resist evaluation through a rationalization that teaching is an art which is so complex that objective evaluation is impossible. Teachers evaluate students, and they themselves are a product of evaluation. Their training, their applications for employment, the renewal of contracts, and the gaining of tenure are wed to evaluation of some sort. Engel suggests that a school board notify the teaching staff that the following policy is in effect beginning next year. Teachers will evaluate themselves and be paid as indicated in points (a), (b), and (c):

(a) 20% of the teaching staff will receive a bonus.

(b) 60% of the teachers will advance per salary scale.

(c) 20% of the teachers will remain at the present step.

(d) Ground rules:

    1. Board will accept the list as presented—no changes.

    2. Top and bottom percentages can vary but must equal to one another.

    3. The contract of any teacher rated in the bottom group for two consecutive years will be terminated.[6]

Under the dictum, teachers and principals would not scream, "We cannot evaluate!" The challenge, "How can we evaluate?" would necessitate a real effort by the faculty to select workable evaluative criteria for themselves.[7]

Teacher Evaluation by Students

Since the teaching process primarily involves teachers and students, rating by the students should be part of teacher evaluation. In 1930, Zax notes, students rated the good teachers as follows: clarity of expression, humor, enthusiasm, insistence on high standards, sympathy, interest in students, expressive voice, cordiality, patience, impressive physique, tolerance, and enjoyment of teaching. Zax believes that:

> . . . good teachers (a) enjoy teaching, (b) are flexible and anticipate the unpredictable happenings in their classrooms, (c) do not feel unduly restricted by regulations, (d) do hope to be further relieved of non-teaching responsibilities, (e) do desire more clerical help, (f) are quite concerned about their communication with students, (g) feel that a lack of knowledge about the individual student underlies their ineffectiveness with certain students, (h) express positive feelings toward problem and non-problem students alike, (i) tend to take student response as a measure of success in teaching, (j) tend to be confident and to hold their views vigorously, (k) are anxious to hear from colleagues, and (l) are anxious to receive supervisory support.[8]

Ratings of teacher effectiveness by seniors with high scholastic achievement and ratings by principals do not agree, although principals tend to agree with one another. Teachers tend to agree more with other teachers and the administration than with the seniors.[9]

Opinions of adminstrators concerning student evaluation of teachers show that: 40 percent were in favor; 42 percent were in opposition; and 17 percent were undecided on the issue: "Shall students evaluate teachers?" Four and one-half percent did involve students in an annual evaluation of teachers. Administrators tend to feel that (1) student evaluation of teachers should be at the teacher's option, (2) students should not be involved in contracting teachers, (3) student evaluations are not valid, (4) since children must attend public schools, they should have an outlet for their opinions, (5) average and below average teachers would object the most to evaluation, (6) students were too immature for objective evaluation, (7) evaluation is a professional judgment and should be reserved for professional personnel only, (8) the student evaluation is too difficult to administer, (9) teachers may adjust their behavior to be socially acceptable to students, for example, to be "good guys" instead of good teachers, and (10) student evaluation would end up being a popularity poll. However, it should be noted that in districts where student evaluation is in effect, 100 percent of the administrators report the program is beneficial to both teachers and students; 10 percent of the administrators further recommend that students as young as fifth graders could evaluate their teachers; while 27 percent of the administrators favor teacher evaluation by students in grades 7 through 12.[10]

What Research Says About Teacher Evaluation

Recommendations stemming from research are (1) the evaluation should be a joint venture of the teacher and the supervisor or principal, (2) the criteria for evaluation should include specific objectives in behavioral terms, and (3) the knowledge of effectiveness provided in feedback to the teacher enables an adjustment in his or her behavior to meet the objective.

The real deterrents to teacher evaluation are: (1) lack of consistency regarding precise criteria for expert teaching, (2) lack of agreement among professionals describing expert teaching, and (3) reluctance of teachers to submit to analysis of their performance.[11]

A study by Washington showed that teachers were not threatened by an evaluation through (1) long term analysis utilizing twenty-five criteria, (2) a "man in motion" study of filmed classroom activity, (3) confidential conferences with the observing team and principal, and (4) providing for planning and completing long range programs of self-evaluation and improvement.[12] Benefits found in this study include improved teacher perception of his or her action, increased constructive criticism of instructional procedures, more adaptable behavior, improved morale among team members, and increased number of conferences which are requested by the observed teacher.

What Is Effective Teaching?

Washington's study reveals: Outstanding teachers tend to be over modest; both teachers and supervisors become expert in observation within a year; educators can be objective and analytical about their actions and at the same time sensitive and adaptable; teachers and principals are willing to express their own behavior, criticize constructively their behavior, and take direct action to change themselves.[13]

The personal traits of the teacher are often used as a basis to measure teacher competency. Defining teacher effectiveness is so complex that it is difficult to use the trait theory to describe the competent teacher. However, according to Miller and Miller, certain personal qualities and professional competencies are associated with good classroom teaching; for example, good teachers personalize their teaching, know their subject matter and related areas, are able to perceive the world from the student's point of view, maintain a neat personal appearance, use English correctly, adjust the program to the ability of the individual student, organize material well, and show enthusiasm in teaching. A questionnaire completed by superintendents, elementary principals, and secondary principals provides the following rank of characteristics. No significant difference existed between the three groups of raters. (+ indicates most important; − indicates least important.)

Personal qualities of teacher:

+ Professional zeal
+ Loyalty and cooperation
   Use of oral and written English
   Social qualities
− Personal appearance
− Voice and Speech
− Punctuality

Professional competency:

+ Knowledge of subject matter in teaching field
+ Classroom management and discipline
   Ability to organize material for teaching
   Ability to organize learning situations
   Evaluation
− Economical use of class time
− Class achievement
− General knowledge and information.[14]

Special note should be taken of the item "class achievement." An interesting shift may be occurring in the rank order of importance of this factor as the whole concept of accountability comes onto the educational scene.

A good teacher must be effective in interpersonal relationships. According to Hamschek, a good teacher is one who (1) can involve feeling in a human process, (2) possess a positive view of his own self image, and (3) is knowledgeable in his subject and is able to communicate that knowledge. He suggests that measuring personality traits may not identify the teacher who most enhances student learning.[15]

Real efforts have been made recently to identify effective teaching in behavioral terms which can be observed and measured. Wagoner expresses the view that board of education members may look at the benefits of contract teaching agreements with outside agencies and may decide to hold teachers responsible for student achievement in the classroom. This policy dictates that discrete measurable objectives be identified and accepted. The fact that private industry places its profit on the line by guaranteeing performance may prompt school trustees to ask, "Why should not teachers do likewise?"[16]

Teacher Evaluation Based on Student Achievement

The concept of judging teaching effectiveness on the basis of product is the subject of considerable current research. One such effort is summarized by Popham.[17] In this research model, an effort was made to identify teachers who could effect educational growth in students. Criteria were selected in advance. Student growth was measured in relation to the criteria selected and not by conventional standardized tests normed to grade level. Grade level norms were judged inadequate for testing the performance of students in contract teaching. In this experiment, teachers taught a total of ten hours and were free to use whatever available material they would choose. Observation was made by the Flanders Interaction Analysis. Experienced teachers were compared to "off the street instructors." The hypothesis stated that a difference would exist in the product from the two groups. This hypothesis was rejected. There was no significant difference between the two groups. Why? Perhaps the tests were not sensitive enough. Perhaps experienced teachers are not particularly skilled in effecting a prescribed behavioral change. Why should they be? What training or impetus have they had to teach for this purpose? Does the research model possess construction validity? Perhaps the experimenters should select teachers who had previously demonstrated the skill compared to a randomly selected group or a group who had not demonstrated the trait previously.

Hyman stresses that student achievement occurs best in an atmosphere which is positive. "A positive climate encourages students to learn. It fosters: (1) further helpful interaction among students, (2) clarifying experiences between teacher and students and respect between people."[18]

Student achievement is highest in classrooms where there is good teaching. Pinkney lists some of the following as characteristics of good teaching: (1) meets the child on his own terms; (2) practices positive thinking; (3) studies and understands the culture of his children; (4) the good teacher refuses to use excuse or place blame on other variables for the children assigned to his classroom.[19]

Broudy reports that in elementary schools the scores on the Minnesota Teacher Attitude Inventory correlate positively with the achievement of pupils who are classified as "affectively" oriented, and does not correlate significantly with students who are classified as "cognitively" oriented. In secondary schools, student teachers who score high on the Minnesota Teacher Attitude Inventory tend to be more effective with noncollege-bound students who are presumed to be affectively oriented. Teachers who score low on the Minnesota Teacher Attitude Inventory tend to be more effective with college-bound students who are perceived to be more cognitively oriented. This research suggests the importance of considering the types of teachers and the types of pupils with whom the teachers are most effective.[20]

Teaching behavior may be observed and recorded in measurable terms. It is debatable whether or not desirable teacher behavior results in greater student achievement. A Skinnerian approach to the problem is reported by Bloom and Wilensky in which teacher behaviors are classified in one of four categories: Information Giving (IG), Response Elicitation (RE), Feedback (F), and Teacher Control (TC). IG refers to teacher supplying information to the student; RE refers to teacher efforts to elicit a response from the students; F refers to teacher feedback behavior to the student response elicited by his RE; TC refers to teacher effort to maintain pupil attention. The observer logs and classifies all teacher behavior for five minutes. Each and every teacher behavior can be tallied in one of the four categories. Following is a comparison of four different teachers (A, B, C, and D) in percentages of time devoted to each behavior:

	IG%	RE%	F%	TC%
A	64	24		
B	34	46		
C	42			
D	43			

Although the effectiveness of a given style cannot be determined from this data, several inferences can be made from an examination of the interrelationship between categories. According to Skinner, the ratio of F to RE should be high for effective teaching.[21]

Micro-Teaching and Video-Taping

While some have advocated that the video-tape used in conjunction with television may be used to save the supervisor time in the supervision of teachers, it is the opinion of the authors that video-tape provides the greatest promise in self-analysis by teachers of their instruction.

Graduate students preparing for supervisory positions or the secondary school principalship are sometimes asked to participate with the "trainee" in analyzing his or her presentation and making recommendations for the second presentation. It is thought that these classroom discussions give students more numerous opportunities to correct their mistakes thereby causing fewer failures when they become teachers.

This is the essence of *micro-teaching* which holds great promise for the education of teachers. However, the use of micro-teaching by principals in their improvement of instruction of their faculty has much less potential since it requires a considerable amount of organization and scheduling. In addition, the demands on the supervisory time of principals to view mini-presentations of the faculty would be considerable. Encouragement of teachers to use the video-tape in their own self analysis, however, has great potential for the improvement of instruction. The following suggestions are made to help principals in organizing for self-analysis of teaching through the use of video-tape:

1. A video-tape machine which is easily portable should be purchased.
2. A video-tape machine which can be operated by the teacher or students is required.
3. Teachers should be assured that tapes will be for their own use in self analysis. (Probably each teacher who desires to use the video-tape machine should have their own tape and keep it in their possession.)
4. The life of the video-tape machine should be anticipated to be about five years, since improved technology will easily outdate the machine.
5. Provisions should be made in the budget for maintenance and repair of the video-tape machine and a repair shop located.
6. The video-tape machine can be used by other organizations such as speech classes, dramatics, athletics, etc.
7. The principal should use the "spinout" approach with the video-tape machine. That is, order one machine for the average-sized secondary school, and let the idea "spinout" to other teachers. Then ask for another machine if the demand is great.

Micro-teaching had its beginning as a Stanford Secondary Education Project in which student teachers taught small groups (three to seven individuals) in short periods of time (three to twenty minutes). It was used at Stanford to provide pre-student teaching experience and as a method for providing research into the teaching process. Since that time, it has evolved into a technique widely used in colleges of education to provide mini-teaching experiences before the assignment of a student teacher.

Micro-teaching generally involves four phases: teach, first critique, reteach, and second critique. The student using this technique usually teaches only one concept to a small group of students. His or her presentation is video-taped and critiqued by a supervisor; often a college professor. After this critique, the concept is taught again, with the student changing the presentation in line with the recommendations of the supervisor. Research has indicated that micro-teaching improves the student teacher in using questions effectively, recognizing and obtaining attending behavior, controlling participation, providing feedback, employing rewards and punishments, and in setting a model.[22]

Micro-teaching, from its beginning in the early 1960s, continues to gain in popularity with teacher training institutions.[23] Video-taping and micro-teaching is also used in foreign countries. One of the authors found on a recent tour that the College of Education of Saarbruken, West Germany, has an excellent micro-teaching laboratory with modern video-taping facilities.

The use of television for improving instruction is not limited to video-tape. A demonstration in which a teacher dissects a frog, for example, can be shown to students in the classroom by television rather than attempting to bring all the students around the teacher to get a closer look. Classroom teaching can also be improved by the use of the video-tape. Speech students may watch a video-tape of their presentation and can observe their posture as well as hear their speech usage.

It is also possible through the use of a video-tape machine to record programs on home television sets to show to classes at a later date, or it is possible to record presentations so that students who were absent can see the presentations later. The possibilities for the use of video-tape in improving instruction are innumerable.

Teaching Centers

Another concept currently being developed in Great Britain which provides promise for the improvement of instruction, is the teachers' centers. Bailey describes these centers as follows:

> Teachers' centers are just what the term implies: local physical facilities and self-improvement programs organized and run by the teachers themselves for purposes of upgrading educational

performance. Their primary function is to make possible a
review of existing curricula and other educational practices by
groups of teachers and encourage teacher attempts to bring
about changes.[24]

The 500 teachers' centers scattered throughout England and Wales are
organized and controlled by the teachers themselves. They are a good
example of one primary criterion of a profession, that of providing for
improvement of the members of the profession.

The teachers' centers provide such programs as: "How children learn,"
workshops on visual aids, and a demonstration on understanding numbers.
The centers also have exhibits of teaching aids and professional literature on
improvement of instruction. Bailey suggests:

Would it not be wonderful if, after years of telling teachers
what to do and where to go, American educational servants and
officials suddenly discovered that the only real and lasting
reforms in education in fact come about when teachers themselves are given facilities and released time to do their own
thing?[25]

The authors believe that the greatest potential for the improvement of
instruction is the motivation which the teacher has from within. The role of
the educational leader is to provide ideas, support workshops, and help the
teacher grow by providing encouragement, time, and environment for
experimentation—a school where teachers can make mistakes. Perhaps the
four-day work week with the fifth day reserved for self-improvement of the
teacher will become popular in our schools of the future.

Interpersonal Relations

There is no question that change in people is necessary before an educational
program can be improved. In recent years, disciples of sensitivity training
have insisted that the false fronts people bear must be broken down before
any real change will occur. As a result, many sensitivity sessions have been
organized either separately, or within the workshop structure, to improve
the instructional program.

These sensitivity training sessions have been designed to help participants discover their human relations strengths and weaknesses. For
example, one group of six persons may be organized in which each member
of the group is exposed to the other five members, and is told his weaknesses
as seen by the rest of the group. Some groups are designed to reject at least
one member of the group with the theory that the person being rejected will
attempt later to correct the weaknesses that led to his or her rejection.

Krafft and Howe write that:

Sensitivity training methods are used to: (1) reduce personal alienation; (2) relieve interpersonal and inter-group tension; (3) learn interpersonal process diagnostic and facilitation skills; (4) "personalize" learning; (5) develop individual and group problem-solving skills; and (6) provide the basis of decision making, leadership training, conflict management, community involvement and various types of organizational development objectives.[26]

As Krafft and Howe indicate, a program of sensitivity training has value if it is carefully planned and is accepted by the faculty and community. No faculty member should be coerced into participating in sensitivity training. Of utmost importance in sensitivity training sessions is choosing qualified persons to lead. A person who has excellent references, is respected, and has been involved in many training sessions may qualify as a sensitivity leader. The purposes of sensitivity sessions should coincide with the plans of the sensitivity leader. The plans of the sensitivity session as well as the objectives should be clear to all participants before they take part in the session. Those uses of sensitivity training methods indicated by Krafft and Howe should be used as a guide in developing this method of providing the necessary atmosphere for change to take place in the school.

If improvement of instructional efforts are hindered by coldness or excessive formality on the part of the faculty, sensitivity sessions may reduce barriers of communication within the group. They may also be useful in helping faculty members realize that other faculty members are human, too, and not nearly as self-centered as they thought. Animosities between faculty members that have developed over the years may be reduced through the use of this method of improving understanding within a group.

If sensitivity sessions can improve the ability of a group to collectively solve its problems, improve its leadership, and reach more effective decisions, then the value of this method cannot be overlooked by the educational leader as a way of improving instruction. However, the authors would like to caution the prospective user of sensitivity training that it has the potential of creating explosive public reaction if not tempered with common sense. The T-group which involves physical contact that may not be in line with the mores of the community should not be used. A person who has little knowledge of this method or who is insensitive to the damage that the lack of propriety might cause the school should not be assigned the leadership of sensitivity training.

Improving Teacher-Student Interaction

The interaction of the teacher and the student is one of the most important criteria which affect the learning process. Without optimum verbal and non-verbal interaction in the classroom, one cannot expect optimum learning.

Amidon and Flanders have given considerable attention to interaction analysis of the teacher and his or her students. In their handbook, they write:

> The primary responsibility of the classroom teacher is to guide
> the learning activities of children. As she helps children to learn
> in the classroom situation, the teacher, as the leader, interacts
> with the children both as individuals and as a group. In the
> process of this interaction she influences the children, some-
> times intentionally with planned behavior, sometimes con-
> sciously without planning, but often without awareness of his
> behavior and the effect of this behavior on the learning
> process.[27]

Interaction analysis has been defined as a system for observing and cod-ing the verbal interchange between a teacher and pupils. The assumption is made that teaching behavior and pupil responses are expressed primarily through the spoken word as a series of verbal events which occur one after another. These events are identified, coded so as to preserve sequence, and tabulated systematically in order to represent a sample of the spontaneous teacher influence.

All verbal communication in the classroom is categorized into either: teacher talk, student talk, or silence or confusion. Flanders' interaction analysis as shown in Table 6.1 consists of categories of indirect influence: (1) accepting, (2) praising or encouraging, (3) accepting ideas, and (4) asking questions. Direct influence is divided into three categories: (5) lecturing, (6) giving directions, and (7) criticizing or justifying authority. Student talk is divided into: (8) responding to teacher, and (9) initiating talk. The last category is: (10) silence or confusion.[28]

Interaction analysis in the classroom may be conducted in one of two ways: (1) by an observer, or (2) by the teacher after taping a classroom ses-sion. The analysis is done by recording at three-second intervals the verbal communication of the teachers and students according to categories as listed above. The category listing by numbers is then arranged in columns on the tally sheet and is referred to as *raw* data. This represents the sequential dimension of the verbal interaction. In order to obtain a frequency measure of the same data, they are tabulated into a matrix.

Flanders believes that learning is enhanced by teachers who use indirect influence in the classroom. He attempts to substantiate this belief by research by himself and his students. The use of interaction analysis is a means for the teacher and supervisor to study the teacher in relationship to direct and indirect teaching.

> Educators have long advocated the use of democratic methods
> in teaching, and research has demonstrated the effectiveness of
> teaching behaviors that are usually classed as democratic. The

Table 6.1
Summary of Categories for Interaction Analysis*

TEACHER TALK	INDIRECT INFLUENCE	1. *Accepts Feeling:* accepts and clarifies the feeling tone of the students in a non-threatening manner. Feelings may be positive or negative. Predicting or recalling feelings is included. 2. *Praises or Encourages:* praises or encourages student action or behavior. Jokes that release tension, but not at the expense of another individual; nodding head, or saying "un hm?" or "go on" are included. 3. *Accepts or Uses Ideas of Students:* clarifying, building, or developing ideas suggested by a student. As teacher brings more of his own ideas into play, shift to Category 5. 4. *Asks Questions:* asking a question about content or procedure with the intent that a student answer.
	DIRECT INFLUENCE	5. *Lecturing:* giving facts or opinions about content or procedures; expressing his own ideas, asking rhetorical questions. 6. *Giving Directions:* directions, commands, or orders with which a student is expected to comply. 7. *Criticizing or Justifying Authority:* statements intended to change student behavior from nonacceptable pattern; bawling someone out; stating why the teacher is doing what he is doing; extreme self-reference.
STUDENT TALK		8. *Student Talk—Response:* talk by students in response to teacher. Teacher initiates the contact or solicits student statement. 9. *Student Talk—Initiation:* talk by students, which they initiate. If "calling on" student is only to indicate who may talk next, observer must decide whether student wanted to talk. If he did, use this category. 10. *Silence or Confusion:* pauses, short periods of silence, and periods of confusion in which communication cannot be understood by the observer.

Note: There is no scale implied by these numbers. Each number is classificatory; it designates a particular kind of communication event. To write these numbers down during observation is to enumerate—not judge a position on a scale.

* Edmund J. Amidon and Ned A. Flanders, *A Manual for Understanding and Improving Classroom Behavior* (Minneapolis: Association for Productive Teaching, Inc., 1967).

focus of much of the writing on educational methods appears to have been placed accordingly on such goals as student self-direction and student participation in the teaching-learning process. Yet there appears to be evidence that the usual programs for teacher education do not produce results consistent with the professed goals of teacher education; that is, teacher education programs generally do not produce teachers who use significantly more democratic teaching methods in the classroom.[29]

Flanders' study of the interaction which occurs in the classroom between the teacher and the student is a most promising attempt to improve the teaching-learning situation. It causes the teacher to focus upon the individual student and to involve the student in classroom activities. It is but one method of improving teaching and should not constitute the only effort on the part of the principal to improve instruction. Learning not only involves teacher-pupil interaction, but independent study, the use of programmed materials, and the use of television and other technology. The interaction of the teacher and student would have little value if neither learned from their experiences.

Classroom Visitations

Classroom visitation can be one of many extremely valuable tools for the principal to use in improving instruction. However, visits by the principal to individual teacher's classes can be very frustrating and upsetting to the teacher. Teachers have a right to be critical of classroom visitation if this is the only tool used for the improvement of instruction and if the visit is made solely for the purpose of evaluating or rating the teacher. The major sources of dissatisfaction and frustration in teaching center on five items: (1) too many duties other than actual teaching, (2) pay too low, (3) large classes and overcrowded rooms, (4) pupils not interested in learning, and (5) disciplinary problems. The principal needs to visit the classroom occasionally to help correct these frustrations and dissatisfactions of teachers.

It should be emphasized that the classroom visit is not made by a superior person observing an inferior teacher. It is not a situation whereby the expert visits the class, discovers what is wrong, then directs the teacher to change certain methods of teaching. Rather the classroom visit is made by an equal with the teacher, first to learn what is going on in the school and the classroom, and second to be helpful to the teacher. The principal, through the classroom visit, might discover something that will help the teacher improve instruction. More than likely, however, the principal will learn something that will be helpful in making him or her a better principal.

The principal must be very careful to utilize the best professional behavior in the use of classroom visits to improve instruction. Before making the visit, rapport with the teachers should be established. He or she should explain to teachers that the purpose of the classroom visit is to: (1) better understand the educational program, (2) better understand teachers, (3) better understand students, and (4) observe the teaching-learning process.

When the principal observes the teaching-learning process, he or she observes the teacher's (1) method, (2) presentation, (3) motivation for learning, (4) assignment, (5) use of teaching and learning aids, (6) discussion or verbal interaction, (7) student interest and attention, and (8) classroom atmosphere. Before making the initial visit, the principal can help establish rapport by making short visits to deliver materials, etc.

Generally, visits to the teacher's classroom should be announced. This is especially true for the first two or three visits during the year. The teacher will probably be most uncomfortable during the first visit. Therefore, it is recommended that the first visit be short, not more than twenty minutes. This is not in line with the recommendations of many writers in supervision, since they advocate that the visitor remain the entire period. The visit should be long enough to observe the teaching-learning process which in some cases may be ten minutes and, in other cases, may be as long as thirty minutes.

A conference, following the classroom visit, should be arranged in an informal setting probably away from the principal's office. Teachers generally feel uneasy being called to the principal's office for the conference. The approach during the conference should be indirect in most cases, with the principal trying to lead the teacher into analyzing himself or herself. For example, if the teacher is sarcastic with students, it is better for the teacher to reveal this than the principal. The attitude during the conference is that of the principal as a friendly colleague who is engaged with the teacher in the cooperative study of an educational activity.

If the principal is to save time for the classroom visit, he or she must arrange a schedule for the visits. Most principals find it too easy to postpone a classroom visit to meet a parent, a salesman, or to run an errand. A schedule tends to force the principal to be involved in the improvement of instruction.

Among other suggestions for the classroom visit, the authors recommend that the principal keep a narrative record of classroom visits. One way to do this is to keep a carbon copy of the notes of the classroom visit, filing the carbon copy and giving the original to the teacher being visited. It is also recommended that the principal remain as unnoticed as possible during the visits, although certain attention will always be paid by students when they know the principal is in their classroom.

While taking notes during the visit is often necessary to avoid forgetting what took place during the visit, the authors frown upon the use of a tape recorder or video-tape machine during the classroom visit. The tape recorder may record something that was embarrassing to the teacher or students, and most likely will prove very upsetting to the teacher. The principal *is* the tape recorder and video-tape machine and should not need additional mechanical aids. The tape recorder and video-tape machine is for the exclusive use of the teacher in self-anlaysis.

Figure 6.2 shows an open ended form to provide a summary of the classroom visit. Figures 6.3 and 6.4 are examples of narratives which have been used to report classroom visits. The principal in the classroom visitation should have in mind a list of learning conditions that promote learning. Gen-

Figure 6.2
Teacher Observation Report

TEACHER'S NAME_____Miss Berry_____SCHOOL_____Outer City Senior High_____

SUBJECT _____English_____ GRADES _____9-10-11_____ ROOM _____78_____

DATE OF VISITATION_____October 2_____ TIME From _____10:30_____ to _____11:00_____

DATE OF CONFERENCE_____October 3_____ TIME From _____2:15_____ to _____2:40_____

TEACHING SITUATION: Teaching was accomplished during the first semester of the school year. Team teaching was the method used in this particular class with Miss Berry and Mrs. Cook working together. The class was composed mostly of low achievers and underachievers in grades nine through eleven. Each teacher met with the class for one and one-half hours.

1. Lesson Plans: Miss Berry used creative planning which was thorough and flexible.
2. Presentation and Organization: Miss Berry's presentation and organization was appropriate. She adapted her instruction to the abilities of her students. She covered the material in a variety of ways.
3. Change of Pace: Miss Berry used various methods on presenting the lesson. She reviewed yesterday's assignment on the chalkboard and developed today's assignment by using the workbook and supplementing the work by using the overhead projector and the chalkboard.
4. Assignment: Miss Berry presented the assignment so that it was clear, concise, and purposeful.
5. Use of Teaching Aids: The chalkboard and the overhead projector were used effectively in presenting the material.
6. Discussion: Students were encouraged to participate, but there was little student response. There did not seem to be adequate teacher-pupil rapport.
7. Classroom Environment: Miss Berry, although using various procedures, methods, and activities, did not have complete control of the class which is so important to learning. There was too much talking and movement of the students. She needed to organize classroom procedures more thoroughly.
8. Comments: Miss Berry displayed skill in oral and written English in her teaching field. She used a variety of materials adapted to the pupils' needs. Her lesson preparation was clear, concise, and flexible. The use of expression in speaking, gesturing to emphasize a point in the lesson and for classroom control should have been exercised more effectively.

   The classroom atmosphere of Miss Berry's class was one of fairness and understanding of individual differences. The organization of classroom procedures should be more thorough for quality teaching as well as improvement in handling discipline problems promptly and effectively.

   Miss Berry's strong point was the preparation of the lesson using current materials and teaching aids.

Figure 6.2 cont'd.

Conference: Miss Berry accepts criticism well for instruction improvement. Miss Berry was aware of the classroom distractons during her presentation. She asked what method would be effective to correct this situation.

Note: Time factor might have been the cause for some of the problems. Each class met for 1–1½ hours.

Recommendation:

1. Miss Berry needs to organize classroom procedures more thoroughly such as:
   a. entering the room quietly
   b. students going directly to their assigned seats
   c. developing the use of proper manners by students at all times during school
2. Discipline and control of class needed improvement. Suggestions for improvement were:
   a. more consistency
   b. voice control of pupils and teacher
   c. handling discipline problems promptly and more effectively by the use of school procedures

My signature signifies that I have observed this evaluation, but in no way indicates that I concur or disagree with the statements contained within this evaluation.

Teacher signature _____

Date _____

Teacher Comments:

Figure 6.3
Observation—Mr. Ferguson

My visit to Mr. Ferguson was not announced and I came into the room while he was teaching. I felt that my presence bothered him for a while but later he seemed to calm down somewhat.

Mr. Ferguson had lesson plans for each day and an outline of what he planned to do for the entire course.

I did not feel Mr. Ferguson was prepared for his discussion on the material the class was covering during the time I was there. He did not seem organized in his discussion.

There was no real change in pace. I felt Mr. Ferguson had good eye contact with the students and led a lot of discussion. I believe a few of the students took advantage of him in some of the questions they asked.

The blackboard was the basic teaching aid used. Also used in teaching the class was simulation of the earth, moon, and sun. Films were also used to help teach the class.

The environment of the classroom was not good. The room was located near a busy road and a lot of noise was a problem. It was an old room and not an adequate room to teach Earth Science. There was one small bulletin board which had only one chart.

I had a conference with Mr. Ferguson following my observation of his class. I expressed my feelings to Mr. Ferguson that he had good interaction with the students but that he may have a discipline problem with controlling the discussion. He expressed his knowledge of the problem but felt confident that he would overcome what problem he had.

Mr. Ferguson was teaching Natural Science at the ninth grade level and had students of both high and low ability. He said he used objective tests and assigned about three chapters a week.

I felt Mr. Ferguson could improve if he would direct his discussion to the entire class and not only to one side of the class. Also, I felt he should direct his questions to one individual and require the remainder of the students to wait their turn. I feel with time and teaching experience Mr. Ferguson can overcome any problems he has and can become an effective teacher.

Figure 6.4

Observation Report—Mr. Black

I observed Mr. Black's United States History class at Inner City High School from 8:45-9:30 a.m. The text being used in the class was *The Making of Modern America.* The class make-up was typical of a summer school session, having both low achievers who were repeating the course and high and average achievers who were taking the course prior to the regular school year.

Mr. Black was adequately prepared for the class. He used a question and answer type discussion very effectively, and attempted to bring many students into the discussion. He took extreme effort to draw out and clarify each topic of discussion. The interaction was excellent and there were no discipline problems evident. I felt that Mr. Black somewhat displayed the very common habit of answering his own question if the first student did not. Although the discussion was very good, I felt that a little change of pace might be beneficial. The discussion lasted the entire forty-five minutes that I observed Mr. Black. He did move around the room well and used his voice very effectively.

The assignment had been given prior to my arrival, but from references to it, I learned that it involved the writing of a short paper on the topic of "Maryland vs. McCulloch."

Mr. Black listed the topics for discussion on the chalkboard. Other than this, the room lacked any type of audio-visual equipment. I learned later that the room was not usually used as a history classroom, and that equipment such as an overhead projector was not available. There were no display boards of any type in the room but I felt that some visual material could still have been displayed to give the room a little more atmosphere.

In general, Mr. Black seemed quite enthusiastic and seemed to like the interaction of the class situation. I felt that he was doing an excellent job under the adverse circumstances. His rapport with the class was excellent.

Mr. Black and I met the following afternoon for a conference. I told him that I felt he had many strong points and showed great promise as a teacher. I praised his enthusiasm. He seemed quite receptive to any advice or suggestions that I could offer. We discussed the tendency he has of answering his own questions at times. I related to him my opinion that this habit tends to hinder interaction. He agreed. I suggested that it might be better to rephrase the question, offer it to another student, or probe a little deeper into the matter before relating to the students the correct answers.

I also suggested to Mr. Black that it is possible to draw out some aspects of a topic in a discussion almost too far. In trying to bring each minute fact to bear, the main concept is sometimes lost. Also, while trying to reach the slower learner in a total class situation it is possible to bore the better students. This suggests that some types of small group and individual work could be very beneficial, and would also serve as a change of pace. Mr. Black seemed interested in this possibility and I feel that he will explore it further. Among the small group and individual activities that I suggested were the panel discussion, individual and group reports, and individual supervised study.

I enjoyed my visit with Mr. Black and I thanked him for allowing me to observe his class.

erally, teacher preparation, learning environment, organization, variety, teacher aids, and student involvement are part of the success of the teacher. A summary of these conditions presented to the teacher after the visit will aid in the success of the supervisory tool.

Figures 6.5 and 6.6 show an example of a traditional classroom observation form and a traditional teacher evaluation form. Because of due process law, accountability, and stronger teacher organization, most school systems have formal written evaluations of teachers. The classroom observation is usually considered as a part of the total yearly evaluation program of teachers.

Teacher Evaluation in Open Concept Schools

Increased individualization of instruction normally occurs in an open classroom. The teacher places more emphasis on providing supporting activities to assist students to effectively utilize the individualized materials available to them. The teacher in the open school should not utilize the same instructional techniques that are found in the traditional classroom. Therefore, it is not appropriate to evaluate the teacher in the open classroom on the same basis as the teacher in the traditional classroom. In the open classroom one usually finds behavioral objectives which specify what the learner is to learn. In the traditional classroom lesson plans normally are developed to assist the teacher to teach, and often objectives utilized do not spell out specifically what the student is to learn.

The teacher in the open classroom may then be judged on how well each student is achieving what he or she set out to achieve. In the open classroom where behavioral objectives are utilized, it is quite important that affective as well as cognitive gains be measured. There is always a temptation to utilize standardized tests to measure student achievement gains. It is more appropriate to utilize a technique that measures the extent to which students learned what they attempted to learn. One must make sure that proper objectives are established in the first place; however, it does not seem appropriate that all students should set out to learn the same thing. This seems to be the assumption when standardized testing is used.

The emphasis on evaluation of the teacher in the open classroom where individualized instruction is utilized is focused more on the output of the learner than the input of the teacher.

Performance Objectives and Teacher Evaluation

The concept of performance objectives as the basis for teacher evaluation has been extensively advocated by Redfern who wrote: "The approach to evaluation which makes the most sense is to focus upon cooperatively deter-

Figure 6.5
Observation Form

FORM 3.23a

AKRON PUBLIC SCHOOLS
Division of Personnel and Pupil Services

OBSERVATION FORM

School _____
Grade or _____
Subject(s) _____

Teacher's Name _____

1. CLASSROOM

	Very Good	Satisfactory	Needs Improvement	COMMENTS
A. Teaching Performance				
Displays knowledge of subject matter				
Demonstrated needed teaching skills				
Speaks clearly, modulates voice				
Makes good use of instructional materials				
Directs a varied, interesting class				
B. Classroom Management				
Plans lessons carefully, makes meaningful assignments				
Maintains a stimulating learning environment				
Utilizes the type of discipline conducive to learning				
Helps pupils develop a sense of personal worth				
Keeps adequate lesson plans, grade books, records				

II. GENERAL

A. Personal Qualities

Dresses appropriately

Maintains poise and displays emotional stability

Handles student problems personally, when possible

Meets all obligations on time

Establishes a consistent pattern of attendance

B. Professional Qualities

Maintains good public relations, works cooperatively with parents

Carries a reasonable share of out-of-class responsibilities

Cooperates with colleagues

GENERAL COMMENTS AND RECOMMENDATIONS

CONFERENCE

Conference held?   Yes _____   No _____

Note: A conference is required when there are two or more checks in the "Needs Improvement" column.

_____   _____
Date   Signature of Principal

THE TEACHER IS TO RECEIVE A COPY OF THIS REPORT

Figure 6.6
Teacher Evaluation

FORM 3.73

A K R O N   P U B L I C   S C H O O L S
D i v i s i o n   o f   P e r s o n n e l   a n d   P u p i l   S e r v i c e s

TEACHER EVALUATION

School _____   Date _____   Teacher's
Years Under My   Total Years of   Name _____
Supervision _____   Akron Service _____   Grade or
    Subject(s) _____

Column (1) to be used by the principal. Column (2) may be used by the teacher in a self- appraisal, using this key: (O) Outstanding (VG) Very Good (S) Satisfactory (NI) Needs Improvement (U) Unsatisfactory. A conference between teacher and principal is required when the teacher has less than three years of service in his present building assignment.

	(1)	(2)
1. Teaching Performance - Demonstrates teaching skills needed for present assignments.		
2. Motivation of Learning - Maintains a classroom situation which stimulates the growth of individual pupils.		
3. Communication - Enunciates clearly in a well modulated voice; uses proper oral and written English.		
4. Sympathetic Understanding of Children - Shows a sincere interest in children and in the solution of their problems.		
5. Pupil Management - Employs procedures that reveal poise, inspires the confidence of pupils, and commands their respect.		
6. Initiative - Has the quality of seeing what needs to be done and is judicious in doing it with or without direction.		
7. School Relationships - Has a cooperative and open-minded attitude in working with others in the solution of mutual problems; respects the opinions, abilities, and contributions of others.		
8. Reliability - Is consistent, dependable, and accurate in carrying responsibilities to a successful conclusion; maintains adequate lesson plans, grade books and records.		
9. Personality - Shows those qualities that make teaching forceful and effective, such as: a pleasant, cheerful disposition, enthusiasm, and an appealing manner with pupils and others.		
10. Personal Appearance - Shows the type of grooming which is neat, attractive, and appropriate.		

11. **Stamina** - Has posture and bearing which gives evidence of energy and vitality in daily responsibilities.

12. **Stability** - Handles situations in a calm, objective manner.

13. **Professional Growth** - Is willing to examine his teaching effectiveness and constantly seeks better procedures.

14. **Community Relationships** - Meets community-school situations with poise, understanding, and tact, resulting in friendly relationships.

15. **Attendance Pattern and Punctuality** - Has a good attendance pattern and meets responsibilities promptly.

Comments and Recommendations by Principal:

Comments by Teacher:

I am aware of the content of this report.

_____ _____   _____ _____
Teacher's Signature   Date   Principal's Signature   Date

OFFICE OF PROFESSIONAL PERSONNEL

mined performance objectives, design a plan of action to achieve the objectives, and to assess the results."[30] The model, developed by Redfern, which appears in Figure 6.7 includes: cooperatively determined inputs, needs assessment, explicit objectives, and significant constraints.

Schools that are currently following this approach to administrator and teacher evaluation involve the faculty in the development of district, school, and individual objectives. This system of evaluation is a part of the total process of management by objectives which in some states is mandated by school accountability legislation.

While the development of school wide objectives which can be measured and which serve as the basis for the instructional program does make a lot of sense, it is not always possible to package desirable educational programs into measurable learning objectives. Evaluating teachers only with measurable objectives may put teaching in a straight jacket of monotonous instructional activity, with little opportunity for individual creativity and initiative.

Schools need purpose, and teachers need to know reasons for their teaching, what they are teaching, and how they expect to reach their instructional goals. However, the evaluation of teachers should not be limited to cooperatively determined performance objectives, but to other factors such as student motivation, student enjoyment, and flexibility of action. Evaluating teachers and administrators by performance objectives may be a large part of the evaluative process, but it should not be the total process.

In Figure 6.8, a simplified model of the evaluation process utilizing performance objectives is presented. This model includes the input, the performance objectives, and anticipated outcomes. In the performance objectives, constraints are listed which may have an affect upon the performance. For example, if one of the objectives involves the achievement of pupils, a most likely constraint for the teacher would be the ability of the pupils. Other constraints might include: materials available, home background, facilities, and teacher experience.

The model also shows what anticipated outcomes might result from the evaluation process, such as improved communication between the principal and the teacher, improved relationships with students, better skill in media presentations, etc. If the evaluative process does not result in improved administration, or teaching, much of the purpose of evaluation has been lost.

Figure 6.9 presents a possible format which can be used to implement evaluation by performance objectives. This format is designed to provide teacher-principal cooperation in developing specific performance objectives. It also indicates how specific objectives are to be achieved, anticipated outcomes for students, and the criteria utilized for measuring the extent to which the specific objectives are achieved.

Figure 6.7
Evaluation of Teacher Performance*
(Model)

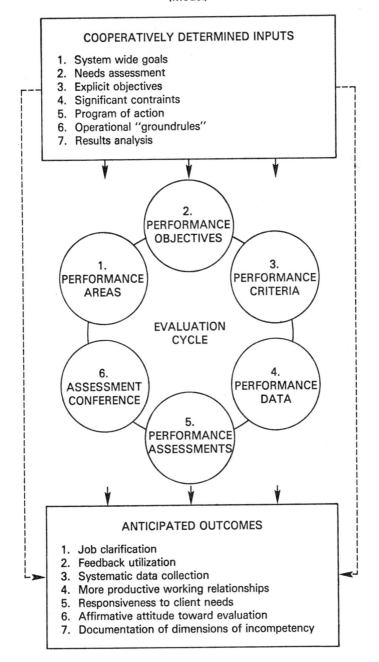

COOPERATIVELY DETERMINED INPUTS

1. System wide goals
2. Needs assessment
3. Explicit objectives
4. Significant contraints
5. Program of action
6. Operational "groundrules"
7. Results analysis

2. PERFORMANCE OBJECTIVES

1. PERFORMANCE AREAS

3. PERFORMANCE CRITERIA

EVALUATION CYCLE

6. ASSESSMENT CONFERENCE

4. PERFORMANCE DATA

5. PERFORMANCE ASSESSMENTS

ANTICIPATED OUTCOMES

1. Job clarification
2. Feedback utilization
3. Systematic data collection
4. More productive working relationships
5. Responsiveness to client needs
6. Affirmative attitude toward evaluation
7. Documentation of dimensions of incompetency

* *American Secondary Education,* Charles L. Wood, ed., September, 1972.

Figure 6.8
Cooperatively Determined Input

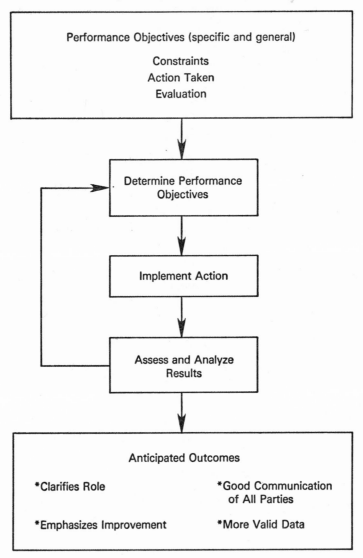

Performance Objectives (specific and general)

Constraints
Action Taken
Evaluation

Determine Performance
Objectives

Implement Action

Assess and Analyze
Results

Anticipated Outcomes

*Clarifies Role

*Emphasizes Improvement

*Good Communication
of All Parties

*More Valid Data

Figure 6.9
Evaluation of Performance Objectives
(Developed Cooperatively with Teacher and Administrator)

Performance Objectives	How Objective is to be Achieved	Anticipated Outcomes for Students	Procedure to Measure Achievement of Objectives

Teachers Signature

Administrator's Signature

Date

Guidelines for Teacher Evaluation

In planning an evaluation program for a particular school, several recommendations are offered. They are as follows:

1. The faculty and administration should synthesize the form appropriate to their need and subject to their mutual agreement. Wherever goals and objectives are set, the statements should be in behavioral terms.

2. The primary purpose of evaluation is to improve instruction. The principal, supervisor, and all persons involved in evaluation should strive to maintain an atmosphere characterized by mutual respect and cooperation throughout the process.

3. All teachers should be familiar with the form and its use.

4. Teachers should have advance notice of a classroom visit for evaluation.

5. Use of the intercom for purposes of evaluation is absolutely taboo.

6. A conference with the teacher being evaluated should be held as soon as possible following the observation period to discuss the teaching situation. The supervisor or principal should maintain a helping posture throughout the conference.

7. The form should be identified by name of school, name of teacher, date of observation, date of conference, rating by supervisor and principal, persons to whom copies are forwarded, and signed by all who participate in the evaluation, including the teacher. The teacher's signature will indicate only that he or she has seen the report and not that he or she necessarily agrees with the opinions or decisions.

8. The teacher should retain a copy if desired.

9. A self-evaluation experience by video-tape should be encouraged periodically throughout the year.

10. A teacher is responsible only to the principal on all matters relating to evaluation. The principal will intervene on all cases questioning the proficiency of the teachers.

11. Persons responsible for the evaluation program should make every effort possible to be adequately informed and to inform their staff regarding current research and development in the evaluation of teaching personnel.

12. The improvement of the evaluation procedure should be the responsibility of a committee appointed for that particular purpose and responsible to the principal.

SUMMARY

Instructional improvement is the primary purpose of the secondary school principal or supervisor. The instructional improvement program is focused upon developing humane educational programs—programs that provide for continuous progress arrangements, stress options rather than uniformity, and occur in humane environments.

Because of changing concepts of instructional techniques and the increased emphasis on individualization, the procedures utilized to improve instruction must change also. More and more reliance will come to be placed upon measurement of achievement of behavioral objectives. This will undoubtedly mean less emphasis on techniques of instruction. More emphasis will be placed on the product and less on the process.

Improving instruction involves changing people, which implies that the principal or supervisor must be aware of the change process. It demands committed leadership that bases decisions upon accepted objectives. The tools of improving instruction include: faculty meetings, classroom visitation, group meetings, workshops, supervisor-teacher conferences, a professional library, university attendance, inter-school and intra-school visitation, use of consultants, pilot projects and the "spinout" approach, micro-teaching, video-taping of teaching, sensitivity training, and teachers' centers.

An important consideration of the inservice education is that it must be a well planned, coordinated program. Teacher involvement is the key element in the foundation of a strong inservice education program. Teachers must be allowed to determine problems to be dealt with and provided opportunities to pursue solutions to the problems delineated. Brainstorming is recommended as a technique in bringing to the foreground problem areas and ideas which may then be focused upon to improve the school.

While the faculty meeting is essential in developing educational programs, meetings are often ineffective because common sense is not used in their preparation and scheduling.

Since evaluation of the effectiveness of teaching is complex and subjective, teachers often resent or resist most evaluative techniques. However, if evaluative instruments are shown to be fair to teachers, and that they have a part in their development, the resentment and resistance often turn to cooperation.

Students should and can be helpful in the evaluation of teaching since they have such a high stake in their teachers' success. Most administrators that have student evaluation programs for their teachers are satisfied with the results.

Certain personality traits are associated with good classroom teaching, such as neat appearance, organization, and enthusiasm. Teaching behavior may be observed and recorded in measurable terms. Objective devices have been recently developed to record teacher behavior.

The primary purpose of evaluation is to improve instruction. Some principles exist for the educational leader to follow in evaluation. One is that classroom visits should be followed by conferences. The intercom should never be used in evaluating teachers.

Micro-teaching, although primarily used as a pre-teaching tool, may be useful in improving inservice teaching as well. Video-taping of lessons which may or may not be used with micro-teaching provides an excellent way for the teacher to self-analyze his or her instruction, with self-analysis being an excellent way to improve instruction.

Teachers' centers are being used in England and Wales to provide the teacher with opportunity to improve his or her profession. These teacher-run centers could serve as a model for similar centers in the United States in which the teacher voluntarily learns new methods of teaching without direction from administrators or supervisors. Sensitivity training provides the educational leader with a tool to break down barriers to change as a result of alienation, tension, and a lack of leadership or decision-making skills within the faculty.

Classroom visitation is a very valuable tool to use in improving instruction. However, the classroom visitation requires great care in human relations. Teacher-student interaction can be improved by the use of interaction analysis which objectively measures the interaction which occurs between the teacher and the students.

NOTES

1. J. Lloyd Trump, "On Humanizing Schools, Point of View and Basic Issues," *NASSP Bulletin* 56:361 (February, 1972), pp. 9–11.

2. Arthur M. Coombs, Jr. et al., *Variable Modular Scheduling Effective Use of School Time, Plant and Personnel* (New York and Beverly Hills: Benzinger, Inc., 1971), p. 1.

3. Don E. Glines, *Creating Humane Schools* (Mankato, Minn.: Campus Publishers, 1971), pp. 70–79.

4. William A. Zeralsky and Enid L. Schester, *New York State Education* (April, 1970), p. 38.

5. R. A. Engel, "Teacher Evaluates Teacher for Pay Differentials," *Clearing House* 45:7 (March, 1971), pp. 407–409.

6. Ibid.

7. M. Zax, "Outstanding Teachers: Who Are They?" *Clearing House* 45 (January, 1971), pp. 285–289.

8. Ibid.

9. Ibid.

10. School Administration Opinion Poll. "Schoolmen Split on Student Evaluation of Teachers," *Nations Schools* 86 (October, 1970), p. 53.

11. E. Washington, "Education Expert Teacher Action Study: A New Approach to Teacher Evaluation," *Journal of Teacher Education* 21 (Summer, 1970), pp. 258–263.

12. Ibid.

13. Ibid.

14. C. Miller and D. Miller, "Importance of Certain Personal Qualities and Professional Competence in Successful Classroom Teaching," *Journal of Teacher Education* 22 (January, 1971), pp. 16–17.

15. D. Hamschek, "Characterization of Good Teachers and Implications for Teacher Education," *Phi Delta Kappan* 50 (February, 1969), pp. 341–345.

16. D. E. Wagoner, "Do You Know Anything at All About How Well or How Much Your Teachers Teach?" *American School Board Journal* 158 (August, 1970), pp. 21–22.

17. W. J. Popham, "Performance Tests of Teaching Proficiency: Rationale Development and Validation," *American Educational Research Journal* 8 (January, 1971), pp. 105–117.

18. Ronald T. Hyman, *School Administrator's Handbook of Teacher Supervision and Evaluation Methods* (Englewood Cliffs, N.J.: Prentice-Hall, Inc., 1976), p. 30.

19. H. B. Pinkney, "Better Teaching: Key to Improving Urban Schools," *Bulletin NASSP* (February, 1977), pp. 30-32.

20. E. P. Broudy, "Notes on the Validity of the Minnesota Teacher Attitude Inventory," *Journal of Educational Research* (October, 1970), pp. 64-67.

21. R. Bloom and H. Wilensky, "Four Observation Categories for Rating Teacher Behavior," *Journal of Educational Research* 60 (July, 1967), pp. 464-465.

22. Robert N. Bush and Dwight W. Allen, "Micro-teaching: Controlled Practice in the Training of Teachers," *Microteaching, A Description* (Stanford Teacher Education Program, Stanford University, 1967), pp. 1-4.

23. Richard N. Jensen, *Microteaching* (Springfield, Ill.: Charles C. Thomas, Publisher, 1974), p. 3.

24. Stephen K. Bailey, "Teachers' Centers: A British First," *Phi Delta Kappan* 53:3 (November, 1971), pp. 146-149.

25. Ibid.

26. Larry J. Krafft and Leland W. Howe, "Guidelines for Sensitivity Training in your School," *Phi Delta Kappan* 53:3 (November, 1971), pp. 179-180.

27. Edmund J. Amidon and Ned A. Flanders, *A Manual for Understanding and Improving Teacher Classroom Behavior* (Minneapolis: Association for Productive Teaching, Inc., 1967).

28. Ibid.

29. Ibid.

30. George B. Redfern, "Evaluating Secondary School Teachers," *American Secondary Education* (September, 1972), p. 7.

7

Development of the Educational Program

The development of curriculum and accompanying instructional materials is a continuous, ever-evolving process. Doll has suggested that several trends appear in the evolution of curriculum when viewing American education from colonial times to present:

1. In the past, ideas have often been developed in private schools, and public schools have then adopted them.

2. Schools and school systems everywhere have frankly copied plans, procedures, and curriculum content from other schools and school systems.

3. New institutions, such as the early academy and the much more recent middle schools, have been established to satisfy unmet needs.

4. Educational principles, such as that of schooling for everyone, have been adopted in substance and modified in detail whenever they have struck a popular chord.

5. Experimentation has occurred, but it has usually been informal and its results have remained largely untested.

6. National committees have determined general objectives, policies, and programs.

7. Psychological and social theories and revelations have turned the efforts of curriculum planners in new directions.

8. American educators have been susceptible to the use of plans, some of them delusive, for making the difficult processes of teaching and learning easier.

9. Even those educational ideas which have been based on the soundest evidence have been adopted very slowly by practitioners.

10. The schools, as an instrument of American society, have been subjected to numerous public pressures, the nature of which tends to change from generation to generation.[1]

Often, the major goal of curriculum development in the past had been to provide the teacher with a rather complete package of instructional materials, including an orientation to their development and use. Thus, it was possible to say that two major work activities generally constituted the production of such a curriculum. One major activity was concerned with the development and preparation of instructional materials, and the other with the process of disseminating information about them.

The preparation of instructional materials frequently centered around determining instructional goals and evaluating them from several points of view, plus establishing the structure to be used in organizing the knowledge to be covered from a given subject matter field. Distinction was made between the long-range objectives one hoped to achieve and certain short steps designed to move one toward those objectives. Once objectives and structure had been determined, initial material development was begun. Identifiable tasks included the preparation of teacher and student materials, audio-visual materials, evaluation techniques, and additional reference materials. After initial materials had been developed they were subjected to a field test or tryout in a selected sample of schools. Upon completion of these operations, final instructional materials were prepared.

The dissemination process began early in a project by outlining the necessary procedures and by selecting schools even before all the material was ready. Teachers and principals were acquainted with the techniques and purposes of the revised curriculum by discussion, class visitations, and such other devices. Lay personnel such as PTA groups were also oriented once the school staff understood the materials.

These fairly well-established steps are still being applied in many areas even though local authorities are not sure of themselves. Part of this hesitancy results from not only university scholars, but others distinguished in their work who prepare courses of study for schools, reflecting advances in many subject areas and including bold ideas about the nature of school experiences. As a consequence, principals faced the dilemma of whether to select the best program available that had been developed by the "experts," or continue local curriculum making efforts. Cooperative efforts between universities and local schools provide a more rational approach to curriculum development and implementation than does separate development and implementation.

ISSUES RELATED TO CURRICULUM DEVELOPMENT

There are a number of different theories and practices popular in curriculum development today. However, administrators must keep in mind that curriculum must first meet the needs of the student. Most administrators agree on the general goals to be sought, but there is considerable difference as to how these goals are to be achieved. Answers to the following questions have a direct bearing on the type of curriculum developed by a school:

1. What is the curriculum?

There are many broad definitions of this term. It may be viewed as a collection of courses or as written courses of study; or it may be considered as all the experiences the student has under the influence of the school. Further, should experiences for students be predetermined by adults or should students assist in determining what they are going to experience? Hass describes the four bases of curriculum planning and planning of teaching as: (a) social forces, (b) human development, (c) the nature of learning, and (d) the nature of knowledge.[2] His definition of curriculum, which goes beyond activities under the direction of the school, is as follows:

> The curriculum is all of the experiences that individual learners have in a program of education whose purpose is to achieve broad goals and related specific objectives, which is planned in terms of a framework of theory and research or past and present professional practice.[3]

2. What should be taught?

Much controversy centers around the content of the curriculum. Should it be made up mainly of specific terms or concepts to be learned, or of material applicable to day-to-day living of students? Another facet of this question is the order in which learning that a particular sequence should be determined beforehand, yet some say that students do not learn that way. Some maintain that sequence and organization are to be found, not in the various courses that make up the curriculum, but in the learner, and that they should determine the needs of the students.

3. Should the demands of society or needs of the individual determine the curriculum?

Some say that since the schools are established by a society to serve its needs, the content of the program should deal primarily with the needs of society. Others maintain that since the business of education is to educate the individual, the curriculum should be built around the needs of the individual. The issue essentially centers around the relative emphasis a school should accord in meeting the needs of the individual and society. The content of the curriculum will not be an "either-or" stand, but will deal with the individual in society. Another aspect of this issue is the question of whether the curriculum should be determined by adult needs or by the student's immediate needs. Some local curriculum committees claim that there are enough concerns common to both student and adult to provide a series of learning experiences that will have immediate significance in the lives of students *and* prepare them to adapt to the changes in the adult world.

4. When and by whom should the curriculum be planned?

This question centers around the problem of the responsibility for determining what the curriculum shall be. Some say it is a specialized job to be done entirely by experts in curriculum planning well in advance of the learning situation. Others believe that the curriculum should be planned by supervisors, teachers, and students on the spot, without any pre-planning. This question will be covered in greater detail in the next section of this chapter, but suffice it to say now that a position between these two extremes must be determined by local curriculum planners.

5. How should the curriculum provide for individual differences?

It is commonly recognized that students vary widely in ability. This has encouraged educators to attempt to devise various means of adjusting their courses to differences in abilities. Here again there are different beliefs as to how this should be accomplished. Some promote the concept of curriculum established in terms of minimum fundamentals, with the main problem being that of helping students of varying learning rates acquire these fundamentals. Another common viewpoint is that students should be grouped according to their abilities, on the assumption that this will reduce the ability range in each group and simplify the job of individualization. A third point of view is that a question-centered, experience-type curriculum permits all members of the group to work together in a common area in which they are interested, with each class member working at his or her own level of academic development and yet contributing to the group enterprise.

6. What is the relative importance of content, method, and materials?

A sound approach by the school recognizes that learning involves the interaction of the three elements: content, methods, and materials. The teacher is the key in bringing these factors together in a meaningful way for the optimizing of the learning environment for the student.

THE PRINCIPAL AND THE CURRICULUM

There are a great many definitions of the word *curriculum*. To many, the word simply means the subjects, academic and nonacademic, that are being taught. In this sense, it is used synonymously with the term *instructional program*. To others, curriculum means a certain pattern of subjects taught within a certain sequence such as the "college preparatory curriculum." Curriculum is also considered by some educators as meaning various sequences of specialization such as the "college preparatory course," the "general course," "vocational course," etc. Still others believe that curriculum includes the sum total of all experience that a student receives in school and all activities related to the school. Included would be subject offerings, activities, and experiences resulting from the everyday interactions emanating from pupil-pupil, pupil-teacher, and pupil-principal relationships.

Doll has indicated that the commonly accepted definition of curriculum has changed from content of courses of study and lists of subjects to all the experiences which are offered to learners under the auspices on direction of the school. He further states that if pupils' experiences are to improve, teachers, supervisors, and administrators must become skillful in curriculum improvement that encompasses the broadened definition of curriculum. According to Doll, curriculum improvement involves understanding the dynamics of changing human behavior and should include input not only from teachers, but also from students and parents.[4]

Principals should remember that no matter how homogeneous their student body may be, there will be real differences among the students. And, regardless of the type of community that the school serves, there always will be some graduates from the high school who will be living in other parts of the country rather than in the local community. The ideal curriculum, then, is one which takes into consideration the previously mentioned conditions and offers diversified subjects and activities. These offerings should be available in sufficient range and degree that each pupil can be challenged and stimulated. Usually, the more diversified the student body, the more difficult this is to accomplish. Of course, if there are plenty of classrooms, sufficient amount of equipment and supplies, professionally qualified teachers for every subject taught, and 100 percent community interest and support for the school, principals would consider curriculum development differently than when they find themselves facing reality.

The curriculum selected should be one that has the best possible offerings consistent with realistic limitations of building sites, equipment, supplies, space, and personnel. Decisions must be reached as to just which subjects are to be in the curriculum and which are to be omitted. This calls for skillful leadership on the part of principals. Such a decision as to what constitutes the "best" program for students is one that is accepted, in the main, by the community.

There will naturally be differences of opinion not only among board of education members, teachers, and administrators, but also among the various community groups. Unanimity will never be secured; but principals must initiate action that will set machinery in motion leading to consensus, acceptance, and understanding of the ultimate program. A truly successful school program cannot be reached unless such consensus is reached. Principals will be tempted to say that they know what really is "best" for students because of their experience in working with such matters; but they must remember that one of their main tasks is not merely to voice personal philosophies and educational theories, but to be an educational leader in the school and community.

As instructional leaders, principals will, from time to time, bring basic issues, questions, and problems to the attention of teachers and laymen. The involvement of diverse groups and the striving for consensus on basic questions is an extremely slow process, but it is a process that inevitably leads to small gains. These gains, however small, tend to accumulate into more important gains and this accumulation spells progress.

The Curriculum Committee

Of course, the real question is how can consensus be attained? Principals are at their best when they can create situations in which people help each other. They can be instrumental in helping to organize a committee in the community known as the "Curriculum Coordinating and Planning Committee." This committee would have on it, in addition to the principal, department heads, staff members, PTA representatives, and others from the community who wish to serve. This curriculum committee should meet at least four or five times within the school year and maybe more often if a special curriculum project is being developed. From time to time, consultants from the local school system and neighboring school systems, and specialists from colleges, universities, and the State Department of Public Instruction should meet with the committee to explain new trends, developments, and research in curricular matters. The committee members should be concerned with types of courses, content of courses, and recommended additions or deletions to the existing program.

The principal must help the committee understand certain ground rules for operating. For example, the committee should be an advisory committee, therefore, one of the functions of the principal should be to discreetly point out advantages and disadvantages to suggestions made by committee members. After the committee has considered suggestions thoroughly, the principal should bring its basic recommendations to the attention of the superintendent of schools or specialized administrative staff. Certain suggestions of this committee can be put into effect without the necessity of action by the superintendent. The principal should use judgment as to the types of recommendations that fall into this category.

The curriculum planning committee is probably the most important committee in the entire school's committee structure; for out of this committee's deliberations, changes may occur in such areas as building and plant planning, kinds of equipment and supplies to be ordered, and the formulation of a general philosophy for the entire school system.

THE PRINCIPAL AND THE CURRICULUM

The principal, as an educational leader in curriculum planning, cannot handle this job effectively unless he or she is an active participant in principals' professional educational organizations and associations. Regular attendance at state meetings should be supplemented with active attendance at national conferences designed to update curriculum development experiences. Also, difficult as it is, the principal should have firsthand knowledge of some of the professional literature which explains the latest research and thinking pertaining to curriculum.

The principal should realize that the curriculum is never a static thing. Never will there be a time when the curriculum is "set" and when it can be said, "That's it!" The curriculum is a continually changing and evolving thing. Therefore, an important aspect of successful curriculum construction is the necessity for a continual evaluation of the program. It is important to have the staff use evaluation instruments from time to time for a self-evaluation of the school program.

The role, then, of the principal in curriculum development is a complex, difficult, and rigorous one. Programs and curricula of other schools or school systems should never be adopted in entirety. It must be remembered that each school and community is unique, serving different students and different populations, and with its own unique set of problems. There is no easy outline or plan to follow that will lead, automatically, to an ideal curriculum. The curriculum is a reflection of an ingredient of American society; namely, the changes in the behavior and thinking of free and independent people. It is the hope, of course, of every administrator that the curriculum should be more than a mere reflection of the times—that it should be a pioneer, a guide, a searchlight showing the way to goals toward which society itself can strive. With the help of the principal, the curriculum can very nearly do just that.

Curriculum Development

Curriculum development can and should be evaluated by the secondary school principal. Such questions as the following should be considered: What new courses have been added in recent years? Has the faculty developed curriculum guides for their subjects? What curriculum changes have been made in recent years to meet the challenges of social unrest, urbanization, mass communication and the affluent society?

Most important in curriculum development is the opportunity which the faculty has for self-improvement. While one of the objectives of the faculty working in the curriculum is to develop a better educational program, the primary purpose is teacher self-improvement through the teachers' more complete understanding of their own subjects and ways to improve the learning of students. Curriculum development is a continuous process which should involve all members of the faculty. It will not succeed without organization and attention from the principal.

Criteria by Which to Judge a Curriculum Plan

Saylor and Alexander provide the following checklist to be used to determine the quality of a school's curriculum:*

1. Are essential data available to the planning groups responsible for the curriculum of the school?

2. Are the goals of the school clearly stated and understood by all concerned? Are the goals sufficiently comprehensive, balanced, and realistic? Is there provision for modifying, dropping, and adding goals as needed?

3. Do the learning opportunities anticipate a progression from dependent, other-directed learning to independent, self-directed learning in accordance with the level of students served by the school center?

4. Do students and teachers mutually understand the specific plans in the total curriculum plan which affect them? Do students participate, as their maturities permit, in making the plans? Do they generally understand and agree as to what is expected of them, and why?

5. Are sets of related major goals grouped accordingly, with the learning opportunities in each set or domain selected for achieving these goals? Have sets of learning opportunities been checked as to their relation to the goals, with gaps and overlappings identified and remedied? Do the learning opportunities seem to be the best possible choices for this group of students at this time to achieve the goals set for them?

6. Within each domain or set of goals and related learning opportunities is there a pattern or patterns reflecting conscious attention to curriculum designing? Are all appropriate and feasible types of learning experiences utilized?

7. Is the plan tailor-made for the particular school center? Are any plans developed externally, adapted to the population and facilities of the school center? Are the learning opportunities planned truly relevant to the educational needs of this population and community?

8. Are demands of external forces screened through a process that keeps them in acceptable balance?

---

* From *Planning Curriculum for Schools* by J. Galen Saylor and William M. Alexander. Copyright © 1954 by J. Galen Saylor and William M. Alexander. Copyright © 1966, 1974 by Holt, Rinehart and Winston. Reprinted by permission of Holt, Rinehart and Winston.

9. Is the total curriculum plan comprehensive? Does it anticipate instruction and evaluation as well as include goals and designs of learning opportunities?

10. Are the responsible planning groups representative of all persons concerned, including students, parents, general public, and professional staff?

11. Does the plan have adequate provision of feedback from students and other concerned groups as well as means for making modification as indicated?

12. Can the plan and each of its parts be explained sufficiently clearly to the students, parents, and other lay persons to be understood by them?

13. Is there some representative council or curriculum evaluation unit or other group or individual responsible for identifying problems and collecting problems identified by others that develop in the planning process? Is there a clear channel of communication of such problems to those who can resolve them and a plan for reporting back to the problem identifiers the resolutions made? Similarly, is there a systematic way of securing, monitoring, and reporting action regarding suggestions for change and innovation?

14. Does the plan anticipate full use of the educational resources of the school center, the community, and the media?

15. Is flexibility built into the curriculum plan by adequate provisions for alternative learning opportunities, instructional modes, and student and teacher options in general?[5]

Individual Differences

It has been estimated that the academic ability of the average tenth grade class ranges from grade five to grade sixteen. Even with students of the same academic ability, there are great individual differences. Therefore, the secondary school must make provision for these differences not only through a broad educational program, but also through various kinds of grouping arrangements to meet the needs of all students. A school with an educational program which provides individualized instruction, is known as the nongraded high school. While the nongraded high school is a worthy goal of all secondary schools, one must be realistic and hope that the high school will have at least some fair and effective plan for meeting the needs of students of all ability levels.

While some ability grouping may be desirable, social stigma will often be attached to low ability groups. Therefore, some classes should be grouped together regardless of ability, while others will be grouped separately, especially such classes as advanced mathematics and developmental reading. Social studies classes which emphasize the discussion of social issues could be grouped heterogeneously. However, students with outstanding ability in social studies should also have the opportunity to be placed in advanced classes. Recent court decisions have raised questions concerning discriminatory practices which may be inherent in grouping procedures.

The following are some advantages of ability grouping:

1. Through homogeneous grouping, the teacher has a narrower range of individual differences.
2. Students that have similar abilities tend to stimulate and motivate their peers as well as teach each other, thus reducing the burden upon the teacher.
3. Students of superior achievement grouped on an ability basis do not feel ostracized or rejected due to their high achievement level. They do not feel the necessity of curbing their efforts and talents in order to conform to "average" class standards.
4. It has been asserted, but not completely verified by research, that homogeneously grouped students can achieve greater insight in problematic situations, progress at a more rapid rate, and learn more when the curriculum is especially designed for this purpose.
5. It is asserted that when a child competes with his intellectual peers, he is less likely to develop a superior attitude as compared to a situation in a heterogeneous class where he is above his peers. Competition with intellectual peers tends to give the child a more realistic evaluation of his or her abilities.
6. Ability grouping is more democratic since the less able student isn't forced to compete with the gifted child.

Some of the disadvantages of ability grouping are:

1. It is impossible to group children homogeneously. A pupil may be grouped high according to reading ability, but ability in other areas may be low.
2. Homogeneous grouping can lead to an elite class. This, of course, could lead to the strengthening of a permanent class structure.
3. Ability grouping tends to encourage teachers to overlook individual differences, since the purpose of ability grouping is to group together those pupils having the least individual differences.
4. Ability grouping is undemocratic since it tends to label and classify students according to bright, average, or dull.

5. There is a strong tendency to have the more able teachers take the bright group, while new or less competent teachers are relegated to the slow groups.

Ease and simplicity of administration, economy, satisfaction of children, teachers, and parents—these and other values all enter into the decision-making process in ability grouping.

The following practices are recommended for the educational leader to use in grouping students:

1. Students are grouped according to the following criteria: teacher judgment, aptitude test scores, past record of achievement, and making provisions for social adjustment.

2. Students are grouped in individual subject areas, rather than "across the board."

3. After students are grouped, materials are utilized which fit the needs of each group. For example, ninth grade students of fifth grade reading ability would be provided with fifth grade equivalent reading materials until they are able to comprehend more difficult materials.

4. The faculty is involved in devising the grouping plan and is solidly behind the methods used in grouping.

5. Students during a large part of their school day are grouped in heterogeneous classes such as physical education, music, problems of democracy, etc.

6. A carefully devised grading system is used which does not penalize either the student in the lower ability groups, or the accelerated groups.

7. Arrangements are made to reduce the class size of the low ability groups. Discipline problems often tend to be multiplied in the low ability groups, and it is wise to distribute the "problems."

8. Careful study is made of ways to handle cases of "misplacement." Care should be also taken to avoid bouncing students from one group to another. Therefore, criteria should be developed which allow for transfer, but avoid a game of "musical chairs."

Articulation of Sequential Programs
Between the Elementary, Middle or Junior High School,
and Senior High School

Too many schools do not give due consideration to the effect their program of studies has on the learning of children at various levels of schooling. The situation is even worse when one considers the articulation between the high school and post-high school training institutions.

Every school should have regular sessions with representatives of other schools within the system to discuss sequence and articulation. The principal should take responsibility to insure that a systematic check on articulation be made periodically. It is also important to make certain that the various subject areas provide for adequate coordination so that students can see the relationships between the various subject areas. Many school systems have a curriculum coordinator who assumes the major responsibility for insuring continuity of the school program. The curriculum coordinator should hold conferences regularly with faculty members to help insure that the overall program has sequence and articulation. The principal of the secondary school should encourage the curriculum coordinator in attempting to provide some order in the school system's offerings. Special efforts should be made to know more about the program of "feeder" schools. Department chairpersons can provide invaluable assistance in improving articulation.

Few schools have any organized program for articulating their offerings with that of post-high school training agencies, namely the college and post-high school training institutions. The secondary school principal can be the key figure in the development of committees to deal with articulation. Such committees should involve teachers, department chairpersons, parents, students, curriculum coordinators, curriculum specialists and building level principals. A committee knowledgeable about the industrial community can be an indispensible aid to insure that the education and training which youth are receiving is relevant to the work-world.

CURRICULAR ALTERNATIVES

No requirements for graduation, voluntary attendance, no dress code, no study halls, no bells, no schedules, no report cards, no counselors, no students assigned to teachers—a high school? Yes, believe it or not, principal Don E. Glines describes his high school in this manner.[6] Selection of educational programs for the principal and supervisor provide a smorgasbord of a wide range of choices ranging from Glines' school to the NASSP model school to the traditional high school with its nine forty-five-minute periods and the large study hall.

Innovation in education which holds great promise for improving learning does not occur in a vacuum nor is it a happenstance. It comes about when there is careful planning of experimental programs based on research. Industry spends some of its income annually on developing newer and improved products. The same kind of investment of the education dollar is needed to improve educational processes.

If effective innovations are developed, there must be experimental schools. These pilot schools would be led by innovative educators who would have great freedom to experiment and carry out new ideas. It is doubtful that the development of pilot schools can be left up to local school districts if effective innovations are to be developed. The university, in cooperation with the state departments of education, should be encouraged to develop experimental schools and programs in cooperation with local school districts.

The NASSP Model School

The National Association of Secondary School Principals has provided leadership in innovative projects during the past two decades which include the differentiated staffing project, the internship for those preparing for the principalship, the beginning teachers' project, and the Model Schools Project.

The NASSP Model Schools project recommends the following division of time for teachers each week:

1. Experience sessions (LGI) (100 pupils
   in each group)   65 minutes
2. Reaction Groups (SGD) (20 pupils in
   each group)   325 minutes
3. Advisory groups   50 minutes
4. Planning, developing materials,
   evaluate, supervise aids, work
   with pupils, etc.   1,250 minutes

                                    Total   1,690 minutes

This project is an attempt to provide more efficient utilization of the teacher's time through such practices as the use of paraprofessionals to accomplish nonprofessional tasks, and to avoid duplication of teaching efforts such as substituting large group instruction for repeating the same presentation to smaller groups. This project is described by Trump and Georgiades as follows:*

I. Basic Goals:

    a. To provide a program with varied strategies and
       environments for learning through which all pupils,
       regardless of differences in individual talents and
       interests, may proceed with gains.
    b. To provide conditions for teaching that recognize dif-
       ferences among teachers and capitalize on the special
       talents and interests of each person.

---

* From J. Lloyd Trump and William Georgiades, "Doing Better With What You Have: NASSP Model School's Project," *NASSP Bulletin* (May, 1970), pp. 109–113. Used by permission.

    c. To define clearly the role of the professional teacher as separate from the roles of clerks, instruction assistants, and general aides.

    d. To separate the principal's role in instructional improvement and general supervision from management tasks that can be done by other persons.

    e. To emphasize in curriculum revision the distinction between those learnings that are *essential* for all pupils, and those learnings which are *specially relevant* for some of them.

    f. To reduce required learnings in all subjects to provide more time for pupils to follow their own interests and talents.

    g. To develop better methods and materials for evaluating changes in conditions for learning, teaching, and supervising, as well as changes in the use of the things of education; also for evaluating the effects of the program on pupils, teachers, and principals.

    h. To utilize school funds, supplies and equipment, and other school facilities differently to produce better results as described under Item "f" *without* necessarily having more of the things of education.

    i. To discover better ways of utilizing outside consultant help not only within a given school but also through audio-visual devices to spread the consultants' talents among other schools.

    j. To analyze the process and the progress of change among schools.

II. Basic Characteristics of the Program:

    a. The principal spends three-fourths of his time working directly with teachers to improve instruction and learning.

       1) He organizes learning for teachers according to the same general principles that he expects teachers to follow with their pupils.

       2) He selects assistants qualified to handle the school's managerial and other tasks only indirectly related to instructional improvement.

    b. Differentiated staffing and other arrangements produce changed roles for teachers.

       1) Instruction Assistants (average of 20 hours per week per teacher) oversee pupils' independent study, etc.;

Clerks (average 10 hours per week per teacher) keep records, etc; General Aides (average of 5 hours per week per teacher) perform tasks *not* requiring competence in subject areas or clerical skills.

2) Teachers are scheduled an average of not more than 10 hours per week with pupil groups (2 hours with large groups, 8 hours with small); the balance of 20 hours, mostly on school premises, is for keeping up-to-date, developing materials, evaluating, conferring and supervising.

3) Most teachers serve a new role as teacher-counselor (helping about 35 pupils *individually* to plan, schedule, and change their independent study time and collecting information about each pupil's progress and difficulties).

4) Teachers work individually in offices or in groups organized by departments or on some other basis.

c. Individualized learning methods emphasize motivation, continuous progress, self-direction, individual scheduling, personalized evaluation, and attention to personal needs and interests, *while maintaining pupil accountability.*

1) Pupils are required, all the years they are in school, to attend 8 hours of motivational presentations and discussions each week in all 8 areas of human knowledge (30 minutes in a large group and 30 minutes in a small group per week in each area). These groups are scheduled by the school office.

2) Pupils have 22 hours per week for scheduling independent study in the school or community (distribution decided by pupils and their teacher-counselors, changeable by them at will with joint approval). A professional counselor or the principal resolves disagreements, if any, between a pupil and his teacher-counselor. These pupil schedules are made, changed, and recorded by teacher-counselors and their secretaries.

3) Each pupil covers required content at his own pace, using specially prepared materials. Much of this work may be done cooperatively in various-sized groups, as established by students themselves.

4) Evaluation for each pupil is in relation to his own past achievement in a variety of educational goals.

Since teachers cannot evaluate every aspect of learning, priorities are established.

5) Attendance of pupils is regularly checked and the amount of each pupil's progress systematically reported by the instruction assistants who supervise independent study.

d. Curriculum revision separates basic, essential learnings from other learnings that mainly are appropriate for pupils with special talents and interests.

1) Materials are organized to provide self-direction, self-motivation, self-pacing, and self-evaluation by pupils themselves.

2) The amount of *depth* and *creative* studies in relation to *required, basic studies* increases with the age and maturity of individual pupils.

e. Improvement of teaching and learning requires that money and facilities be utilized differently.

1) Financial input is analyzed in terms of gains (product output) in the foregoing Items "a," "b," "c," and "d" (principal's role, teaching roles, individualized learning and curriculum revision). Improvements in those areas do not necessarily cost more.

2) Most conventional classrooms become learning centers (both kinds: *study* and *work*) for independent study; a few rooms are divided for small-group meetings and for teacher offices and workrooms; a few spaces are needed for large-group instruction (motivational presentations).

3) Priorities for new construction or for purchase of supplies and equipment are based on what will produce the most good for the most pupils, in terms of the goals of the teacher-learning methods in the Model.

f. Increased emphasis on evaluation is essential to provide feedback for directing further improvements, and to produce confidence in the changes.

1) The emphasis is on behavioral changes when evaluating individual pupil progress.

2) Analyses will reveal changes made in conditions for learning, teaching, supervision, curriculum development, and the use of funds and facilities in school and community.

3) The effects of the changes on pupils and teachers en masse, on principal and assistants, and financial efficiency will be measured.[7]

In order to implement the Model Schools Project, Trump and Georgiades suggest:

1. Keep a log of what the principal now does and suggest to his superintendent how he can change to implement the model.
2. Set up an instructional system for teachers to implement the model.
3. Organize a faculty study center for faculty independent study concerning the model and student independent study.
4. Conduct several discussion sessions with teachers concerning the model.
5. Help teachers develop continuous progress programs and individualized instruction packages.
6. Reduce the amount of time teachers talk to classes (not more than twenty percent).
7. Abandon the conventional schedule for a week, once or twice a year to permit pupils to study or work on subjects of their interest.
8. Develop a series of mini-courses.
9. Reduce overcrowding by introducing more independent study.
10. Tear out some walls, add some walls to accommodate various size groups.[8]

The Nongraded School

For more than four decades, teachers have been encouraged by professors of education and educational administrators to individualize their instruction. Yet, they were never given the tools necessary to be more than "group" teachers, with the exception of ways to group classes to deal with more individual needs. Teachers are accused of being textbook teachers, or subject matter specialists. Educators can hardly expect teachers to work with individuals as long as their responsibility and supervision is extended over twenty-five to thirty-five pupils with varying abilities.

In order to cope with individuals in the heterogeneous class, teachers are encouraged to provide enrichment materials for the fast learners and less difficult materials for the slower learners. The traditional ratio of thirty to one prevails; however, some energetic, and in many cases, harried teachers really accomplish some individual instruction. With the nongraded school concepts, the educational leader can give teachers the organizational tools necessary to provide for the individual needs of their pupils.

The nongraded school is based upon the concept of continuous progress. That is, so far as possible, students progress at their own rates of development. The nongraded school differs from the graded school in that pupils of the graded school spend a year in a particular grade or subject regardless of their ability, motivation, and interest; whereas in the nongraded school pupils are assigned "grade levels" and subjects on the basis of their achievement. This is illustrated on the following pages.

Figures 7.1 through 7.6 show that, instead of emphasizing time as the prime determinant of the completion of a certain amount of work,

Figure 7.1
Promotion Steps of the Graded Elementary School

					Grade 6
				Grade 5	
			Grade 4		
		Grade 3			
	Grade 2				
Grade 1					

Figure 7.2
Continuous Progress, Nongraded Elementary

Skill Level 1	Skill Level 2	Skill Level 3	Skill Level 4	Skill Level 5	Skill Level 6
a b c d	a b c d	a b c d	a b c d	a b c d	a b c d

Possible Length of Time to Complete Skill Levels

Fast Learner	5 years
Average Learner	6 years
Slow Learner	7 years

Figure 7.3
Promotion Steps of the Graded Middle School

		9th Year Subjects
	8th Year Subjects	
7th Year Subjects		

skill levels are emphasized. Thus, the child beginning his formal education would begin with skill level "A." And as he completed skill level "A" to the satisfaction of the teacher and achievement test scores, he would proceed to skill level "B" and so on until he completed the six skill levels. The chart shows that the fast learner may complete all six

Figure 7.4
Continuous Progress, Nongraded Middle School

	Skill Level 1	Skill Level 2	Skill Level 3
Social Studies	a b c d	a b c d	a b c d
Mathematics	a b c d	a b c d	a b c d
English	a b c d	a b c d	a b c d
Science	a b c d	a b c d	a b c d
Exploratory Subjects	a b c d	a b c d	a b c d

Length of Time to Complete Skill Levels

Fast Learner	Two and One-Half Years
Average Learner	Three Years
Slow Learner	Three and One-Half Years

Figure 7.5
Promotion Steps of the Graded High School

12th Grade Subjects

11th Grade Subjects

10th Grade Subjects

Figure 7.6
Continuous Progress, Nongraded High School

	Biology	Chemistry	Physics	Advanced Science*
Science	a b c d	a b c d	a b c d	a b c d
English and Literature	English 1 a b c d	English 2 a b c d	English 3 a b c d	English 4 a b c d
Foreign Languages	1 a b c d	2 a b c d	3 a b c d	4 a b c d

*Skill levels

skill levels in five years, and would begin his middle school studies at this time, probably in the same elementary school. On the other hand, the slow learner may require seven years to complete the six skill levels. However, both the fast learner and the slow learner would remain in the elementary school for six years while the fast learner would complete his seventh level of the elementary school.

The only reason for the nongraded school is the possibility of an improved instructional program for the student. Research has clearly shown that humans who are given certain freedom in the conduct of their own lives will achieve at a higher rate than those under highly structured organizations. While many ingenious teachers and administrators have developed ways to beat the system within a rigid organization, many others have become its victim. It is true that the traditional graded school is an administrative convenience. It serves as a means in which school administrators and teachers can provide custodial care of the students. Nongraded schools are often feared by administrators because they need constant attention and may provide occasional "hot seats" for the principal. Nevertheless, the nongraded school does provide the daring principal an opportunity to experiment, to be flexible, and to improve the quality of the educational program.

It is logical to classify children for learning on the basis of their achievement rather than the grade which reflects their chronological age. Standardized achievement tests show clearly that the learning ability of students fifteen years of age may range from as low as ten years to as high as that of college sophomores. It is just as fair to force a student whose achievement level is that of a ten-year-old to compete with a student whose achievement is on the college level, as it is to force a 100-pound boy to wrestle a 200-pound boy. The nongraded school allows for students to compete with their peers in achievement. It also provides for slow learning students to experience success, which is almost impossible under the traditional grading system.

One of the greatest problems in breaking away from the lockstep of the graded school is the lack of appropriate curriculum materials. Some courses, such as mathematics, foreign languages, and the sciences lend themselves to a more logical sequential organization than other subjects, such as social studies, art, and the practical arts. In many subjects, chronological age and maturation are important factors, such as in physical education and the practical arts. For this reason, homogeneous grouping according to mental achievement should not always be the primary factor in grouping learning arrangements. Therefore, the curriculum makers must develop a set of sequential learning steps in each subject area.

Grades such as A, B, C, D, and F would not be given in the nongraded school, but rather records would be maintained upon the successful completion of each step in a particular subject area.

Organizing the Individualized Learning Program

The vast majority of learning for an individual takes place independent of the teacher, yet most of our schools are organized to prevent the opportunity for independent learning. The teacher is typically scheduled with his or her students most of the school day and is either expected to be conducting a lecture or discussion, or supervising study.

Trump writes:

> . . . schools continue to require much more than students need or want. Efforts to reduce these requirements are met with loud protests from many segments of our society. . . . Will the future bring enlightened, massive efforts in all of the areas of school concerns to identify what is essential for everyone to know, to do, and the appreciations that are needed?[9]

With the report by Weinstock that the young aren't as young as they used to be, there is need for more independent study activities for secondary school youth. Weinstock reports that the first appearance of menses in girls is now occuring two to five years earlier; that at the turn of the century growth for men stopped at about age twenty-six, but today there is little growth after age seventeen or eighteen. She also reports that more than one-fourth of the girls are not virgins at the time of graduation from high school, and illegimate births have doubled since 1940.[10]

The need for alternate programs and independent study activities in American schools is well documented. Coping with changing youth and a changing society will necessitate the principal developing inservice programs for independent study and alternative programs outside of traditional school patterns.

The success of independent study programs is directly related to adequacy of the school's learning resources center. Laboratories are also important, as well as individual work spaces or stations. Audio-visual materials, typewriters, photo copiers, art studios and shops, available for student use, are also essential to a successful independent study program.

Independent learning can be thought of as learning which takes place away from groups or under the teacher's direction. Such study can consist of structured assignments, a research project, or a contract plan between the teacher and the student. The success or failure of any attempt to expand the independent learning of students depends upon at least three factors: careful planning; the human, material, and physical resources available; and the maturity level of students.

Sufficient study time which permits students some degree of freedom from constant supervision is essential for effective learning. Students in independent study should be given free access to resource centers, open classrooms, open labs, etc.

In successful independent study programs, students meet with teachers in small groups to discuss how they can facilitate their learning and how to effectively use resource centers, laboratories, etc.

One procedure to individualize instruction involves the development of learning activity packages which spell out activities which would assist the student to learn a certain concept. Normally, a pre-test and a post-test are available to measure progress. It is necessary for the teacher and the student to interact periodically concerning progress being made.

Ritter reports the use of the dial access system for independent study. Students may obtain an audio- or video-tape of a lesson by dialing a certain number. A student may obtain these tapes whenever and as often as needed. Ritter's school has 107 dial access carrels. In his first year, 250 students enrolled in individualized courses in English, Social Studies, Mathematics, and Journalism. Teachers were given a maximum of 15 students a period to work with in independent study. Teachers were allowed to prepare their own schedules as follows:

> As the students are released to work independently, the teacher's "schedule" becomes whatever it needs to be. He can schedule seminar discussion groups by period or by special interest because of the blocks of time now available to both teacher and student. He can schedule individual conferences. He is accessible to students who "just drop by" to ask a question. He has time to study the student's records, work and progress; diagnose his needs and prescribe materials for him. He can schedule his own "free" periods. (In actual practice, the independent study teachers rarely take a "free" period.) He may insist that a student report at regular times, even every day, if he feels a need for this. In short, the teacher has the freedom and the responsibility to schedule learning activities according to the needs and abilities of the students at a particular time. Experience has shown that students need to report to a teacher anywhere from daily to once every two weeks.[11]

Independent study is a necessary part of the secondary schools' continuous progress program. Everson describes her continuous program in junior high school mathematics as an attempt to provide students with successful experiences according to each one's ability:

> The teachers have been willing to try to become guides on the sidelines rather than the "all-knowing lecturers in front of a class. . . ."
>
> How does our Continuous Progress operate? Units containing behavioral objectives, directions, pre-test, appropriate learning activities, optional learning activities and self-test are provided for the concepts included in the course outline. A child

reads the objectives and directions and takes the pre-test if he so desires. If results of the pre-test indicate that the child already has an understanding of the concept, he does only the learning activities needed to strengthen his skill. Answers are posted around the room, and the child checks his own work. . . . If the student has achieved satisfactorily, his instructions will be to proceed to another unit; if the student has not mastered the concept, his instruction will include explanation and more practice work of the same kind.[12]

While independent study is an essential component of any learning program, most schools are encouraging students to become more dependent as they progress through school. This is in opposition to the known development of human beings from infants to adults. Psychologists and other human behavioralists tell us that as a person matures, he or she demands more self direction of personal affairs.

Unless schools take deliberate steps to provide students with more choices of actions, the school can become rather restrictive—not only in the educational program offerings, but in the daily living procedures students must follow in the school. Students who must follow rigid class schedules, obtain passes to move anywhere in the building, must be accountable to some adult at all times of the day, and must dress and act in specified ways, are not provided with opportunities for self direction.

Education which seeks to provide guidelines to adolescents rather than lectures and knowledge can be most effective in developing reasoning and mature adults. Some examples of independent study activities include the following:

1. Correspondence study.
2. Programmed instruction.
3. Contract.
4. Released time from regular classes.
5. Individually planned studies.
6. Seminar type groups working with common topics.
7. Independent study as part of a regular class.
8. Before and after school independent study.
9. Vocational or work experience programs.
10. Regularly scheduled independent study classes such as art, industrial arts, music, etc.

Secondary school leaders cannot implement independent study activities unless they have the endorsement of their faculty and students, and have at least a minimum of facilities. Independent study is an essential part of the nongraded school, and as such, will need a well-developed learning resource center as previously described.

The school also needs laboratories for various independent study projects including a science, vocational, and in some instances, an agricultural or marine laboratory. The ingenious school leader may develop other laboratory facilities outside of the school in business, industry, and college locations. Some have advocated the use of computers to assist in analyzing student performance information in order to permit more effective individualized instruction based on student needs, interests, and abilities. This technique has been labelled Computer Managed Instruction (CMI). Systems of Computer Managed Instruction give the teachers information necessary to choose relevant instructional activities for meeting each student's learning needs and will also perform the routine clerical tasks of monitoring student progress.[13]

Computer Assisted Instruction

Several experimental programs are being conducted throughout the United States in which the computer is used to assist the instructional efforts of the teacher. The computer has an advantage over programmed textbooks, machines, etc., in that many students can use the same program through the computer. Through the use of the typewriter and visual devices such as the television screen, immediate feedback can be obtained by the student of his or her response to a question or some other work assignment. A computer can be programmed so that it has the capability to provide the student and teacher a diagnosis of student needs in this particular assignment. It can also be utilized to solve complex problems which require many intricate steps.[14]

A review of the research on computer assisted instruction (use of the computer for direct instruction of students including the four modes of drill and practice, problem solving, simulation, and tutorial) revealed the following:

1. All studies have shown normal instruction supplemented with CAI to be more effective than normal instruction alone.

2. When CAI was substituted, in whole or in part, for traditional instruction, nine studies showed that CAI students achieved more than non-CAI students, while eight studies found little or no differences. Three studies showed mixed results.

3. From the evidence available, it cannot be concluded that any mode of CAI is consistently more effective than other modes.

4. Several studies have shown that even though CAI does not always result in greater achievement, the time it takes students to learn is reduced.

5. Even though students may learn more or may learn more quickly through CAI, there is some evidence that they may not retain as much as traditionally taught students.[15]

While the use of the computer in assisting instruction has advantages in improving and increasing learning, the main disadvantage at the present time appears to be its great cost. However, some feel the money is available but that the public must be convinced of the financial feasibility of CAI.

Open Study Halls

The open study hall is an attempt to remove the disadvantages of the traditional large study hall with its bleak conditions of no study materials, rows and rows of chairs, etc. The large study hall provides an institutional-like atmosphere for the secondary school student. It symbolizes inhumaneness in the school. Many schools have retained these study halls to enable teachers without study hall responsibilities to teach a larger load of classes. The result has been an overloaded teacher and, in a great many instances, a chaotic study situation for students.

The open study hall provides for students who want to complete their assignments. It frees from the study hall those who desire other types of activities such as socializing in the student commons, visiting the library, or completing an independent study project.

The open study hall, as indicated, requires an extensive learning resources center with individual study carrels as well as a well-developed student commons center. In addition to these facilities, the secondary school leader must develop a plan that provides for teacher supervision of independent and individualized student study. The open study hall gives the teacher an opportunity to provide individual help, therefore, the teacher must arrange time appointments with students, etc., to insure that the individual help is given. Study centers or study labs must be established in all subject areas. A mathematics study center, for example, would have adding machines, calculators, slide rules, reference books, etc. A social studies center would have a wide variety of reference books, paperback books, maps, etc. Each of these study centers would be manned by a teacher, or teachers, so that help may be provided when needed.

Differentiated Staffing

It is rare to find a secondary school in which there is not some form of team or cooperative teaching being practiced. Administration of standardized tests is a cooperative effort of the entire faculty. Often, noon recreation is a cooperative responsibility of the faculty. Differentiated staffing as a partial concept of the secondary school is not new. What is new, for many schools,

is the idea of complete differentiated staffing in all secondary school subjects. Dempsey and Smith state:

> The goals of differentiated staffing are clear: The improvement
> of teaching (instruction), individualization of instruction, better
> utilization of the unique abilities of individuals (teachers and
> pupils), the provision for an upward-mobile career in the class-
> room for teachers, a mode of operation which begins with the
> strengths of a teacher, the placement of a person at the level at
> which he functions best, an increase in specialization, the
> involvement of teachers in decision making, and a provisional
> to allow teachers to police and regulate their profession.[16]

A differentiated staffing model, according to Dempsey and Smith, may
include the following:*

> *Educational Technician.*   The Educational Technician performs
> the routine tasks of the classroom, relieving the teacher of these
> lesser duties. His function varies, depending on the subject area
> or grade level in which he works. His job includes such routine
> tasks as ordering supplies, developing bulletin board displays,
> mixing paints, record keeping, duplicating materials, typing,
> playground supervision, setting up materials for laboratory
> experiments, or any number of other activities essential to the
> process of the classroom.

> *Academic Assistant.*   In most models the Academic Assistant is
> seen as a non-tenured person with at least two years at a recog-
> nized college. His work with students and teachers in the
> instructional program involves the use, the preparation, and the
> evaluation of materials. He could be responsible for maintain-
> ing clerical materials and supplies, grading papers, and giving
> specialized instruction in remedial enrichment areas, directed by
> a member of the professional staff, as well as supervise student
> study and be responsible for resource-centered activities.

> *Staff Teacher.*   The Staff Teacher is the core of the educa-
> tional program and his strength lies in his ability to communi-
> cate with students, work with parents, and effectively imple-
> ment the goals of the educational program. He must be an
> accredited teacher and have at least one academic degree. He
> would be given the usual ten month teaching contract with a
> salary based upon a regular salary schedule. The Staff Teacher
> spends 100 percent of his time in classroom teaching. He must
> be able to plan daily for groups, meet individual student needs,

---

* From Richard A. Dempsey and Rodney P. Smith, Jr., *Differentiated Staffing* © 1972, pp.
13–17. Reprinted by permission of Prentice-Hall, Inc., Englewood Cliffs, New Jersey.

keep classroom control, maintain pupil rapport, select and organize materials, confer with pupils and parents, effectively utilize educational assistance, function as a member of a teaching team, and make use of his opportunities to grow professionally.

Senior Teacher. The Senior Teacher's primary responsibility is the application of curricular innovations to the classroom. He modifies new ideas and works out the details for implementation. From his work emerge refined, sound, and practical curricula ideas ready for immediate implementation.

The Senior Teacher must have demonstrated excellence as a teacher, and must continue to teach, though on a limited basis. He must have manifested leadership capabilities and be considered a master practitioner, with a great deal of experience and training, who remains vital and imaginative. The Senior Teacher must know the most recent developments in teaching and his subject/skill area.

It is proposed that the Senior Teacher spend most of his time in doing what is most needed—teaching effectively. He might conceivably be on an eleven or twelve month contract and spend about 50 to 60 percent of his time in class. The remaining 20 percent of this time might be spent on staff development and inservice education programs, workshops and seminars.

Teaching Curriculum Associate. The Teaching Curriculum Associate's primary responsibility lies in curriculum development. Using the most promising educational trends, he could develop new curricular material which might eventually become part of his district's or county's educational program. He should be able to conduct sound research, demonstrate an understanding of the learning process, and utilize instructional resources efficiently. The Teaching Curriculum Associate could contribute to the development of new methods and new programs of education. He must be able to organize materials in ways that will be meaningful and amenable to classroom use.

The Teaching Curriculum Associate, like the Senior Teacher, is first a teacher. He would spend some of his time teaching, since everyone in the instructional program above the Staff Teacher must first be a teacher, and the rest of his time as follows: The Teaching Curriculum Associate develops new curricula, and works with Senior Teachers in pilot programs in actual classroom situations. He conducts inservice programs and attends workshops, conferences, and other meetings. By refining and revising curricula with the Senior and Staff Teachers he keeps programs up to date and teachable. He might as well work with the same teachers on school programming and scheduling.

The Teaching Research Associate.   The Teaching Research
Associate would keep pace with the very latest developments in
his educational field or fields. Expected to read and investigate
widely, he would bring to the staff a constant flow of ideas
culled from research centers, universities, forward-looking
school districts, and innovative schools. He must be able to
critically select those ideas and materials most valid and practical for the program of instruction under his survey.

Working on a twelve-month contract, the Teaching Research
Associate would spend about 60 percent of his time in the classroom. His salary would be near the top of the expanded salary
schedule. His activities would include the establishment and
maintenance of a continual program of research and evaluation
in curriculum development and new teaching methodologies. He
should read reports of related research, conduct inservice
classes and workshops, attend research conferences, and work
with the Teaching Curriculum Associate in developing curricula
which incorporate the latest research. He would coordinate the
efforts of all teachers along with his other responsibilities.[17]

Peer Teaching

Peer teaching is a method whereby students teach each other various concepts in the educational scene. Those of us in the teaching profession realize
the truth in the statement: "The best way to learn a subject or a concept is to
teach it." Thus, peer teaching not only helps the student doing the teaching,
but the learner as well. The potential of learning which can be released in a
secondary school through this method is staggering. The ratio of teachers
can be increased from 25:1 to 20:1 to 1:1, the ultimate in secondary schools.
The secondary school leader should take a careful look at this idea to
improve the learning environment in his or her school.

With the increase in student freedom, individualization of the secondary school, and developing a more humane school, peer teaching provides
many exciting opportunities to release the total learning potential within a
secondary school.

The Learning Resources Center

Much has been written about the learning resources center, the media center,
the instructional materials center, etc. All writers have generally agreed that
it is the center of the learning process in the secondary school. Some have
advocated that it be larger than the gymnasium. However, regardless of its
size, its importance, its location, etc., it has no value unless it is utilized by
the student and faculty. In the authors' opinions, in the humane school, the

learning resources center would be of two types: the central center for the entire school and the center for each general subject area.

A central learning resources center with a large number of study carrels, student stations, etc., is more efficient than the traditional library with its round tables and no student access to materials. A learning resources center for mathematics, social studies, etc., separate from the central learning resources center has two advantages. It allows teachers to develop their own center as well as work with students in their field, and it separates students so that they have greater privacy in their learning. For the most part, the individual study carrels would be located in the subject learning resources centers.

Neagley, Evans, and Lynn predict that the school of the twenty-first century will not be a school as we know it, but a learning center. Each home will also have a learning center which will be connected with the central learning center. This twenty-first century school will have the following characteristics:

1. No standard classrooms.
2. A few large group instructional areas.
3. Several seminar rooms.
4. Computerized home learning centers.
5. Visual screen on the home learning center.
6. Student interaction with the central computer and student learning progress diagnosed.
7. Periodic conferences with his teacher to review the student's progress.
8. Large group lectures by scientist teachers.
9. Periodic seminar sessions with varying groups to discuss problems and share ideas.
10. Ability of the home learning center to bring in films, tapes, slides from the learning bank.
11. The library as we know it now is a central area with printed materials, etc., recorded on the computer which can be recalled for use on the home learning center.
12. Individualized program without failure.[18]

The secondary school leader should keep the future in mind when shopping for learning materials and a learning resources center. While the authors favor subject area learning resources centers as well as a central learning resources center, the following characteristics of the learning resources center could be utilized in both.

The learning resources center would include equipment and materials that can be used by students and teachers. Some materials may be kept primarily for teachers, while others would be kept for students. But both groups could utilize both types of equipment and materials. The director of the learning resources center would be a person who is well-qualified in the cataloging of books and materials, as well as in the use of audio-visual materials and all types of learning materials.

The learning resources center would include:

1. A wide variety of books and periodicals shelved so that there is easy access to students and teachers.
2. A wide variety of films and filmstrips with the same easy access to students and teachers.
3. Study carrels, both wet (containing facilities for audio-visual and electronic equipment) and dry (without audio-visual and electronic equipment).
4. A wide variety of viewing equipment such as 16mm film projectors, loop film projectors, tape recorders, television to view video tapes, etc.
5. Provision for production of teaching and learning materials such as overlays for the overhead projector, copying machines, cameras to prepare slides and photographic equipment, etc.

The staff of the learning resources center has a complex task in obtaining materials and equipment, distribution of this equipment, and coordinating various kinds of media programs. Brown and Norberg lists the work of the learning resources staff as follows:

1. Participating in the planning of instructional programs with respect to printed and audiovisual material, instructional devices, media and systems.
2. Coordinating the selection and organization of collections of instructional materials for students and professional library resources for teachers.
3. Circulating instructional materials.
4. Coordinating the selection, processing and distribution of textbooks.
5. Planning and producing instructional television and radio broadcasts and closed-circuit television programs in cooperation with appropriate curriculum or other committees.
6. Coordinating the use of instructional television and radio services.
7. Planning, designing, and preparing instructional materials such as graphics, photographs, slides, filmstrips, motion pictures, recordings and programmed materials in cooperation with teachers.

8. Circulating appropriate printed, broadcast, and other information to schools and the lay public to acquaint them with the services, facilities and materials of the educational media program.

9. Consulting with teachers and school administrators to identify instructional problems or opportunities related to the use of media and materials and to assist in solving problems or exploiting opportunities.

10. Planning and coordinating a variety of in-service training activities to assist teachers in the effective use of instructional media and materials.

11. Participating in the planning and design of school buildings and facilities to ensure the most effective and efficient use of technological resources in teaching.

12. Promoting and coordinating appropriate experimentation and research to ascertain the values of various instructional materials, techniques, and media and to develop better ways of using them.[19]

In most secondary schools, as one can see from this list of responsibilities of the learning resources center staff, the task is too difficult for one professional. Most schools would have a coordinator of the learning resources center, an audio-visual specialist, a book and periodicals specialist, and a specialist on television and electronic machine operation. Nonprofessionals such as a secretary and a repairman would also be desirable.

Even though a secondary school has an excellent learning resources center, it may be ineffective since students and teachers may not know how to use it. It is important that the secondary school leader have a well planned inservice program for the use of the learning resources center. Included in the inservice program would be a description of various kinds of instructional aids that teachers can use in their instruction.

Teachers may provide assistance in ordering equipment and supplies for the center if they are given the opportunity to visit displays and other resources centers to become acquainted with the possible uses in their classes. It is seldom that material will be ordered without the teacher's endorsement. The secondary school leader must visit centers and displays, and become acquainted with the instructional aids that are available. The inservice program acquaints the faculty with a wide variety of available media and instruction in the utilization of materials in the school's learning resources center.

The old library, with its neatly stacked books, central desk for checking out materials, and a large open room with open or circular tables, is as outdated today as the graded school. The nongraded or continuous progress school, with its flexibility and increased learning vitality requires a dynamic resources center for learning. The learning resources center not only contains a large collection of books and magazines, but a wide variety of material and electronic aids. The North Central Association lists the following as *progress criteria* for the instructional media program:

> Professional Staff hold a Master's Degree in Library Science and/or Audio-Visual and are provided with sufficient technical assistance to adequately perform services.
>
> A minimum collection of 6,000 books, or 10 books per pupil for larger schools is provided.
>
> Independent study spaces (carrels) are provided for a substantial number of students along with rooms for small group discussions.
>
> Careful study is made of advances in electronic learning devices and appropriate efforts are made to incorporate them for use in the library facility. A modern information retrieval system should be an important objective of the faculty and administration.
>
> Teachers' offices are in close proximity to the library in order to foster easy communication.[20]

The learning resources center is the key to success in the nongraded school since it provides the spaces for independent study as well as the materials and equipment which the student needs for individual learning. The design for the study carrel and the physical arrangement for the learning resources center, provides for a variety of learning activities for individual study. The learning resources center not only houses the school's collection of books, films, film strips, etc., but includes individual student study carrels with electrical outlets for use of various media. Some study carrels would include computer terminals for computer assisted instruction.

The design for the learning resources center provides for a student lounge, where a student may relax and socialize with fellow students. The design provides easy access to various kinds of electronic aids as well as books and periodicals. One benefit of this design for the learning resources center is the provision for an efficient and attractive learning environment in which the student can use the discovery method of learning by questioning, gaining new skills, and exploring through research of the materials available in the learning center. This design promotes the idea of the teacher utilizing a variety of books and materials instead of being forced to rely upon a single textbook for the instructional program.

The principal should be concerned with the proper selection of materials for the learning resources center, instruction in the proper use of these materials, and the supervision of the learning center. The faculty is the primary resource to utilize in the selection of materials and equipment. However, the successful implementation of the center, through instruction to students in the proper use of materials and supervision, is dependent upon the director of the learning resources center. The director of the center is a competent librarian, who also has training in the use and distribution of audio-visual aids. The librarian in the learning center not only becomes an expert in holding and dispensing materials and equipment, but also can train lay personnel in the operation of many complicated pieces of the electronic equipment. While many librarians are not trained in the use and care of electronic equipment, the principal can provide this instruction by sending the librarian to various instructional media training sessions given by commercial companies or the local university.

The design of the learning center includes provisions for large spaces needed for production areas, storage areas, and individual study carrels. It should be the largest and most comprehensive room of the school, including the gymnasium.

SUMMARY

Curriculum development must be based on student needs. While meeting local needs is of prime importance, state, regional, and national needs must be considered. Faculty and students must be involved in the development of curriculum since they will become the implementers and consumers of what is developed.

The authors have presented criteria by which to judge a curriculum plan. Also included were some curriculum alternatives which they feel will assist the secondary school principal and supervisor in meeting the changing needs of secondary school students. Increasingly, educators will be held accountable for the success of their supervision, administration, and instruction. Accountability begins with developing objectives of education that are accepted by the community, faculty, and students. Measurable objectives and their resulting accountability focus upon students and their learning, not upon teachers and their teaching. Forty-five minute periods of time for teacher talk, or student-teacher discussion is no longer sacred. What is sacred is the student and the guidance of time that he or she needs to accomplish certain tasks.

More and more educational leaders are advocating increasing independent study as a method of improving student achievement and the learning environment. Computer assisted instruction provides a mechanism to assist in the individualization of instruction. The open study hall is also being discovered to be at least as good as the closed study hall. It results in improved student discipline as well as promotes independent study. Differentiated staffing has many advantages and certain features of this plan can be implemented in every secondary school.

The concept of peer teaching, a method whereby students teach each other various concepts, has exciting possibilities for releasing the teacher for other learning activities.

The nongraded school is becoming more and more accepted as the ideal model for the secondary school. This is based on the concept of continuous progress which encourages students to progress at their own rate of development. The continuous progress school usually develops units of instruction which contain behavioral objectives, directions, pre-test, learning activities, and several self-tests. As students complete one unit, they progress on to the next unit, and so on. The freedom from pressures and the emphasis on the individual are the key advantages of continuous progress. Humans generally will achieve at a higher rate if they have a degree of freedom to conduct their own lives. While the nongraded school may provide an occasional "hot seat" for the principal, the advantages of an improved learning environment for youth are well worth the effort.

Essential to the nongraded continuous progress school is a well-equipped learning resources center in which the student will find spaces for independent study, materials and equipment to reinforce studying, and a wide variety of reading materials. The learning resources center also provides for a student lounge, where a student may relax and socialize with fellow students.

NOTES

1. Ronald C. Doll, *Curriculum Improvement: Decision Making and Process* (Boston: Allyn and Bacon, 1974), pp. 12–13.

2. Glen Hass, *Curriculum Planning: A New Approach* (Boston: Allyn and Bacon, Inc., 1977), p. 6.

3. Ibid., p. 5.

4. Doll, *Curriculum Improvement,* pp. 22–24.

5. J. Galen Saylor and William M. Alexander, *Planning Curriculum* (New York: Holt, Rinehart and Winston, Inc., 1974), pp. 44–45.

6. Don E. Glines, *Creating Humane Schools* (Mankato, Minn.: Campus Publishers, 1971) pp. 11–20.

7. J. Lloyd Trump and William Georgiades, "Doing Better With What You Have: NASSP Model School's Project," *National Association of Secondary School Principals Bulletin* (May, 1970), pp. 109–113.

8. Ibid., pp. 114–118.

9. J. Lloyd Trump, "The Future In American Secondary Schools," *American Secondary Education* 6:2 (March, 1976), pp. 4–7.

10. Ruth Weinstock, *The Greening of The High School* (New York: Educational Facilities Laboratories, Inc., 1973), p. 19.

11. Myron W. Ritter, "Individualized Study In Coatesville," *National Association of Secondary School Principals Bulletin* (November, 1970), pp. 70–78.

12. Margaret Everson, "Recipe For Continuous Progress," *American Secondary Education* (June, 1971), p. 13.

167

SUMMARY

13. Carol Dagnon and Dennis W. Spuck, "A Role For Computers In Individualizing Education—and It's Not Teaching," *Phi Delta Kappan* 58:6 (February, 1977), p. 460.

14. John J. Hirschbuhl, "CAI—A Right Hand and a Third Arm," *American Secondary Education* (March, 1972), p. 20.

15. Judith Edwards et al., "How Effective Is CAI? A Review of The Research," *Educational Leadership* 33:2 (November, 1975), pp. 147–153.

16. Richard A. Dempsey and Rodney P. Smith, *Differentiated Staffing* (Englewood Cliffs, N.J.: Prentice-Hall, Inc., 1972), p. 7.

17. Ibid., pp. 13–18.

18. Ross L. Neagley, N. Dean Evans, and Clarence A. Lynn, Jr., *The School Administration and Learning Resources* (Englewood Cliffs, N.J.: Prentice-Hall, Inc., 1969) pp. 5–7.

19. James W. Brown and Kenneth D. Norberg, *Administering Educational Media* (New York: McGraw-Hill Book Company, 1965), pp. 285–286.

20. *North Central Association Policies and Standards for the Approval of Secondary Schools* (Commission on Schools, Boulder, Colorado, 1977), p. 33.

8

Evaluating the Education Program and Student Progress

Program evaluation should be designed to determine if needs are being met at the following five levels:

1. *Individual.* The more one works with faculties, students, and lay people, and the more one reads the literature of sociologists and those concerned with human relationships and learning, the more it becomes apparent that the key to improvement of an individual's performance and behavior is self-desire for improvement. Individuals will more likely seek self-improvement when they realize the educational program is designed to meet their needs. Therefore, it is vital that individual student needs be assessed and met as nearly as possible.

2. *Local Community.* Each community has unique needs which can be met through the educational program available in the schools located within the community. From these local needs, purposes and objectives are developed for the school. These purposes and objectives of the local school set the stage for evaluation of the school program. The administration and faculty should frequently return to the purposes and objectives to question whether or not each phase of the school program is fulfilling an overall objective.

3. *State.* Education has been reserved as a responsibility of each state. As such, each state has developed requirements which must be met for the general welfare of all within that state. Schools normally are checked using some type of inspections and/or annual reports to verify if they are meeting prescribed state curricular standards.

4. *Regional.* Educators have voluntarily joined together on a regional basis to seek better coordination and higher standards of quality for the educational programs they offer. The quality standards developed on a regional basis have served to stimulate self-improvement in educational

programs. The North Central Association recognizes the importance of the program evaluation by requiring each member school to submit an annual report concerning their educational program and to be reevaluated at least once every seven years. Regional program evaluation has been found to:

a. Provide direction for the school.

b. Raise the level of the school's awareness of its strengths and weaknesses.

c. Encourage the school to evaluate and improve programs and instruction.

d. Provide another point of view for the school through the observations of the visiting team.[1]

5. *National.* While the United States Constitution does not mention education; it has been deemed important that the general welfare and common defense of the country be safeguarded. Several national professional organizations and committees have established standards they believe to be worthy of consideration for adoption as criteria to judge the effectiveness of the educational program at the local level.

The remainder of this chapter will deal with factors which influence the educational program at the building level. Practical techniques related to program evaluation are also given.

Accountability

The issue of accountability in education has gained widespread support in recent years. A major project entitled "Cooperative Accountability Project" was initiated in April of 1972 to develop an accountability system that would serve as a model for state education agencies. The project was financed by funds provided under the Elementary and Secondary Education Act of 1965 (Public Law 8-9-10, Title V, Section 505) with Colorado as the administering state. The headquarters are located in the Colorado Department of Education, State Office Building, 201 E. Colfax, Denver, Colorado, 80203. The other states involved in the project are Florida, Maryland, Michigan, Minnesota, Oregon, and Wisconsin.

The following five specific aims of the project have been identified:

1. Legislative Mandate—An examination of the laws and directives of the several states (and authorized groups within the states) dealing with accountability.

2. Criterion Standards—An examination of such standards as data requirements necessary for accountability, and the state of the art in measuring pupil performance in various areas.

3. Models Identification—A determination of the common needs in

accountability, and the choice of a number of models that may be adopted in states and local districts.

4. Role Expectations—Identification of the roles in accountability to be played by various participants and decision makers: state and local educational administrators, expert consultants, legislators, parents, pupils, patrons, the community, and subgroups within it— teachers and other school staff.

5. Reporting Practices and Procedures—Analysis of the methods and techniques already in use or that may usefully be put to use in reporting to the various audiences concerned with accountability.

National Assessment

National Assessment of Education Progress was a project of the Education Commission of the States. Project planning began in 1964 while actual administration of the National Assessment exercises in the schools began in the spring of 1969.

The following are excerpts, questions, and responses taken from a document entitled, "Questions and Answers about the National Assessment of Educational Progress."

a. What are the goals of National Assessment?
   The two major goals are:
   1. To make available the first comprehensive data on the educational attainment of young Americans.
   2. To measure any growth or decline which takes place in selected aspects of the educational attainments of young Americans in certain subject areas.

b. Does this mean you are gathering data on specific school districts that will allow you to compare the effectiveness of different schools and districts?

   No, the sample is not drawn in such a way that we can make any statements about individual schools, districts, or even states. The smallest area we can talk about is a geographic region. For National Assessment purposes, the country is divided into four regions—Northeast, Southeast, Central, and West.

c. How does the Assessment gather data to determine the educational attainments of Americans?

   First, it is necessary to determine what the educational system is trying to achieve. These objectives are identified through the efforts of both school and non-school people, and are to meet three basic criteria. These are that they must be:

1. Accepted as educational tasks by the schools.
2. Considered important by scholars.
3. Considered desirable by other thoughtful citizens.

Second, questions and tasks, called exercises in National Assessment's terminology, are written to determine how well these objectives are being achieved. Third, the exercises are administered to people selected through random sampling procedures throughout the country.

d. Are all these areas being assessed each year?

No. Other than the first year, two subject areas are assessed each year. The assessment plan is:

Cycle 1

March 1969–February 1970	Science, Writing, Citizenship
October 1970–August 1971	Reading, Literature
October 1971–August 1972	Music, Social Studies
October 1972–August 1973	Math, Science (second Assessment)
October 1973–August 1974	Writing (second Assessment), Career and Occupational Development
October 1974–August 1975	Citizenship (second Assessment), Art

Cycle 2

October 1975–August 1976	Reading and Literature (second Assessment)
October 1976–August 1977	Music and Social Studies (second Assessment)
October 1977–August 1978	Math (second Assessment), Science (third Assessment)
October 1978–August 1979	Writing (third Assessment), Career and Occupation Development (second Assessment)
October 1979–August 1980	Citizenship (third Assessment), Art (second Assessment)[2]

National assessment was the first major attempt to evaluate education on a nationwide basis. It remains to be seen what the success of the endeavor was.

Follow-Up Studies

The follow-up study of dropouts and graduates provides an excellent means for principals to use in determining the success of their educational program. Forms which may be used in these follow-up studies appear in Figures 8.1 through 8.3. The follow-up study should be more than a distribution of questionnaires to graduates and dropouts. Personal interviews with graduates and dropouts should also be made. The questionnaire is often returned by those who are highly satisfied with the school, or highly dissatisfied. Therefore, a more meaningful evaluation of graduates' and dropouts' opinions will be obtained through use of both the questionnaires and the interview technique. Grade reports from colleges and work reports from industry or other employers will be extremely valuable.

The evaluation of the dropout study may reveal that dropouts felt an alienation toward the school. In an attempt to correct this, the principal may expand the intramural program or provide activities which attract the potential dropout. Or it might be necessary for the principal to arrange for special classes for pregnant girls. The principal may find it necessary to add developmental reading and courses which allow the low achieving student to experience success, since many dropouts have experienced little more than failure in much of their education.

Academic Inventory

While the emphasis in providing creative educational programs for the gifted has lessened in the past few years, there appears once again to be renewed interest. The purpose of the academic inventory is to determine how well the school is doing in guiding its gifted students in the selection of more difficult subjects.

Principals may find that the more academically talented students are shying away from the tough courses because the grading is too low. Principals may have to do some arm twisting, or even transferring of the teacher if they find the gifted students are penalized with low grades when they take the more advanced courses. Of course, the ideal situation would be to eliminate grades or marks entirely from the school. This would encourage students to take courses which fit their ability and desires rather than those which add prestige to the family name or increase the possibility of a scholarship.

Standardized Tests

An evaluation of the success of the school program can also be accomplished through a study of the results of various kinds of standardized tests given students. Standardized aptitude tests can be compared with the results

Figure 8.1
*Follow-Up Study of Graduates**

Categories	Boys	Girls	Total	
			Number	Percent
Schools leading to a bachelor's degree				
Other schools beyond secondary school				
Professional, technical and kindred workers				
Farmers and farm managers				
Managers, officials and proprietors				
Clerical and kindred workers				
Sales workers				
Craftsmen, foremen, and kindred workers				
Operatives (machines, trucks), miners, kindred workers				
Military service				
Service workers				
Laborers				
Homemaker				
Unemployed				
Unknown				
Total				

* "The NCA Guide for School Evaluation, A Workbook for the Self Study and Team Visit," 3rd ed., 1976 (Boulder, Colorado, Commission of Schools, North Central Association), p. 91.

Figure 8.2
Analysis of Students Who Have Withdrawn From the School*

REASONS FOR WITHDRAWALS	Boys	Girls	Totals	
			Number	Percent
TRANSFERS				
1. Transferred to another school; change of residence				
2. Transferred to another school; no change of residence				
Total for school transfers				
DROP-OUTS				
1. Left because of school failure				
2. Left because of other problems in school				
3. Left because of financial pressure				
4. Illness				
5. Pregnancy				
6. Marriage				
7. Left because of lack of interest in school				
8. Expelled				
9. Reason undetermined				
Total for school drop-outs				
PRESENT STATUS OF DROP-OUTS				
1. Returned to this school				
2. In attendance in another school				
3. Working full or part-time				
4. In the military				
5. Housewife				
6. Unemployed				
7. Unknown				

Notes:
1. This survey is to cover the period from September 1 of last year through September 1 of this year.
2. Place each drop-out in only one category, even if two or three seem to apply.
3. Indicate the source of your data for these tables.

* "NCA Evaluation Guide for Secondary Schools, A Workbook for the Self Study and Evaluation Review," 2nd ed., rev., 1974 (Boulder, Colorado, Commission of Schools, North Central Association), p. 59.

Figure 8.3
Computation of Enrollment Stability of the School*

---

1. Number of students who were enrolled in the earliest grade in this school in _____(1)   _____

2. Number of students who entered the school in _____(1) and remained to graduate last year.   _____

3. Number of students who entered the school in _____(1) and subsequently transferred to other schools.   _____

4. Number of students who entered in _____(1) and who subsequently withdrew (dropped-out).   _____

5. Number of students who entered in _____(1) who still are in school, not having graduated last year.   _____

6. Percentage of students who entered in _____(1) and remained to graduate last year. (Item 2 divided by Item 1.)   _____

7. Percentage of students who transferred from the school before graduating. (Item 3 divided by Item 1.)   _____

8. Percentage of students who dropped out of school from this class. (Item 4 divided by Item 1.)   _____

9. Percentage of students who are still in school, not having graduated last year. (Item 5 divided by Item 1.)   _____

Notes:

1. Before completing this form, insert in the six spaces marked (1) the year that last year's graduating class entered the school.

2. This table does not concern itself with those students who transferred into the school. Hence it is not a survey of all the students who graduated last year, but of those who came to the school with the class at its point of entry some years back.

* "NCA Evaluation Guide for Secondary Schools, A Workbook for the Self Study and Evaluation Review," 2nd ed., rev., 1974 (Boulder, Colorado, Commission of Schools, North Central Association), p. 60.

of achievement tests to determine whether students are achieving up to their predicted ability. While the intelligence test has been misused in the evaluation of individual student's predicted ability and actual achievement, it does have value when the results for a *group* of students are compared with their results of standardized achievement tests. These comparisons may provide a key to the correction of some weakness in the school program.

However, there are many factors involved which should be considered in the evaluation of the school based upon standardized tests. First of all, is the faculty teaching the same concepts that appear on the achievement tests? If they are, should they? What are the backgrounds of the students? Are teachers teaching for the tests? Do the tests provide an inventory of values which the faculty considers important?

In other words, the achievement tests should not determine the curriculum of the school. Rather the needs of students as determined by local industry, state, national and international opportunities, teachers, and the community should be the primary considerations in developing the curriculum. This is why the faculty self-study of the curriculum is so important.

Personnel Relationships Which Affect Educational Programs

The principal can evaluate the administrative structure of his or her school through the use of faculty, students, university personnel, and lay people within the community. Areas of evaluation of the administrative structure would include:

1. Relationships between administrators and teachers.
2. Relationships between the principal and superintendent.
3. Relationships between the administration and students.
4. Departmental heads structure.
5. Assistant principals—their responsibilities and their morale.
6. Policies, procedure, and structure of the board of education, or in the case of the private school, the governing body.
7. Staff and student morale.
8. Instructional staff—are they competent? Are they teaching in their major fields?
9. Who appoints or recommends faculty members for employment? The principal? The superintendent?

Relationship Between Principal and Teachers

The relationship between the teacher and the principal should be one of mutual confidence. The principal may evaluate this relationship by conversations with the teachers, parents, and students. Questionnaires which the principal may use in the evaluation of this relationship as well as the morale of the faculty appear in Figures 8.4 and 8.5.

Relationship Between Principal and Superintendent

The principal and the superintendent must be compatible if the school is to be administrated under optimum conditions. The superintendent must enhance the morale of the principal whenever possible. This can be accomplished through providing adequate secretarial help and support in time of undue attack from parents, teachers and, more recently, the students themselves. On the other hand, the principal must support and protect the superintendent from unfair attack. The principal is an administrative officer and, as such, has responsibilities for enforcing policy which may not be popular with some teachers.

Figure 8.4
*Teacher Opinionnaire**

Section I: Operational Procedure and Organization

Please indicate to what extent each of the statements below characterizes your school, using the following scale:

A—rarely   B—sometimes   C—frequently   D—very frequently

_____ 1. Teachers spend out-of-class time (unscheduled periods and after school) assisting students with study problems.

_____ 2. Classes are regularly and periodically visited by supervisors or administrators.

_____ 3. Routine duties interfere with the job of teaching.

_____ 4. Teachers regularly use unscheduled time (preparation periods) for class preparation and instructional improvement.

_____ 5. Administrative and supervisory personnel are available to assist teachers with instructional problems.

_____ 6. Faculty meetings generally deal with important education problems.

_____ 7. Teachers are informed of the results of a supervisor's or administrator's classroom visit.

_____ 8. Counselors aid teachers with difficult instructional and emotional problems their students may have.

_____ 9. Discipline problems are dealt with in an appropriate manner.

_____ 10. Teachers frequently assume individual responsibility for the general operation of the school, apart from their immediate classroom responsibilities, as a matter of professional obligation.

_____ 11. Teacher suggestions for new programs and procedures are encouraged and supported by the administration.

_____ 12. Faculty meetings are mainly principal-announcement meetings.

_____ 13. Teachers participate in policy and decision making regarding curriculum and instruction.

_____ 14. Program changes and policy are imposed from the top without consulting teachers.

_____ 15. Students are given a large measure of freedom in utilizing their own class time.

* "NCA Evaluation Guide for Secondary Schools, A Workbook for the Self Study and The Evaluation Review," 2nd ed., rev., 1976 (Boulder, Colorado, Commission on Schools) pp. 28–29.

Figure 8.4 cont'd.

Section II: Teaching and Working Conditions in the School

Please rate each of the items by using this scale:

A—excellent   B—satisfactory   C—unsatisfactory   D—very poor

_____ 1. The availability of school supplies for classroom work?

_____ 2. The adequacy of the library collection for instruction of your classes?

_____ 3. The recency and quality of textbooks (primary reference materials) for your classes?

_____ 4. Your teaching load, both in number of students taught and number of preparations?

_____ 5. The physical facilities for the faculty (lounges, cafeteria)?

_____ 6. The extent and type of non-teaching assignments given you?

_____ 7. The provisions for student control in the school?

_____ 8. The adequacy of clerical assistance for the teachers?

_____ 9. The professional growth opportunities provided by the district (in-service programs, travel funds, etc.) for teachers?

Section III: The Climate of the School

Please note your perception of the following factors, using this scale:

A—better than average   B—average   C—below average   D—poor

_____ 1. The general level of student behavior in the school?

_____ 2. The general attitude of the students towards the school?

_____ 3. The general attitude of the students towards the teachers?

_____ 4. The morale of the teachers in the school?

_____ 5. The degree of cooperation among the teachers in the school?

_____ 6. The general attitude of the teachers towards the administration?

_____ 7. The general attitude of the administration towards the teachers?

_____ 8. The parents' attitudes toward the teachers in the school?

_____ 9. The respect accorded to teachers in the community?

_____ 10. The degree to which teachers know what is going on in the school?

_____ 11. The lack of bureaucratic sterility in the school?

_____ 12. The sense of involvement teachers feel in the school?

_____ 13. The degree of educational excitement *you* feel in the school?

_____ 14. The degree to which the school's statement of purposes (philosophy) actually helps determine the school's program and procedures?

_____ 15. The school administration's openness (receptivity) to change?

_____ 16. The staff's openness (receptivity) to change?

_____ 17. Which of these designations best characterizes the general climate of the school in reference to its approach to students?

_____ permissive   _____ balanced   _____ regimented

Figure 8.4 cont'd.

18. Which of these following statements best characterizes the extent of educational change and renewal in this school?

_____ There is no educational/curriculum change in the school.

_____ There is little educational/curriculum change in the school.

_____ There is a moderate amount of educational/curriculum change in the school.

_____ There is much educational/curriculum change in the school.

_____ There is too much educational/curriculum change in the school.

Please provide the following information about yourself:

Sex: Male _____   Years of teaching experience: Total years _____

          Female _____   In this school _____

Date _____   School _____

Figure 8.5
Teacher Satisfaction Scale

Please indicate on the attached sheet the degree of your personal satisfaction with the following items, using 1 as very unsatisfactory, 2 as unsatisfactory, 3 as satisfactory, 4 as very satisfactory, and 5 as highly satisfactory. Thus, 1 represents the lowest degree of satisfaction, while 5 is the highest.

1. The principal's use of my teacher talents is _____.
2. My own personal sense of achievement at this school is _____.
3. The principal's success in working with me as a teacher is _____.
4. The principal's personal interest in me as a human being is _____.
5. The personal relationships among the other teachers and the principal in this school are _____.
6. The casual social relationship between the principal and me is _____.
7. Whenever I make a mistake which becomes known to the principal, my feeling toward him or her is _____.
8. Whenever a parent criticizes me to the principal, my admiration for the principal is _____.
9. Whenever I take sick leave, the principal's acceptance of my explanation of the absence to me is _____.
10. Whenever I ask for time off, the principal's reaction to it is _____.
11. My success as a teacher with my pupils is _____.
12. My personal friendship with my pupils is _____.
13. My desire to continue at this school on an indefinite basis is _____.

Relationship Between Principal and Students

In the eyes of many students, anything that is wrong with the school is the fault of the principal. The principal who takes student criticism of the school personally is likely to spend many sleepless nights during the school year. The principal can evaluate the attitude of students toward the school and administration through conferences with students and by the use of questionnaires.

Attending meetings of the student council provides the principal with opportunity to keep in tune with student attitudes. At first, this may inhibit the student council in their deliberations, but when they find that the principal is human and interested in their concerns, they will no longer be inhibited by his or her presence. The student council provides the principal with the best "hearing aid" concerning student opinion and problems.

The principal should strive to make the student council the single most important student activity of the school. The principal's discussions in student council will enable the members to keep in tune with administrative problems. If the student council is to be truly representative, barriers such as grades, etc., must be eliminated for student council representatives.

A student inventory of attitudes can be obtained periodically, probably at least twice each year. A questionnaire can be supplemented through interviews of students in the principal's office. It is good for students to know that they can be invited to the principal's office for reasons other than discipline. It is great therapy for both the principal and the students to become better acquainted with each others' problems.

Departmental Heads Structure

The principal cannot do all things for all persons on the staff. The department head provides the organizational structure which allows teachers to work with a small group in their own subject area. The department head can give the beginning teacher advice on the teaching of a particular subject, which in most cases is more effective than the advice of the principal. Curriculum matters, as well as ordering materials, sharing rooms, sharing instruction, etc., can be handled by the departmental head.

In the evaluation of the departmental structure, the principal should ask such questions as: Does the department head have free time to perform duties as the department head? Does the department head have a reasonable amount of freedom to develop his or her department? Are regular meetings conducted by the department head? Does the principal attend some of these meetings? Is there special provision by the principal to organize meetings of all department heads within the school? Is the department head structure so bureaucratized that teachers must go through the department head before they can confer with the principal?

The authors recommend that the following principles be used in the development and use of the departmental structure within the secondary school:

1. That the principal appoint the best qualified teacher as department head.
2. That the departments be established along subject lines rather than grade lines.
3. That the departmental head be given responsibility for developing the curriculum within his or her department, coordinating the ordering of supplies and equipment, serving as a consultant to the teacher on instructional problems, and serving as representative on the principal's advisory council. Ample time must be provided for the department chairperson to perform duties.
4. That the department head has no responsibility for rating teachers. Although it would be unreasonable to expect that the principal would not consult with the department head in recommending tenure, transfer, etc., for teachers within the building, the principal should protect the teacher-teacher relationship which the department head and teachers should have. It is a relationship of an experienced and capable teacher assisting the inexperienced teacher.

Assistant Principals

Evaluating the utilization and responsibilities of the assistant principal, and providing him or her with esteem and the opportunity for self-actualization, are essential for a good secondary school. The faculty, students, and parents can be involved in evaluating the role and success of the assistant principals.

Many regard the assistant principal as a training position for the principalship. In many cases this is the situation. However, there may be assistant principals who desire to make a career of their present position. Whether it is a career position or a training position has little effect upon the nature of the responsibilities. The assistant principal assists the principal in the administration of the school. The assistant principal relieves the principal of routine duties that cannot be handled effectively by nonprofessional personnel.

This is not to say that the assistant principal is relieved of any responsibility for classroom visitation and other such responsibilities which demand a high degree of professional training. Where there is but one assistant principal in a school system, he or she will be assigned a small amount of time to supervise teachers. However, in the larger secondary school, one assistant principal may be assigned primarily to student affairs, another to administrative affairs, and another to the improvement of instruction.

The authors recommend that the following considerations be made in the evaluation of the assistant principal and this position:

1. Are the assistant principal's duties and responsibilities clearly outlined which aid in avoiding misunderstandings among the professional and nonprofessional staff?

2. Are the special qualifications the assistant principal possesses being properly utilized by the principal?

3. Is the assistant principal part of the administrative team of the school?

4. Is the assistant principal kept informed of the administrative decisions and problems of administration within the school?

5. Could the present duties be handled by a good secretary? If this is true, perhaps the position could be eliminated, or perhaps the assistant principal could be involved in instructional improvement?

6. Does the assistant principal have the backing of the principal when making decisions?

7. Is adequate secretarial help provided so that the assistant principal may devote work activities in line with professional training and the needs of the school?

8. Does the assistant principal have opportunities to attend professional meetings?

Policies of the Board of Education or Governing Body

The board of education or governing body of the secondary school usually has broad powers in determining the nature and administrative organization of the school. It is the governing body's responsibility to provide the financial resources necessary for the educational program, to employ personnel, and to evaluate the results of the total educational effort. The North Central Association requires that member schools "shall have administrative and supervisory personnel, for effective operation of the program. The administration of the secondary school has the necessary autonomy and authority to provide the leadership needed to accomplish improvement of instruction with the staff."[3]

It is essential that the board of education does not interfere in the administration of the secondary school. Of course, if in the majority opinion of the governing body, there is a feeling that the principal is incompetent or in need of leadership improvement, they have every right to discharge the principal or ask for an improvement, after proper hearing with the principal. However, the board relies upon the professional judgment of the superintendent in these matters.

The North Central Association regards the following as desirable conditions for board-staff relationships:

1. Board members are familiar with and accept the tenets of "A Code of Ethics for School Board Members" as published by the National School Boards Association.

2. Board members are given the opportunity to attend meetings of the NSBA and to visit other school systems to observe effective practices. Their participation in NCA evaluation activity is encouraged.

3. The use of ad hoc citizens' committees for specific purposes and to assure improved communication between the school and the public is recommended. Use of standing board committees is discouraged.[4]

Staff and Student Morale

Evaluation of faculty and student morale is a continuous process which the principal accomplishes through interviews and questionnaires. Figure 8.5, previously illustrated, is a sample questionnaire which the principal may use. This questionnaire is not standardized and does not give the principal any standard for comparison with faculties of other school systems. However, any rating which is below average calls for action on the part of the principal.

Figure 8.6 is a Decision-Making Autonomy Profile developed by one of the authors for a regional accrediting association. A survey of the faculty concerning their own involvement in decision making will help the principal improve faculty morale.

Figure 8.6
*Decision-Making Autonomy Profile**

Generally, decisions concerning curriculum, teaching method, student control, school program, and the like should be made as close to the operational level as possible. It is evident that the effectiveness of the school increases as professional decision making becomes a shared responsibility and concern of the staff, rather than being completely centered in the principal's suite or the district office.

Obviously, not all decisions should or can be made at the faculty level. Moreover, some concerns are not so vital to the professional vigor of the school as are others. The purpose of this profile is to determine the existing decision-making process within this school and to obtain a reading on what various segments of the school consider the preferred situation to be.

You are asked to give thoughtful consideration to the items on the profile, then mark your responses clearly. Do not sign your name on this sheet.

In completing the profile, you are to place an X along the continuum line from "Not Involved" to "Determines Final Decision" according to your view of the present situation. On the same line you are to place an O indicating the degree of involvement you think it would be *desirable* for you and your colleagues to have in this specific area of decision making.

---

* "The NCA Guide for School Evaluation, A Workbook for The Self Study and Team Visit," 3rd ed., 1976 (Boulder Colorado, Commission of Schools, North Central Association), pp. 80–81.

Figure 8.6 cont'd.

For example, if you are a teacher and you feel you are only partially involved in major decisions concerning classroom discipline, you would place an X somewhere near "Partially Involved" on the line. If you think that as a classroom teacher you should be making specific recommendations in matters of classroom discipline, you would place an O accordingly. Thus the line for Classroom Discipline would read:

	Not Involved	Partially Involved	Make Specific Recommendations	Determine Final Decision
1. Classroom Discipline		X	O	

If the desired situation coincides with the prevailing condition, simply place the X and O together.

Upon completion, connecting the X's with black lines will give your conception of your present autonomy profile. Connecting the O's by red lines will yield your conception of what the optimal situation should be. The coincidence or divergence of these two profiles will be significant, especially on particular items.

Please use an X to denote the existing situation, as you see it, and an O to indicate what you think the situation should be.

Item	Not Involved	Partially Involved	Make Specific Recommendations	Determine Final Decision
1. Classroom Discipline...........................				
2. Overall School Discipline.......................				
3. Employment of Teachers........................				
4. Transfer of Teachers...........................				
5. Promotion of Teachers..........................				
6. Teacher Assignments...........................				
7. Teacher Schedule..............................				
8. Teacher Evaluation.............................				
9. Extra-Curricular Duties.........................				
10. Salary Schedule...............................				
11. Personnel Policies.............................				
12. Professional Leave.............................				
13. Professional Travel.............................				
14. School Schedule...............................				
15. School Calendar...............................				
16. In-service Program.............................				
17. Contract Negotiations..........................				

Figure 8.6 cont'd.

Item	Not Involved	Partially Involved	Make Specific Recommen- dations	Determine Final Decision
18. School Policies..				
19. Use of Educational Aides...				
20. School Procedures..				
21. Content Taught...				
22. Textbook Selection...				
23. Program of Studies...				
24. Subject Testing Program...				
25. Standardized Testing Program.......................................				
26. Student Promotion Standards..				
27. Student Final Grading..				
28. Teaching Materials and Equipment...................................				
29. Selection of Library Books and Media................................				
30. District Budget...				
31. Individual School Budget...				
32. Department Budget...				
33. Student Activity Budget..				
34. Student Transportation..				
35. School Lunch Program...				
36. Remodeling of Building..				

Please indicate your position in the school

_____ teacher   _____ department head   _____ asst.

_____ principal   _____ other (please specify)   principal

Date _____   School _____

A principal of a modern school building with plentiful equipment and supplies, and eager and professsionally competent teachers, is well on the way to achieving high student morale. In this situation, morale will often be high in spite of the principal. On the other hand, a principal of an ill-equipped, old school building, even though staffed by excellent teachers, may find keeping morale high is a difficult assignment.

Therefore, high or low morale on the part of teachers and students may not always be due to administrative control of the school. The principal who finds low morale in his or her building should not take it personally, but consider many factors including the nature of the building and the nature of the student population. Regardless of whether the principal knows better or not, the students and faculty should be made to believe that the principal feels that they and the school are the best.

Instructional Staff

The instructional staff can be evaluated according to professional education completed, highest degree completed, assignment to major subject field, professional attitude, travel of the staff (especially foreign language and world history teachers), and success in teaching.

Some desirable conditions for the development and improvement of the professional staff as listed by the North Central Association include the following:

> . . . Three fourths or more of the faculty members are assigned to teach only in their major field of preparation.
>
> The school system is making efforts to continually strengthen its professional staff through a professional program which reimburses faculty members for advanced training, curriculum work; and travel to improve their experiences or to observe innovations being tried in other schools.
>
> Para professional personnel are provided to relieve teachers of non-teaching duties. Every teacher has regular access to clerical and secretarial help for those routine tasks which can be satisfactorily handled by sub-professional help.
>
> Every teacher has regular access to clerical or secretarial help in accomplishing the routine tasks which can be satisfactorily handled by sub-professional help.
>
> The governing board has adopted the policy of requiring teachers to earn the Master's degree of 30 semester hours of graduate credit within a period of at least seven years of service in their system. The provisions of this policy become a part of each teacher's contract at the time of employment and require that work in the teacher's major teaching field be included in the graduate program.
>
> Various levels of teacher ability are recognized such as master, regular, and beginning teachers, and appropriate assignments are given each type.
>
> The ratio of pupils to teachers and other professional staff members in high schools is less than 20 to 1.[5]

EVALUATING AND REPORTING STUDENT PROGRESS

Schools should be a place where students can achieve at their maximum level of capability. Parents and students alike, for the most part, are very interested in the student's level of learning. They both want to make sure the education students are receiving is of the highest possible quality. It is imperative that principals know where the school desires to go and where the school is in terms of quality education. Information concerning the current level of achievement can provide beneficial input as to how much one has yet to achieve.

Issues Related to Evaluation and Reporting of Student Progress

An issue that causes much frustration among students, and may indeed cause some to exhibit aggression and thus result in discipline problems, centers around grading. Probably one of the most controversial aspects of marking is the purpose of marks. Some of the common reasons for giving marks are:

1. Motivating students to achieve.
   a. Reward for achievement.
   b. Punishment for failure to achieve.
2. Informing the students and parents of the progress achieved.
3. Assisting the determination of future course selections and future vocational selections.

One of the major problems faced by teachers is the interpretation of what a mark really means. Questions related to this problem are:

1. Should grades be used to enforce discipline or should citizenship grades be given to reflect classroom behavior?
2. How should class attendance affect grades?
3. Should grades be given on the basis of effort in relation to ability or should level of ability be disregarded?
4. What type of marking system should be employed?
   a. Percentage
   b. Curve grading
   c. Letter grading
   d. Pass/Fail
   e. Rank order scores
   f. Percentile rank
5. What percent of the course grade should each of the following be worth?
   a. Final test
   b. Periodic tests
   c. Homework
   d. Class participation
   e. Special projects
6. Should extra credit for extra work be given?
7. What policy should be adopted regarding failing grades?

8. Does "tough" grading insure quality teaching and learning?
9. What should be the basis for grading in courses that are designed to foster the development of certain attitudes?

Grades, in and of themselves, probably are not too reflective of the quality of the educational program. The search for a solution to the accountability problem has resulted in educational proposals which could have implications for the grading systems. Concern about the quality of education being received has prompted interest in exploring such plans as performance contracting and the voucher plan.

Performance Contracting

Performance contracting simply stipulates a certain level of achievement for a certain cost. The question then becomes one of who is to measure the level of achievement and how. Of further concern is the level of performance that is desired and what knowledge should be tested. In other words, grading now becomes a matter of looking at group performance. If the group performs well enough, the contract is fulfilled. Of course, individuals can still be tested and graded.

The results, to date, concerning the success of performance contracting have not shown it to be highly successful. Many of the initial contracts existed between private companies and local school corporations. Further refinement of procedures or more direct involvement of local staff members may result in more success of performance contracting in the future.

Voucher Plan

The voucher plan purports to foster competition between schools to provide better quality education. The voucher plan gives parents the opportunity to select the school of their choice within the school corporation by giving them a voucher which has a value approximately equivalent to the cost of education for their child. This plan could result in problems in achieving desired racial balance. However, some schools have stipulated they will accept students in such a way as to achieve racial balance. They do this by specifying the percentage of each racial or ethnic group they will accept and when the desired quotas are reached, they will accept no more students that fall into that category. In addition to racial balance, teachers and principals may feel compelled to consider how their grading standards may affect the desire of students to enroll in their school.

Testing and Grading

Increased emphasis on accountability has provided added incentive for those who are strong believers in testing to "push" their cause. Those who are most inclined to be learner-centered argue that teaching becomes merely preparing for tests if testing is emphasized. Those who favor testing feel that students need to become acclimated to the reward system that grades provide since our economic system is built upon competition. However, many students are not convinced of the reward of grades, thus, grades are not effective motivations for them.

Is quality education measured by the grades students achieve? In summarizing his feeling concerning marks, Ebel says:

> Marks are necessary. If they are inaccurate, invalid, or meaningless, the remedy lies less in de-emphasizing marks than in assigning them more carefully so that they more truly report the extent of important achievements. Instead of seeking to minimize their importance or seeking to find some less painful substitute, perhaps instructors should devote more attention to improving the validity and precision of the marks they assign and to minimizing misinterpretations of marks by students, faculty, and others who use them.[6]

The controversy surrounding the advantages and disadvantages of testing and grading has not been resolved, nor is it likely to be in the near future. However, it is worthwhile to explore and discuss various facets of testing and grading.

For a more detailed discussion of these topics, the authors recommend *Alternatives to Tests, Marks, and Class Rank* by David A. Gilman (Terre Haute, Indiana: Indiana State University Curriculum Research and Development Center, 1974).

Test Analysis

A principal can increase confidence in testing if he or she arranges for inservice programs for improving teachers' use of tests. The following types of analyses provide teachers with valuable information concerning the worth of their tests:

1. *Item Difficulty.* The percentage of students who answered the item correctly.
2. *Discrimination.* The number of students in the upper 27 percent who answered the item correctly minus the number of students in the lower 27 percent who answered the item correctly divided by 27 percent of the total number of students who took the examination.
3. *Reliability.* Indicates the extent to which each person would score approximately the same on subsequent tests when using the same or similar tests.
4. *Validity.* Indicates the degree to which a test actually measures what it is designed to measure.

Students should be given statistical information concerning the test which provides them with an idea of how well they did on the test. Such statistical information as the following is helpful:

1. *Mean.* Computed by adding all the scores and dividing by the number of scores.
2. *Median.* If the number of scores in the group is odd, it is the middle score. If the number of scores in the group is even, it is a point halfway between the two middle scores.
3. *Range.* The difference between the highest and lowest score in a set of scores.
4. *Percentile Rank.* Indicates the percent of scores which fall below a particular score.
5. *Standard Deviation.* A statistical measure which indicates how a set of scores are dispersed around the mean.
6. *Z-Score.* Indicates the number of standard deviations a score is from the mean.

Alternative Testing Methods

Criterion Referenced Tests. This approach to testing specifies a minimum level of acceptable performance by students on a test. This procedure implies that students have not adequately learned the material unless they are able to meet the specified level of acceptable performance on the test. It is important that these tests be constructed to measure specifically what is to be learned.

Self-Scoring Tests. This type of test is usually multiple choice and utilizes a procedure whereby all choices are covered in some fashion. Students are asked to continue selecting a choice until the correct answer is revealed. A common test of this nature requests students to erase the material covering their desired choice. The more wrong choices, the higher the score and thus, the lower the grade on the test. This technique provides students with immediate feedback on the correctness of their response.

Standardized and Classroom Testing

Demands for more comprehensive and refined techniques of evaluating educational efforts have led administrators and teachers to employ a variety of strategies. One set of strategies uses informal approaches. Here, the teacher, mainly through classroom observation, appraises the performance of students in recitations, special projects, and regular homework assignments. These observations are important evaluation tools even when much of the teacher's evaluation of progress is based on the formal testing program. In the more formalized approach, the testing program is divided into teacher-made tests and the standardized test.

No doubt the most widely used procedure in determining student progress is the teacher-made test. While many teachers produce very fine tests, it has been repeatedly demonstrated that the reliability and validity factors quite often leave much to be desired.

Due to the problems associated with assessment of student progress by utilizing observation and teacher-made tests, standardized testing programs have come into prominence. Since all conscientious teachers are concerned with the progress of their pupils in achieving the objectives on instruction, many have turned to standardized testing strategies.

These tests afford the principal an impartial basis for judging how well the students are attaining worthwhile educational goals. The principal is necessarily concerned with the changing character of the student body and with the appropriateness of the school's curriculum for students of different levels of ability. Standardized test results provide much needed data for sound consideration of both these matters. The principal will find objective test data information of considerable value in discussing with parents the nature of the school's educational program as well as the specific attainments, or abilities, of individual students. The prudent principal will not use test results as a basis for evaluating the efficiency of teachers, for he or she will realize that so many factors influence the achievement of students that it would be hazardous to ascribe either unusually good performance or unusually poor performance solely to the efforts of the teacher.

When thinking about the overall advantages in choosing standardized or teacher-made tests when both may be used with equal validity, the following should be considered:

1. The standardized instrument provides an independent, objective criterion which will not reflect the biases of the individual teacher.
2. Although the best teacher-made examinations are adequate to appraise the relative achievement of pupils within a single class, only the standardized instrument, through the provision of comparative norms, permits the assignment of a relative rank to any given pupil among students within a larger and more representative population.
3. The standardized tests, due to commercial competition and large sales volume, will usually represent a very economical form of testing.
4. The extensively detailed preparation and research which are devoted to item construction and test validation by commercial test producers are more likely to result in more reliable instruments than is normally possible in the classroom.

Standardized achievement tests are also definitely superior to all others in certain aspects of instructional programming which are divorced from course evaluation. They are of particular importance in determining the instructional placement of transfer students, and for determining readiness for higher levels of sequentially structured instructional programs.

Their value is greatly increased when test results have been cumulated over a period of years, since trends may be discernible; and, marked digressions from the established pattern of development may possibly indicate a need for more intensive diagnosis and remediation. If compensatory treatments are initiated, alternate forms of achievement tests may be used for the assessment of improvements resulting from their introduction.

The proper administrative uses of the results of testing constitute the greatest single opportunity for the schools to meet their responsibilities to children and society. Because the average or median test results with which the superintendent's office deals are usually based on adequate samplings, these measures are usually highly reliable and valid. Thus, they provide accurate information for the guidance of administrative and supervisory officers. Test results reveal such important facts as:

1. The level of mental maturity or intelligence is disclosed for a school system as a whole, and for the individual schools; they suggest the level of achievement which should be attained by the district as a whole, and the variations which should be expected among schools.

2. Test data reveal what is actually being accomplished, where the schools are strong, and what subjects, areas, or grades are weak; this information suggests where administrative and supervisory services are most needed.

Principals have an obligation to make sure that testing does not become overemphasized. This can be accomplished by surveying teachers to determine how many tests are given each semester, and how much weight is given to tests in relation to other class assignments that affect the final grade.

Alternative Ways to Evaluate and Report Student Progress

Letter Grades. A, B, C, D, F grades have been the traditional way to indicate to students the extent to which they have achieved. It has always been difficult to reach agreement as to just what each letter means in terms of the level of achievement. Some teachers use a "normal curve" method to determine the number of students who were to receive each letter grade. This would mean that the same number of students would receive a grade of A, as received a grade of F, etc. Other teachers use a percentage or point system to determine where the cut-off on the A, B, C, and D grades would be.

Those classes which are ability grouped cause specific grading problems because some teachers feel students in a low ability group should not receive above a D, while those in the upper group should not receive below a B. Teachers have experienced motivation problems with those students who know they could not receive above a certain grade or below a certain grade.

Dual Marking System. Some educators advocate the use of a dual marking system. One mark represents the student's level of achievement in relation to that of other students in the course. The second mark represents the student's achievement in relation to personal ability. In other words, the second grade represents a measure of how close the pupil is performing to the level at which personal ability indicates he or she should be performing.

Performance-Based Evaluation. This technique involves reporting to students the extent to which they have mastered behavioral objectives which have been specified by the teacher. Normally, students are required to successfully complete a minimum number of objectives. Letter grades are usually not given; however, a system of awarding certain letter grades for specified levels of achievement could be developed.

Contracts. The contract method involves developing a set of activities for an individual or a group and specifying the grade which can be earned for successful completion of that specified set of activities. The development of the activities could be a joint effort between the student and the teacher. Students can decide the grade they want to try for and then reach agreement with the teacher as to how they are to achieve that grade. This technique provides for individualization of instruction.

Pass-Fail or Pass-No Pass. The pass-fail system encourages students to explore areas of knowledge which they might avoid because of fear of receiving low marks if the traditional marking system were used. Removing the threat of low grades and setting the level of achievement necessary to pass allows students to spend time in courses that really interest them and fit their needs. The pass-fail system would also permit the creative student to explore areas of knowledge beyond what might be required for the traditional A grade.

Narrative Reports. This method normally does not involve providing a letter grade, but does give a narrative description of student progress. This description is usually done for each subject and may be developed from a listing of characteristics related to student progress. It is possible to utilize computers to print out selected comments by each teacher. Parent-teacher conferences can be utilized to discuss the narrative reports or they may be mailed to the students and their parents.

A Point Value System for Promotion. L. J. Des Pres, Superintendent of Schools of South Callaway R-Z, Markane, Missouri, reports on a grading system which eliminates the philosophy of nonpromotion or giving F's. Students receive percentage scores for all final course grades. The percentage scores for each course are divided by 10. This figure represents the point value the student has earned for that course. Each student must achieve 120 points a year in order to graduate in four years. The individual point values of each course are added together to determine how many points the student has earned toward the required 120 a year, if he or she is to graduate in four years. A student could receive such a low percentage score for a course that traditionally the course would have to be repeated because the percentage would have been considered an F. At South Callaway R-Z, the student simply adds the point value of this particular course with that of all courses and he or she is not required to repeat the course.[7]

Instructional Objectives

In order to solve the grading dilemma, we must first become concerned about informing students exactly what we expect them to know. A grade by itself does not tell much about what a student learned.

Most teaching is directed toward goals which often are global and sometimes vague in nature. Therefore, one of the first things teachers and administrators must do is to establish instructional objectives which are clearly specified. That is, they must be spelled out in such a way that they provide definite directions for students in:

1. what is expected of the student in the way of student achievement
2. how the teaching-learning process will be conducted in order to obtain the objectives
3. how the student will be evaluated

Educators have been urged to express objectives in terms of learner behavior. An instructional objective may be operationalized by describing either the specific observable behavior in which the student is to engage, or the products which the student will produce. Many educators feel the exercise of too much operationalizing of objectives leads to teaching of minute, fragmented bits of information which become rather insignificant. While this caution should be observed, it should not preclude the practice.

Teachers and administrators have utilized various methods for selecting appropriate educational objectives, ranging from those objectives suggested by textbook authors to the teacher's own conception of what is most worthy of consideration. However, in recent years, increased attention has been focused on taxonomic analysis as a starting base. This classification system has been widely circulated in the educational community through the works of Bloom et al.[8]

The three realms into which the taxonomy has been divided are referred to as the cognitive domain, the affective domain, and the psychomotor domain. In the cognitive domain the concern is with the intellectual response of the learner; while the affective domain relates the attitudinal, emotional, and value judgment responses of the learner. In the psychomotor domain the physical responses of the learner become important, particularly in the performance of certain types of manipulative operations. For a full breakdown of the three domains, the authors recommend the work of Bloom and his associates.[9]

With these domains forming a classification of objectives to be achieved, one should then consider levels of performance to be accomplished.

The first major task is to identify the terminal behavior that is expected of the learner. This is the beginning of writing a behavioral objective. Mager has stated that instructional objectives should also describe the conditions leading to the terminal behavior and then specify the criteria of acceptable performance.[10] All three conditions are important in the development of instructional objectives. But in the final analysis we must focus on what end behavior we might reasonably expect of our students.

This may be supported by the additional notion that a better learning environment is further advanced when learners are encouraged to assist with the evaluation of their progress and educational goals are made clear. Student involvement also facilitates methods of instruction which are more easily fitted to the interests, aptitudes, and abilities of the individual student. Such arrangements bring more effective and lasting results, for not only the principal and teacher are involved and concerned about meeting objectives, but so is the student. In the final analysis, it is the reporting of student progress to the involved learner which provides him or her with the personal feedback to more readily modify behavior, which is the essence of good teaching.

The successful program for reporting student progress will employ diverse methods for students to evaluate their own work. Such procedures materially aid the student to discover personal strengths and weaknesses and frequently suggest appropriate remedial procedures.

To illustrate the growing concern for students to take additional responsibility for appraising and reporting their own progress, the Model School Project sponsored by the NASSP has indicated that the student is best served by self-appraisals of continuous growth along a learning sequence. This means in the MSP approach students are informed of performance objectives.

Questions raised by students and parents relating to what is really happening in the schools and what is expected of the students are answered in a variety of ways. They include newsletters, composite progress reports, awarding of credits as they are earned, and telephone contacts with the home. Special projects and other affective developments are recorded and noted in the students' permanent records.

In an effort to humanize the school and curricula, all feedback possible is provided to student and parents from the individual testing programs, reinforcement activities, interdisciplinary experiences, cognitive comparisons (pre- and post-tests), teachers' planning programs with students, and the student's own evaluation of the program.

Competency Tests and Graduation Requirements

There has been increasing public concern that a high school diploma does not really insure that the holder is able to perform minimal basic skills. This attitude has encouraged the use of tests of competence to insure a basic level of skill performance in various areas before a standard diploma is awarded.

There is some concern as to what happens to students who do not qualify for a competency based diploma. The following suggestions have been advanced as ways to recognize those who have spent four or more years in high school but who still lack certain competencies:

1. special diplomas
2. certificates of competency
3. diplomas with endorsements certifying that the student has (or has not) met specified competencies
4. certificates of attendance.[11]

Guidelines for Improving Evaluation of Student Progress With Marks

Once the marking system has been developed and instituted, the following suggestions are offered to reduce the possibility of student frustration concerning marks:

1. Teachers should be assisted in developing course outlines which give the course objectives stated in concrete terms. Students should be given a copy of the outlines at the beginning of the course. The outline should contain the procedure used to determine final course grades. This procedure should spell out exactly what the student is expected to do in the way of daily assignments, tests, etc. These outlines can best be developed by the various departments. They should be revised periodically based on the results achieved by students completing the courses.

2. An evaluation of all marks assigned by teachers should be undertaken and published for use by the teacher involved. An evaluation of all marks given in each course should be undertaken, and finally, an evaluation of marks given by departments should be carried out. Department chairpersons can provide valuable leadership in the evaluation of marks and the subsequent use of these evaluations. The various evaluations must consider the ability of the students taking the various courses.

3. The reporting of marks to students should be done at consistent intervals, and a system should be developed which does not require the return of the report card to the school. All final course grades should be recorded in a permanent record in a manner which does not require extensive copying of grades.

4. An analysis of marks should be conducted which shows a comparison from year to year. The same should be done for achievement test scores.

5. Tests used by teachers as a basis for assigning marks should be analyzed to determine their reliability and validity. Using tests with a low reliability or validity as a basis for assignment of marks cannot be justified.

6. Sufficient evidence should be gathered to insure an adequate basis for the assignment of a mark. A one-test course does not adequately support this principle.

7. Teachers should be given adequate time to conduct discussions with students and parents concerning the marks received by students.

SUMMARY

The building principal is the most important individual in setting the climate for meaningful curriculum development. Evaluation of the present curriculum can set the stage for further curriculum development. Standards established by state departments of public instruction, regional accrediting agencies, and national level agencies can provide assistance in evaluating current educational programs. Follow-up studies of students, standardized tests, evaluations of school staff and administration, and evaluation of the extent of articulation between the various grade levels should be utilized to assist in the evaluation of the curriculum.

Grades or marks, as they are now commonly called, have been used in the past to motivate students. The intent was not so much to let students know where they were so that they could progress further, but to threaten them to achieve or receive a low or failing mark. The movement toward more individualized instruction has resulted in marking systems designed to show students how much they have achieved in terms of the objectives they set out to achieve. Energy expended on the development of instructional objectives would probably be more worthwhile than that spent on deciding how to "grade" students. If the traditional grading pattern is utilized, then a periodic analysis of how those grades are determined, and a comparative analysis of the actual grades given should be undertaken. This information should be relayed and interpreted to students.

NOTES

1. K. Forbis Jordan, "Program Improvement Through School Evaluation," *Educational Leadership* 34:4 (January, 1977) p. 274.

2. "Questions and Answers about the National Assessment of Educational Progress," (Denver: Education Commission of the States, 1973), pp. 1–6.

3. North Central Association, *Policies and Criteria for the Approval of Secondary Schools,* 1977 (Boulder, Colorado, Commission of Schools), p. 8.

4. Ibid., p. 15.

5. Ibid., p. 25.

6. Robert L. Ebel, *Essentials of Educational Measurement* (Englewood Cliffs, N.J.: Prentice-Hall, Inc., 1972), p. 315.

7. L. J. Des Pres, "Grading System That Really Works," *School and Community* 56 (May, 1970), pp. 12–13.

8. Benjamin Bloom et al., *Taxonomy of Educational Objectives: Cognitive Domain* (New York: David McKay Co., Inc.), 1961.

9. Ibid.

10. Robert F. Mager, *Preparing Instructional Objectives* (Palo Alto, Calif.: Fearon Publishers, 1962).

11. Scott D. Thomson and James B. Clark, *Competency Tests and Graduation Requirements* (Reston, Va.: The National Association of Secondary School Principals, 1976), p. 18.

9

The Development and Operation of a Student Activities Program

Numerous terms such as cocurricular, student activities, extracurricular, and extraclass activities have been used to describe those educational activities students engage in outside of prescribed in-class time. Each title has a justifiable reason for its use; however, the term *student activities* will be used throughout this chapter.

Student activities have moved from being considered a frill, to being tolerated, and finally to receiving active support. The educational value of student activities has been realized. Activities of this nature should supplement the in-class activities. Most educators have come to the realization that all needs of students are not met by in-class instruction. There still exists, though, debate as to how extensive the student activity program should be.

Robert Buser, with the cooperation of the National Association of Secondary School Principals, conducted a study of schools which had developed "outstanding student activity programs." The following three paragraphs discuss the findings of this study.[1]

Many new clubs, councils, and seminars are oriented toward increased involvement in the pressing problems of society. These include ecology clubs, peace clubs, life discussion seminars, black culture clubs, minority councils, councils on world and human relations, women's liberation groups, drug seminars, and exploratory education periods during which students can schedule any class of their choice. New leisure-oriented clubs include horseback riding, sky diving, out-of-doors, folk music, skiing, scuba diving, weight training, and art and music. Some of the more novel school-community service activities include volunteer service to homes for the aged, voter registration drives, anti-pollution and clean-up days, and tutoring services.

"Outstanding" ways of involving students in the day-to-day decisions facing schools include: student representatives on the faculty advisory boards, student-faculty grievance committees, student membership on the principal's advisory committees, student advisory boards, bi-racial committees, student council representation on the boards of education, student senates, senior administration day, student-administrator discussion groups, and consultative councils.

Schools reported changes in both interscholastic and intramural athletics. Additions to the interscholastic sports programs were in the areas of gymnastics, wrestling, golf, tennis, soccer, swimming, and cross country for both boys and girls. Intramural programs were expanded for boys and/or girls. Some schools instituted coeducational student and faculty sports. The schools in the study reported the activities they dropped as well as the ones they added. Those dropped by order of higher frequency were: traditional subject area clubs such as math, hobby clubs like chess or camera, assemblies, school dances, class plays, and pep clubs.*

The fourth edition of the Evaluative Criteria for the Evaluation of Secondary Schools published by the National Study of Secondary School Evaluation lists the following major categories under the heading of the student activities programs:

1. Student government
2. School assembly
3. Workshop and service activities (for church related schools)
4. School publications
5. Music activities
6. Dramatics and speech activities
7. Social life and activities
8. Physical activities (does not include regularly scheduled physical education classes)
9. School clubs[2]

Issues related to each of these listed categories will be discussed in this chapter. To serve as guidelines for discussion of these various student activities, the following questions are presented which represent issues a principal must deal with when considering student activities.

1. What are the values and objectives of the activities?
2. Are the activities geared to the students' needs and interests?
3. What are the principal's responsibilities?
4. How are the sponsors selected?
5. What are the sponsors' responsibilities?

---

* From Robert Buser, "What's Happening in Student Activities in the Schools of the Seventies?" *The Bulletin of Secondary School Principals* 55:356 (September, 1971), pp. 1-9. Used by permission.

6. What are the organizations, if any, which govern these activities other than the high school?
7. What are the regulations for becoming a member of these groups?
8. By what means are the rules and regulations for each activity formulated and by whom?
9. How are the activities financed?
10. Who is responsible for handling the finances?
11. How are the activities scheduled?
12. What are the legal aspects of student activities?

The principal should develop answers for each of these questions for each area of student activities. General guidelines related to the organization and administration of the activity program are discussed in the next section of this chapter. Specific guidelines for the major categories of student activities listed previously are presented in the remainder of this chapter.

ORGANIZATION AND ADMINISTRATION OF THE ACTIVITY PROGRAM

The administrative and organizational duties of an activity program seem to automatically fall on the shoulders of the principal, as chief administrator of a particular building. Idealistically, the principal should have time to spend each day for supervision of activity programs. But time in many schools does not permit this. There is a need for a "director of activities," especially in the large secondary schools of today, because the responsibilities of the principal are constantly becoming greater. The principal, as chief administrator, advises or delegates authority to the director of activities, but maintains the necessary overall control and power of veto.

What person does the principal appoint as director of activities? Funds may not be available to hire a specialist in activity program supervision. If the principal can appoint a member of the staff the improvements may be great. An assistant principal or interested staff member may be the ideal solution to the improvement of the activity program.

The person selected to become director of activities should be familiar with (1) student, faculty, and community needs; (2) the supervision practices and personality of the principal; and (3) the present program of activities.

Once the appointment is made, the principal must work to further orient and induct the director of activities to the needs and improvements the principal perceives. Both principal and director should agree upon the following seven aspects of the organization of the activity program:

1. The principal maintains overall control of the program and power to veto.

2. The director should be allocated time each day for activities program work.
3. The director and principal will develop a "central planning committee" and the director will work with sponsors in inservice training type gatherings.
4. The director should spend part of this time supervising and evaluating activity sponsors by a predetermined evaluation system as based on written and verbal objectives.
5. All activities must have an interested sponsor.
6. Some type of evaluation is essential to constant improvement.
7. The program should be varied to meet the needs and interests of as many students as possible (as studied by the central planning committee).

Activity sponsors should be the core of the central planning committee. With them, the director of activities begins to work toward improvements. The function of the director and central planning committee is the development of policies, both operational and administrative, under which the program will operate. The committee, with the director as chairperson, is responsible for:

1. Developing a written statement of beliefs on the philosophy of student activities. This should be accepted by the faculty, principal, superintendent, and the school board.
2. The establishment of guiding principles of organization and administration of student activities.
3. The formation of policies concerning:
   a. the selection, training, and supervision of sponsors
   b. the publicizing of the program to pupils, parents, and community
   c. maintaining an activity calendar
   d. financing and accounting system for safeguarding funds
   e. establishment of a calendar of activities for the following year
   f. formulation of methods and procedures for objective evaluation
   g. membership and participation
   h. determining criteria for fund-raising activities
   i. addition or elimination of activities
   j. suggestions for scheduling of activities

Regulations for Participation in Student Activities

The following alternatives or combination thereof can serve as examples of ways to regulate participation in student activities:

1. A point system which assigns a certain number of points to each student activity is used in many schools. Following are some of the purposes:
    a. Distribute more evenly the opportunities for participation.
    b. Prevent the student from overloading.
    c. Equate activities where credit is allowed or required.
2. Simple limitation is the simplest method of limiting participation in activities, stating the number a student may belong to.
3. A system of major activities and minor activities where all the activities are put into the group, and a student can only be in a certain combination of the two.
4. The group system is when the activities are put into classifications like sports, academic, service, general, social literary, music, and dramatics. The student then can only belong to one activity in each classification.
5. Other consideration or requirements for being in activities are:
    a. Does participation lower a student's marks?
    b. Shall the student with low grades be allowed to participate?
6. Some other methods of encouraging participation are:[3]
    a. Award activity points or honor points.
    b. Requiring the participation of the students in the extraclass activities.
    c. Allow academic credit for participation.
    d. Awards for participation:
        (1) Letter or emblem.
        (2) Certificate of merit.
        (3) Public recognition.
        (4) Appointment to position of honor.
        (5) Special privileges.
        (6) Banquets.
        (7) Trips, etc.

Financing of the Student Activity Program

As a guiding principle, the expenses involved in participating in any student activity and in the total program of a school year should be set at a figure which will permit 90 percent of the students to participate without financial strain.[4]

Standards for student fund-raising enterprises include the following:

1. Efficiency
2. Businesslike methods
3. Fairness

4. Moral acceptability
5. Legitimacy
6. Educational soundness
7. Noncompulsiveness
8. No exploitation
9. No competition with local merchants
10. A sense of value[5]

Alternative money raising activities are:

1. Admission fees
2. Variety of events
3. Sales of goods and services
4. The School Store
5. Gifts and donations (No gifts to the school generally, or to any particular organized activity, or to any individual students will be solicited or accepted from any individual, or business, or other organization except as they are approved by the principal and recommended by the parent-faculty council and the student association board.)
6. Dues and special levies
7. Student fees
8. Public taxes used by the board of education.[6]

STUDENT GOVERNMENT

The success of the entire activity program, and indeed the entire school, probably correlates very closely with the extent to which the student governing body operates successfully.

The educational leader of the secondary school has suddenly found that he or she is no longer the omnipotent administrator, but one who must listen to students demands, confrontations, walkouts, sit-ins and other signs of student activism. Students are insisting upon the right to be seen and the right to be heard.

Weak student councils, authoritarian administrators, and poor communication between the principal and students are obsolete in the dynamic secondary school of today. Sabine received the following answer from a student when he asked the question:

If you were invited to make a speech to the principal and teachers of the high school you attended, what would you say?

I would tell my high school principal how much I wanted to learn and how my desire was vanquished. I would mention the

silly backward rules which inhibit social and academic development. I would ask the students to leave quickly, before they are
turned into mice too meek and too well trained for anything
but a dreary existence.[7]

Principals and teachers must be concerned about student interests so
that the desire to learn will not be vanquished, so that rules are relevant,
meaningful, and acceptable to adolescents.

The key to good student-personnel relationships is a dynamic, worthwhile, and effective student council or government. Student councils in
many schools have little to do with student government. They often are involved in such tasks as selling apples and candy at noon hour, arranging for
a student council dance, or other such social functions. An effective student
council that channels student desires into action and actually promotes
educational change will most likely eliminate violent student activism.

In a study of fifty junior high schools, Wilt found that none of their
student councils were responsible for approving all club activities including
athletics. Fifty-two and nine-tenths percent of the schools approved all club
activities except athletics. The following table indicates the principal's opinion of what the student council should do.

Table 9.1
What Should the Job of the Council/Government Be?*

	Response	*Percentage*
Operate Student Court	14	28
Prepare Student Handbook	32	64
Recommend New Courses	21	42
Evaluate Class Instruction	2	4
Recommend Changes in Instructional Methods	13	26
Promote School Spirit	48	96
Plan School Social Events	48	96
Plan School Fund-Raising Projects	30	60
Make Recommendations on Hiring Teachers	0	0
Organize Student-Lead Courses for Non-Credit Subjects	8	16

* From Bruce Wilt, "Survey of the Student Councils of Fifty Junior High Schools in Ohio"
(Unpublished Master's Problem, The University of Akron, 1971).

Wilt concluded in his survey that:

1. Principals consider the student council to be nothing more than a social committee for the school.

2. Principals consider the role of the council in discipline, curriculum, administration and community relations to be minor.

3. Students show little interest in the student council.[8]

In a study of students in one large state, 90 percent of over 1,000 students surveyed felt that they should be involved in determining curriculum change. A majority of these students also felt that they should be a part of determining discipline in the school and that the dress code and rules of conduct should be a joint consideration of students and administrators.[9] The student government can help alleviate these felt needs by providing for curriculum involvement and development of rules of conduct within the school.

If the student governing body is to function in a manner most beneficial to students, faculty, and administration, the student governing body must be more than a rubber-stamp organization. It must be permitted to originate proposals, debate the issues, and carry through with the programs that are developed.

Guidelines for the Operation of Student Government

Several factors concerning the operation of the student governing body must be considered in the determination of what makes a student governing body successful. The authors present the following guidelines to assist in the development of a successful student governing body.

1. Some person other than the principal should serve as a sponsor for the student governing body. The sponsor should be selected by the principal with assistance from the faculty and students. It is quite important that the students perceive the sponsor as a person who is capable of fully comprehending their point of view. The sponsor should have enough rapport with student council members to seriously consider all aspects of actions they propose. This should reduce the necessity of vetoing final proposals by the council.

2. The principal should have veto power over student council proposals, but should exercise extreme caution in exercising that authority. Frequent communication between the student governing body, the administration, council sponsor, and faculty will assist in avoiding the use of veto power.

3. Final action on proposals initiated by the council should not be taken until at least the next regularly scheduled council meeting. Perhaps at least a week or two is an adequate time lapse. It may be wise to provide for a longer period of time lapse and the development of a procedure to hear all sides concerning major proposals of the council. This allows time for interaction of all concerned parties and will result in a more desirable proposal.

4. The student governing body probably should not be burdened with an undue number of fund-raising projects. It may be best to sponsor one major fund-raising project to finance the council or specify that a certain portion of funds raised by the individual classes be allocated to the student council.

5. Council members should be elected in such a manner as to adequately represent all segments of the student body. This may mean election from classes rather than clubs. Club membership may not adequately represent the student body.

6. The president of the student council should be elected by the student body as a whole. The other officers may be elected by the council members or by the student body as a whole. The student body should feel that the student council represents its point of view. Their involvement in the election of the president will assist in fostering this feeling.

7. Candidates for student council should actively campaign for their positions. Written guidelines should be established which specify procedures to be followed in conducting a campaign. Candidates for student council should be required to circulate petitions and give a speech before an assembly in order to be nominated as a candidate.

8. The only defensible position when establishing criteria for eligibility for student council is that the student be a bonafide member of the student body.

9. The number of members on student council should not exceed that which makes it impossible for all to feel they are able to actively participate in the affairs of the council. If the number exceeds thirty-five or forty, it may be wise to consider the formation of two councils representing upper and lower class levels, and establish a common executive board for the two councils.

10. The constitution for the student council should be in a written form, adopted by the student body as a whole, and verified by the board of education.

11. The council constitution should specify the areas which it has jurisdiction over and the extent to which it has final say. All areas in which the council can act only in an advisory capacity should be spelled out.

12. The student council should meet on a regular basis. Meetings longer than ninety minutes will usually not lend themselves to efficient dispensation of the business at hand. Provision should be made to schedule student council meetings just like any class is scheduled. Students should not be asked to miss class time to attend council meetings.

13. The officers of the student council should function as an executive body and meet as often as necessary. No official action should be taken by this body, and the essence of all discussions should be reported in writing to the student council as a whole.

14. All students should be notified of the time and place of all student council meetings. Room should be available for all those who desire to attend the meetings. In order to provide for the orderly conduct of the council meeting, an agenda should be developed prior to the meeting and adhered to. The agenda may provide for a time period for presentation by those who are not members of the student council.

15. The proceedings of each student council meeting should be published within two days following the meeting.

16. Perhaps the use of standing committees and ad hoc committees to consider issues related to their area of concern, which meet outside of the time alloted for council meetings, would expedite the orderly transaction of business during council meetings.

17. The council should periodically conduct an inventory of all students to determine issues it should deal with. Student council members could also set-up a "rap" session either daily or weekly to seek student opinion.

18. The student council should establish itself as a budget agency for all classes and clubs. This will insure that an equitable distribution of finances is made. It must be made clear that the council should not be the agency which receives and distributes funds, but it should be an agency which is involved in the approval of annual budgets for the various clubs and classes. The receiving and distribution of funds should be made through the central treasurer. Any change in the initial budget request should be acted upon by the council.

19. The student council should be permitted to present proposals to the school board after all approved procedures on the building level have been followed.

20. The student council should make provision for a human relations committee.

21. The student council should establish policy concerning the role of the student council in cases of student disorders.

22. Student court systems run by students entirely are not recommended. An appeals procedure which involves students should be established to provide students who have been disciplined with a place to be heard if they feel they have not received a fair hearing of their case. The appeals body should only be able to recommend. This body should assist in reducing the number of cases which are referred to board action.

23. The student council should develop an instrument to periodically evaluate the entire student activity program. This should include an analysis of the cost to an individual student of participating in the activity program.

24. The student council should periodically solicit student opinion as to the worth of the actions it has taken.

INTERSCHOLASTIC ATHLETICS

A major question that arises concerning interscholastic athletics is that of the purpose of athletics. Difficult questions such as the following are often raised:

1. Are athletics for competition or to develop cooperation?
2. Should one play to win and be judged only on such results?
3. To what extent should eligibility for participation be restricted?

Objectives of interscholastic athletics should contribute to the educational purposes of the school by providing participants the following:

1. Opportunity to learn new games.
2. Improvement in playing skills.
3. Development of physical vigor and of desirable habits in health, sanitation, and safety.
4. Opportunity to make real friendship with squad members.
5. Opportunity to meet and visit people in different communities.
6. Develop and observe good sportsmanship.
7. Association with athletic coaches, contest officials, teammates, and opponents.
8. A chance to enjoy one of the greatest heritages of youth—the right to play.
9. The general public participating as spectators can enjoy wholesome recreational activities.

Participation of women in interscholastic activities has become a major issue. Titles VI and VII of the 1964 Civil Rights Act and Title IX of the 1972 Education Amendments Act dealt with sex and race discrimination and have been utilized as a lever to encourage broader participation by females in interscholastic activities. Many questions have also arisen concerning equality of pay between male and female coaches. Schools must insure that they are in compliance with the federal guidelines relating to these issues. Title IX coordinators in school systems can be of valuable assistance to the principal.

Organizations other than the high school, which govern interscholastic activities are:

1. The National Federation of State High School Athletic Associations. The basic purpose of this organization is:
    a. The protection of the athletes
    b. Recommending minimum eligibility requirements
    c. Developing award limits
    d. Recommending semester attendance limits
    e. Writing of playing rules
    f. Developing standards for the cost and approval of athletic equipment
2. State High School Athletic and Activity Association. The purpose includes:
    a. Health—To organize, develop and direct an interscholastic athletic program which will promote, protect, and conserve the health and physical welfare of all participants.
    b. Education—To formulate and maintain policies that will safeguard the educational values of interscholastic athletics and cultivate high ideals of good sportsmanship.
    c. Competition—To promote uniformity of standards in all interscholastic athletic competition.

Educationally, the only acceptable source of support is the board of education which, through its resources, supports all educational ventures of school. However, the following list presents alternative ways to secure finances:

1. Admission prices
2. Season tickets
3. Student activity on general organization tickets
4. Student fee plan
5. Contributions
6. Special projects[10]

Guidelines for the Administration of the Athletic Program

The following summary statements provide general guidelines for the operation of an interscholastic athletic program:

1. Interscholastic athletics should not be overemphasized to the point that the intramural program suffers in its development. The existence of a strong athletic program indicates a desire to support this kind of activity. This support can also be utilized to develop a strong intramural program. It seems wise to build on the strength of the athletic programs to develop a strong intramural program rather than try to degrade the athletic program.

2. Provision should be made for competition by both boys and girls.

3. Provision should be made for individual sports as well as team sports.

4. Specific objectives related to goals of education should be developed for the athletic program. Periodic evaluation should be made to determine the extent to which these objectives are being met.

5. Careful consideration should be given to the criteria of eligibility for participation in order to insure participation by the maximum number of students.

6. Participants in athletics should not be excused from participation in physical education classes. Physical education classes should be designed to provide experiences related to skills development in addition to that which is found in athletics.

7. The community must continually be informed of the real purpose of interscholastic athletics. The development of an intramural program that involves adults of the community will provide a balance between the athletic program and the intramural program. Perhaps a cooperative arrangement with the city to provide recreational facilities and programs for all age groups will provide further evidence.

8. Most state high school athletic associations have established eligibility requirements. Interscholastic athletic programs should be based on educational value; therefore, eligibility requirements should not be so stringent as to eliminate those who could gain from participation.

9. The ideal financing arrangement would involve support from taxes as other educational programs are supported. However, not all states permit athletics to utilize tax money, thus, other sources of revenue must be secured. A central treasurer should be responsible for periodic financial reports. Many states have specific budgeting practices that they specify should or must be used.

10. The principal should insure that a plan be developed which permits adequate crowd control at athletic events. This plan should be well understood and supported by all who are involved. For some situations it may be necessary to utilize local law enforcement personnel to assist with crowd control. There should be a mutual understanding of the manner in which

crowds in general and unruly persons are to be dealt with. Emergency evacuation procedures should be established.

11. The principal, along with the athletic staff, must insure that race and sex discrimination do not occur in the interscholastic athletic program.

12. It is particularly important to establish clearly who will be in charge of the interscholastic program. While normally, the building principal is the person who assumes the responsibility for effective functioning of the athletic program, an athletic director can perform many duties such as hiring officials, scheduling games, securing and maintaining equipment and facilities, and insuring eligibility of contestants which will relieve the principal of these duties.

13. A systematically developed budget should exist to provide proper balance in the athletic program. Continued monitoring of the receipts and expenditures should assist in maintaining a balanced budget.

14. A guiding principle to determine the extent to which interscholastic athletics should be provided for junior high school age students is:

    a. Physical education should receive first consideration in the athletic program.

    b. A well planned and well administered program of intramurals should complement the physical education program.

    c. The third phase of the junior high school athletic program should include a few extramural contests involving teams selected from among the intramural teams to compete against similar teams from other schools.

    d. If a junior high school provides adequately for physical education, intramural, and extramural activities, it may offer additional opportunities for those pupils with superior athletic abilities to compete in a limited number of interschool contests with teams representing other junior high schools.[11]

15. An advisory athletic council which may consist of representation from all levels of administration, coaches, faculty members, student body, and patrons, with the principal serving as chairperson, could be of invaluable assistance in providing recommendations concerning establishing goals, evaluating the athletic program, and solving problems.

INTRAMURAL ACTIVITIES

Intramural activities refer to those physical activities which occur under the guidance of the school outside the regular scheduled physical education classes and interscholastic activities, with no grades or credits given to students. These activities should provide students with a chance to experience recreational activities which assist in the development of sound bodies and enough skill and interest to be useful in later life. Intramural activities can be an extension of a well-rounded physical education program and coordinated with the community recreation program. The emphasis should be on providing a variety of activities and insuring maximum participation by students with intramural events held both during and after school. Personnel should be assigned and paid for conducting these activities. Activities such as camping, boating, golfing, swimming, tennis, bowling, bridge, chess, and team sports should be provided.

Perhaps the intramural activities programs could be set up to encourage parental participation, at least in some activities. Primarily the activities should be scheduled for students, but parents may find this kind of involvement beneficial to establishing rapport between themselves and their children and the school.

A truly coordinated intramural program existing between the schools and the community will call for some dedicated planning by both agencies. This planning should result in a more economical and efficiently run program. Planning should eliminate unnecessary duplication of facilities and equipment.

SCHOOL PUBLICATIONS

The student newspaper and the yearbook quite often raise the issue of freedom of expression and censorship. Students question the right of the sponsor and the principal to exercise censorship.

The faculty member in charge of these activities should be highly skilled and knowledgeable of law concerning libel. The faculty sponsor should be given adequate time to perform expected functions. This duty should be part of the sponsor's regular load and should not be assigned in addition to a regular teaching load.

If students are aware of the laws concerning libel and are instilled with a sense of responsibility that is a part of freedom of expression, the problems for the principal are probably lessened. Editorial boards composed mainly of students along with the faculty sponsor and other faculty members can serve the function of reviewing documents prior to publication. Students should be allowed free discussion of issues of vital concern to the school.

The student staff should be allowed adequate time, money, and space to publish the newspaper. The responsibility for the publication of the newspaper should reside largely with the faculty sponsor. It should be kept in mind that excessive repression of expression in the school-sponsored newspaper may result in the publication of an underground newspaper. One principal in a school with an underground newspaper offered school facilities for its publication. The long term result was a merger of the underground and regular school newspaper with greater freedom of student expression. Since the key to the success of school publications is the sponsor, the principal must use careful judgment in his or her appointment.

With a mature, common sense approach by the sponsor and recognition by the faculty and administration that students want free expression within legal limits, exciting, effective school publications can be developed.

SCHOOL ASSEMBLIES

The student council should establish a committee composed of faculty and students to be in charge of school assemblies. This committee should be responsible for determining what kinds of programs are suitable for the student body. The committee should secure lists of programs available and attempt to match the selected one with student interests. A variety of different types of assemblies should be planned, ranging from pep rallies, motion pictures, and panel discussions to special performances by talented performers.

The committee should present their recommendations to the student council for its final approval. Also, the committee should assist the administration and staff in discovering ways to insure courteous student behavior at assemblies.

The student council should develop an annual budget that specifies the anticipated income and expenditures for assemblies. Also, it is helpful for future reference to keep a record that indicates the success of the various types of programs.

DRAMATICS AND SPEECH

Because of the degree of skill needed to perform in speech and dramatic areas, skilled staff members should be available to provide students with the training they desire. The speech and drama activities can provide for a very worthwhile extension of scheduled classroom activities. However, students should not be required to enroll in speech and drama classes in order to participate in these activities. Preparation for contests should not be given undue emphasis in this area. Many local programs can be presented in speech and dramatics that do not require the time and perfection needed to win top ratings in contests.

The student council, the student council sponsor, and the dramatic and speech sponsors should all have some latitude in determining appropriate speech and dramatic activities to present. Variety in the area of speech and drama activities is essential. Activities such as: (1) one-act plays, (2) three-act plays, (3) debate teams, (4) extemporaneous speaking, and (5) radio and television presentations are just a few examples.

It is important that adequate finances be provided for needed materials and equipment if the dramatic and speech activities programs are to be successful. An annual budget should be developed specifying expected revenues and expenditures.

MUSIC ACTIVITIES

The major questions involved in dealing with music activities center around whether grades and credit should be given and how much emphasis should be placed on contests and performances. The decision as to how much emphasis should be placed on contests and performances is also highly related to the time and effort required to finance music activities. The principal should make every effort to insure that music courses be offered as electives open to all students. Also, the principal should insist that music courses not overemphasize the performance aspect to the extent that students do not develop an appreciation for music of all types. Furthermore, courses in music should explore music theory. It is essential that students be given an opportunity to study music found in contemporary society.

The authors conclude that the following guidelines should be applied to the music area.

1. Elective courses that are organized to develop an appreciation for music rather than emphasize performance should be offered. Perhaps giving students a chance to elect to take this type of course either for a grade or on a pass, no-pass basis would encourage student enrollment.

2. Instructional activities which are directed toward cumulating in performance should not be graded in the traditional sense. Perhaps a pass, no-pass could be utilized to serve as granting credit, if the granting of credit is deemed desirable. The rationale for granting credit for performance activities in music is probably no more justifiable than granting credit for participation in athletics.

3. Guidelines must be established which set forth the policies governing travel, expenditures, and public relations activities that the organized music groups participate in. The lack of these specific guidelines will most likely result in an overemphasis in performance activities. Lack of guidelines may also cause conflict between parent groups who assist in fundraising activities for music groups and the principal and staff who attempt to maintain a proper balance in the music program. Community organizations may utilize organized music groups to such an extent that it interferes with other activities that participants would like to engage in.

4. Specific job descriptions should be spelled out for faculty members who function in the music area. It is essential that they understand how much time they are expected to spend, what groups they are to direct, and what is expected of them during summer months.

SOCIAL LIFE

A principal must make an analysis of activities and experiences available for students to provide opportunities which will allow them to function well in social settings. Provision for small group interaction during the school day can assist in the social development of students. Formal activities such as dances, banquets, attendance at school functions, etc., can also assist in this development. Parents can play an important role by providing their assistance at social functions.

Opportunity must be provided for students to learn and experience those things which are accepted as socially desirable at various social functions. This may mean providing learning experiences in dancing, eating at formal occasions, speaking in front of groups, etc.

The principal should evaluate the total experience the students undergo to insure the development of well-rounded individuals. The social life aspect can be incorporated in the regular curriculum and in the daily operation of the school as well as being a part of the student activity program.

SECRET SOCIETIES

Terms such as fraternity, sorority, secret society, and Greek letter society, have all been used; but the definition given by Illinois Legislation in 1919 defines secret societies as "any club program, or organization, no matter how high its ideals and how worthy its program, and no matter whether it meets at school or in the homes of its members, to which eligibility is on the basis of a favorable vote of the members, it is a secret society."[12] Regardless of the name given to a secret organization, the public schools cannot sponsor such groups, as courts in decisions of long standing have ruled them to be unjustifiable. All groups under the control of public school boards must have open constitutions which relate to the many aspects of organizational membership and operation. Thus, discrimination and secret practices must be avoided in student activity programs.

Hence, student organizations should not be allowed to select their own membership in the manner in which private secret clubs do. To allow this type of selection to take place in schools would provide an environment that does not contribute to the ideals of a democratic society.

SUMMARY OF GENERAL GUIDELINES
FOR ALL STUDENT ACTIVITIES

1. Student activities should be developed as a result of genuine interest by students. This can be accomplished by conducting a periodic inventory of student interests.

2. The student activities program should provide for balance between the various kinds of activities. For example, the time and money spent on the athletic program should not be excessively out of line with that spent on other student activities. There should also be balance within various activities such as the intramural programs. Activities for girls and boys should be in balance, team activities should not be over emphasized in relation to individual activities, etc.

3. Student activities should have educational values that students can draw upon throughout their life.

4. The student activities program should reflect democratic ideals.

5. Student activities should be scheduled so that maximum opportunity is available for participation by all.

6. Procedures should be established which insure that a few students don't monopolize the student activities that are available.

7. Adequate faculty supervision should be provided. Students must be involved in the selection of faculty sponsors.

8. Each organized student group should submit their charter to the student governing body for approval. This charter should include objectives and operating procedures of the organization. Each charter should be reviewed annually by the student governing body to determine that objectives are being met.

9. Student participation in student activities should not involve excessive cost to the individual or the school.

10. Financial accounting systems for student activities should be established in accordance with good bookkeeping procedures. All accounts should be centralized through one designated school treasurer. Organizations should be required to develop budgets and to utilize a system of vouchers for payment of bills. Each organization should be required to develop periodic (perhaps monthly) financial statements.

11. Careful consideration must be given to the establishment of criteria for membership in each student activity. Scholastic requirements for membership may tend to restrict from membership those students who could benefit most from participation. Students should not be allowed to select and/or restrict membership in their organization.

12. The student activity program should be evaluated periodically for:
    a. Optimum educational value
    b. Satisfying student needs
    c. Providing carry-over values
    d. Economical use of the student's and the school's time.

NOTES

1. Robert Buser, "What's Happening in Student Activities in the Schools of the Seventies?" *The Bulletin of Secondary School Principals* 55:356 (September, 1971), pp. 1-9.

2. "Evaluate Criteria for the Evaluation of Secondary Schools," (Washington D.C.: National Study of Secondary School Evaluation, 1969), pp. 261-270.

3. Harry C. McKown, *Extracurricular Activities,* 3rd ed. (New York: The MacMillan Co., 1962), pp. 604-609.

4. Robert W. Frederick, *The Third Curriculum* (New York: Appleton-Century-Crofts, Inc., 1959), p. 161.

5. Ibid., pp. 161-164.

6. Ibid., pp. 164-178.

7. Gordon A. Sabine, *How Students Rate Their Schools and Teachers* (Washington, D.C.: National Association of Secondary School Principals, 1971), p. 4.

8. Bruce Wilt, "Survey of the Student Councils of Fifty Junior High Schools in Ohio" (Unpublished Master's Problem, The University of Akron, 1971).

9. Barbara Everett Bryant, ed., *High School Students Look at Their World* (Columbus: R. H. Goettler and Associates, 1970), p. 55.

10. Charles E. Forsythe and Irvin A. Keller, *Administration of High School Athletics* (Englewood Cliffs, N.J.: Prentice-Hall Inc., 1972), pp. 229-232.

11. Ibid., p. 343.

12. McKown, *Extracurricular Activities,* pp. 242-243.

10
Developing Desirable Student Behavior

For the past eight years the Gallup Poll has measured the attitudes of Americans toward their public schools. Discipline has been cited seven of the past eight years as the most important problem of public schools.[1] Probably no one single issue has been of more recent concern to principals than the matter of student behavior, or the commonly used term *discipline*. Of late, the principal's authority has been seriously challenged.

Principals are expected to have ready-made solutions. The parents and board of education cannot understand why the principal does not become more strict. The students wonder why the principal has been so strict in the past.

There is evidence to suggest that one must first understand the cause of the problem so that the cause may be dealt with rather than the symptoms. This chapter deals with possible causes of the student behavior problem and possible solutions to these causes. The necessity of developing rules and regulations in school and the pros and cons of various methods of enforcing those rules and regulations is also discussed. Guidelines for the development of an effective discipline program are presented.

DISCIPLINE

A term that has commonly been used synonomously with student behavior is discipline. *The Dictionary of Education* lists four definitions of discipline that apply to the student. They are as follows:

1. The process or result of directing or subordinating immediate wishes, impulses, desires or interests for the sake of an ideal or for the purpose of gaining more effective, dependable action;

2. Persistent, active, and self-directed pursuit of some considered course of action in the face of distraction, confusion, and difficulty;
3. Direct authoritative control of pupil behavior through punishments and/or rewards;
4. Negatively, any restraint of impulses, frequently through distasteful or painful means.

Further concepts associated with the definition of discipline include preventive, corrective, punitive, and democratic.[2]

These definitions reflect and increase most people's confusion in thinking about discipline. With the variety of definitions, teachers still use it in different ways. There are mainly three different ways teachers talk about discipline. First, teachers refer to the degree of order we have established in a group. Secondly, teachers define discipline as not the order we have, but the trick by which we have established order. And the third way teachers commonly use the word discipline is special ways of enforcing order by punishment.

After seeing many different definitions of discipline, administrators must decide what goals we expect it to attain. Discipline is always connected with a goal or purpose. Individual discipline is often thought of as an organization of one's impulses for the attainment of a goal; while group discipline demands control of impulses of the individuals composing a group for the attainment of a goal which all have accepted.

Discipline in the Past

For most of the years of American education, fear of the rod was a major instrument of student discipline. Infliction of physical pain was justified on the same grounds as were the harsh penal codes of the day for adults. "Fear was conceived as the only force which would make men amenable to dominion . . . It was natural (to believe) that children, too, should be controlled by violence or the threat of violence."[3]

A historian of childhood, Phillippe Aries, has traced the great change in educational style that took place between the late Middle Ages and the seventeenth century, from a comradely association of teachers and learners to prison-like schools where "the birch became the mark of the schoolmaster . . . the symbol of the subjection in which (he) . . . held his pupils."[4] Thus, a humiliating disciplinary system—whippings at the master's discretion—became widespread in schools in Europe. The American colonists, coming from a land where flogging had become common in schools, took it for granted that corporal punishment would be used to control the children in the schools they established in the New World.[5]

The children in pre-revolutionary America suffered not only pain of the flesh, but the tormenting threat of eternal damnation. A catechism told the child he would be sent down to an everlasting fire if he were naughty. Evangelist preachers told the child that he was born sinful and graphically described what awaited him in the afterworld. This repressive attitude toward life, this insistence on conformity to a moral and ethical code based purely on religious sanction, was naturally reflected in the colonial schools and in the discipline of children.[6]

The libertarian ideas and the humanitarian movements of the eighteenth and nineteenth centuries were slow to overcome the authoritarian spirit that still prevailed in schooling of the young. Though whipping posts and other harsh instruments of adult punishment gradually disappeared, the tradition of the rod remained fixed in the educational practice. The Reverend Francis Waylaid, President of Brown University, expressed the prevailing view in a public address in 1830, "it is the duty of the instructor to enforce obedience and the pupil to render it."[7]

Even Horace Mann, who crusaded during the 1830s against excessive application of corporal punishment, did not approve of abolishing it altogether.

The pros and cons of corporal punishment have been debated for years. And corporal punishment never quite dies as an educational issue. However, corporal punishment hardly presents itself as the answer to the disciplinary problems of the schools of today.

Discipline Related to School Board Policy

In formulating a philosophy of discipline, the principal's role is one of advisor to the school board. The role as a consultant demands that the principal be continually involved with faculty, students, and patrons to develop a clear understanding of their attitudes. Hence, the principal's informed advice can be given to the board which will lead to policies related to discipline that will be effective. Formulating school discipline policies is a legal function of school boards. In light of recent court decisions it is very important that school boards act with reasonable exercise of their authority. The recent court decisions have tended to restrain the school from exercising many of the forms of control over student conduct which it and the community formerly accepted as normal and proper. But whatever their outcomes are, the impact of court decisions relating to control of student behavior is felt more immediately and heavily by the building principal than by anyone else in the administrative or teaching hierarchy.

It is worth mentioning at this point that some states have policies on school discipline which must be followed by local school boards. However, even when the state outlines school discipline policies, there is usually a degree of freedom, which permits the community to handle certain local problems.

The authority of the boards of education to make policies relating to various aspects of student behavior has always been challenged to some degree. However, in the last decade litigation and legislative action relating to student rights of all kinds has increased; which resulted in more definitive guidelines relating to student rights. Reasonable exercise of authority by school boards that provides adequate student due process continues to be an extremely important factor in court decisions.

Discipline Related to School Rules and Regulations

While it is the function of the school board to formulate policies, the principal is charged with the responsibility of implementing these policies. It is imperative that the principal insure that the rules and regulations developed to implement these policies do indeed reflect the intent of the policies concerning discipline. Rules and regulations concerning discipline adopted at one building level should receive the approval of the board once it is determined there is no conflict between policy and the rules. In order to insure more effective implementation of rules and regulations, those affected by the rules and regulations must be involved in their formulation. Teachers and students will more willingly accept rules and regulations to which they are committed.

As the leader or head, the principal must take the lead in promoting a positive approach to discipline. To do this, the principal must be aware of the factors and practices that aid in developing good behavior patterns in schools. Lawrence E. Vredevoe, in his "Third Report on a Study of Students and School Discipline in the United States and Other Countries," indicated the practices that students and teachers believe to be most successful in developing good teacher-student relationships do not differ in size, location, or composition of the student body. In Vredevoe's report, the schools selected as being representative of the best citizenship and teacher-student relationships, had the following common practices:

1. There was an understanding and apparent recognition of the purposes and values of the standards and rules in force by faculty and students.

2. Emphasis was placed on self-discipline by teachers and students.

3. Good citizenship and conduct were characteristic of the faculty as well as the student body. Courtesy, consideration, respect, professional dress and manner, and good speech were practiced by faculty members.

4. Standards and rules were subject to review and change, but were enforced until changed by due process.

5. The emphasis in treatment of all discipline cases was on the individual involved and not the act. This represents a

significant change in the past fifty years. Today's society is more concerned with the transgressor than the crime.

6. Students could expect fair but certain reprimand or punishment for violation of rules and standards.
7. The punishments meted out were fitted to the individual rather than the transgression.
8. Faculty and students cooperated in establishing, maintaining, and revising rules and standards.
9. The program was challenging to all groups.[8]

There are certain legal considerations which must be taken into account when formulating school rules and regulations. The principal is legally responsible for student discipline from the time the students leave for school until they arrive back home. The principal, therefore, has the responsibility to formulate rules and regulations to control the students' behavior on their way to and from school.

Courts generally recognize the principal as one who stands "in loco parentis" with the students. With this recognition, the principal has the rights and responsibilities of the parent. However, even this legal aspect is changing in recent years. Courts are insisting that the right to search students' lockers and personal clothes is dependent upon a clearly understood policy by all students. If students are led to believe that their locker is private, a search of their locker would be illegal.

The concept of the civil rights of the student has been used in recent years to restrict the authority of school officials in controlling student behavior. More and more courts are recognizing that the school must consider the rights of students in the development of rules and regulations. Courts are upholding students' rights to wear long hair, unorthodox clothing, arm bands, etc., if these actions do not upset the rights of others to a peaceful and organized education.

Philosophical Considerations Related to Discipline: A Point of View

In dealing with discipline and the adolescent on the secondary level, we must be prepared to change with the times and with changing conditions. Discipline, along with all other aspects of school life, is a changing phenomenon, reflecting the rapidly shifting community scene today. Policies relating to discipline often become outmoded. School regulations, like city statutes, become anachronisms with changing conditions. Thus, policy evaluation and policy formulation become a continuous problem.

Teachers and principals in the more difficult schools may long for the autocratic methods of keeping order and forcing obedience that were available to the schoolmasters in earlier times. But even if today's students would submit to the harsher disciplines of the past, those methods would hardly suit the goals of modern education. The old disciplinary procedures served a society that held submission to authority to be a prime goal of childhood education. Today the ideal product of the mass schooling system is expected to possess an independent mind and a cooperative spirit—traits not likely to flourish in an atmosphere of institutional coercion.

Students have a right to be made fully aware of what is expected of them and not be subject to the whim of the individual personality of any member of the staff or administration.

When students break a rule or regulation, or when they display inappropriate or disturbing behavior, disciplinary action may be required. Any disciplinary action undertaken should seek to foster in the students that sense of responsibility which accompanies freedom. In order to do that, the schools in dealing with disciplinary problems should: (1) understand that students can learn from mistakes made; (2) develop a sense of cooperative effort to solve the problem rather than an attitude that suggests a struggle of students against faculty and administration; (3) help students understand and control their own behavior; (4) deal with the underlying causes of the problems not just the symptoms; (5) strive to prevent the problems from occurring.

In some cases an individual student may not be capable of and/or willing to understand and control his or her behavior. Likewise, the school may not always be able to deal with the underlying causes of a behavioral problem or prevent that problem from occurring. It is for such reasons that penalties are necessary to control behavior. The school should administer penalties that are in keeping with the nature of the behavioral problem. They should be administered as soon after the incident as possible, allowing for a rational cooling off period if necessary. The penalty should be one that the school feels is just and at the same time one that can be successfully imposed.

Underlying Causes of Discipline Problems

Schools must handle discipline problems responsibly if they wish to have students take responsibility for their own actions. Strict enforcement of rules and regulations or doling out prescribed punishments from a rigid penal code is not necessarily dealing responsibly with discipline problems. Although either tactic *may* force students to change their behavior, neither of them effectively deal with the problem. To effectively deal with the problem, the underlying causes of the behavior have to be identified and dealt with.

Identifying the underlying causes may be a difficult task. Oliva has divided the causes of adolescent behavior problems into six categories:

(1) causes originating with the child, (2) causes originating
within the child's group, (3) causes originating with the teacher,
(4) causes originating with the school, (5) causes originating
with the home and community, and (6) causes originating in the
larger social order.[9]

In order to effectively determine causes, students must feel that the
school environment is receptive and that the faculty and administration are
genuinely concerned about the welfare of students. If the climate in the
school is not open-minded, students are not likely to volunteer much information dealing with the underlying causes of their problems.

In attempting to identify causes, the principal and/or teacher might ask
questions relating to any one or more of Oliva's categories. Is the student
physically or mentally incapable of behaving in a certain manner? Is the student emotionally upset? Is his or her peer group competitive, hostile, etc.?
Does the teacher humiliate the pupil in front of the class? Does anyone listen
to the student when he or she has a complaint about the school? Do the
pupil's parents think that school is a waste of time? Is he or she worried
about finding a job when the unemployment rate is so high?

After identifying the cause(s), then a course of action can be undertaken. The school might see to it that the student gets medical or psychological attention. The principal might talk to the teacher about his or her
interaction with the student. Someone from the school might visit the student's home and talk to the parents, or the parents might be invited to the
school.

In addition to dealing with the causes of a specific behavior problem the
school has a responsibility to try to prevent these problems from occurring.
Annual workshops could be held for teachers to improve their skills. A committee could be set up by the principal whereby students could have input
into decisions concerning disciplinary procedures, dress codes, etc. Services
could be provided by the school to help students deal with common concerns
such as job placement. Establishment of career centers where information is
available that describes the types of jobs available and the qualifications
needed to hold that job would provide valuable assistance to students.

It would seem wise to establish some format to give students a chance to
discuss current problems of the larger social order such as war, integration,
politics, etc. Some procedure to deal with these types of issues on short term
notices should be established. Students seem to be sensitive to this kind of
issue and may feel compelled to express their point of view on such things as
the day-to-day actions taken by those in governmental offices on the local,
state, national, and international level.

It may be necessary to establish "sound off" sessions operated under
some guidelines to assure some type of orderly procedure. Students must be
assisted to understand how they can best make their actions produce effective results. This procedure may often avert student walkouts, sit-downs,

etc. It is important that students know how to take some type of democratic action rather than resort to actions which really only serve to alienate them from those who could provide some assistance.

It is quite important that the principal recognize the importance of analyzing the pattern of underlying causes of discipline problems. This pattern and the resolution of the underlying cause may indeed provide the key to preventing many discipline problems from occurring.

CORRECTIVE MEASURES

It is not always feasible to deal with the underlying causes of behavioral problems. A simple breaking of a rule or a regulation may not be related to underlying causes other than short term boredom or restlessness. In such cases, corrective measures may be necessary for control purposes.

Some corrective measures are more effective than others. A few may be helpful in identifying the causes of the problem. Most are punitive in nature, however, and at best force a student to conform to the rules.

In administering some corrective measures legal limitations must be observed. These limitations basically come in two forms: (1) statutes passed by state and federal legislatures, and (2) judicial decisions handed down from states and federal courts. Statutes passed by the United States Congress and decisions handed down from the United States Supreme Court apply to school districts within the nation. Statutes passed by state legislatures apply to school districts within that state. Decisions made by courts other than the United States Supreme Court affect those school districts under the jurisdiction of that court. Some decisions rendered apply only to the specific case ruled upon, but can be used as a guideline in other cases. In addition to statutes and judicial decisions, the school board, working as an arm of the state, can make policies which legally limit the implementation of some corrective measures.

Some corrective measures follow:

1. The reprimand is the most common device and the one most frequently resorted to by a teacher. If administered calmly and without the heat of anger, it can be very effective.

2. The pupil-teacher conference can be a most effective means of getting to the bottom of misbehavior. The conference can have overtones of punishment, however, when the pupil is forced to remain after school for the appointment. This can be a very real punishment in itself if the student works after school or takes a bus.

3. Another popular device, as old as education itself, which has met court approval is "staying after school-detention." Many schools have

abandoned detentions completely because it appears that detentions only annoy the student and do not get to the root of the problem. Also, it is very difficult to assign certain punishments in the form of hours of detention to certain misconducts.

4. Enforced labor is sometimes used when a student has written his priceless witticisms on the basement wall or defaced any school property. Usually the student can see the justice in being required to wash the entire wall.

5. Fines are sometimes used in schools for certain adult-type offenses like damaged books or failure to return books to the library. However, principals should be aware that the courts have not looked with favor upon fining students without an alternative punishment such as the legendary "ten dollars or ten days." Principals who exclude a pupil for failure to pay a fine for which no alternative is offered, are on dubious ground if the matter goes to court.

6. It may be necessary for principals to use corporal punishment in order to quell a disturbance, obtain possession of weapons, defend themselves, or protect persons or property. Since the courts hold that the teacher or principal stands *in loco parentis* with students, they have also upheld the right to use corporal punishment, if it is reasonable and accomplished without malice. However, the use of the paddle or other physical means as punishment tend to be undesirable practices and should be used with great care after other more constructive avenues have been pursued.

7. As the science of behavior modification develops, it appears that operant conditioning is useful for correcting serious misbehavior. However, some indicate that it works better for children below grade six since a larger number of teachers are involved with the student beyond that level.[10] Blackwood advocates operant conditioning as a method of improving behavior in the classroom. He sees corporal punishment as an attention-getting device for many students. He writes:

> Attention is one of the strongest and most misused of stimuli.
> It is a powerful payoff for most children. A disruptive child
> usually reacts to attention even more strongly than other
> children. The reinforcing attention can come from other
> children or from the teacher. However, there is something
> especially powerful about teacher attention. It is so powerful
> that a rowdy child often prefers unpleasant attention to being
> ignored. If you scold a child, criticize him and lecture him, you
> may think you are punishing him, but chances are that you are
> paying off the misbehavior with the most valuable currency
> around.[11]

Ackerman indicates that operant conditioning is based on reinforcing desirable behavior and providing no reinforcement for undesirable behavior.[12]

8. It sometimes becomes necessary to exclude a student from classes (suspension) for more than one day. Generally, courts uphold the right of the principal to suspend students from the school or classes. Suspension is a serious step on the part of the principal and should be taken only as the last resort. Sometimes suspension is an ineffective corrective measure because the student would rather be out of school than in school. An assignment to special classes is a far better alternative. Some states spell out in the law maximum number of days that a student may be suspended from school. Many states indicate suspension is for a "reasonable" length of time, which often is assumed to be three days.

9. Alternatives to suspension have come to the forefront recently because suspension alone only removes the problem from the school setting for a period of time, but does not solve the problem for the student who was suspended. Some of these alternatives involve a "center" concept within the school where students will be sent for diagnosis and treatment of the problem. Most centers have someone on duty at all times so students may receive attention immediately and not have to wait until someone such as a dean or assistant principal is available. The treatment generally involves a team effort to assist the student in solving his or her problems. The team could consist of guidance staff, teachers, deans, psychologists, principals, assistant principals, and subject matter specialists.

10. The school code reserves the right of expulsion to the school board. A parent of an expelled student has the right to appeal to the board of education. Provisions for alternative instruction must be made if the student is within the age limits of compulsory education.

STUDENT DUE PROCESS

There is an increasing concern for the pupils' rights to due process in expulsion procedures. A law was passed in Indiana recently that described the rights and responsibilities of students, teachers, principals, superintendents, and school boards in student suspensions, expulsions, and exclusions. The following is a summary of the due process aspects of the law.

1. Teachers and other school personnel have the right to take reasonable action to carry out the educational function he is in charge of, however, teachers and other school personnel do not have the right to suspend students from school. They do have the right to exclude students from any educational function within the supervision of a teacher or any other school person-

nel, but may not exclude students for more than one day without the approval of the principal or his designee.

2. Each principal within the school or school function under his jurisdiction may make written rules and establish within standards governing student behavior and take reasonable action to carry out any educational function. However, all rules, standards, or policies adopted by anyone other than the school board are not effective until they are reviewed and approved by the superintendent and until they are presented to the governing body. Further, no rule or standard is effective until a written copy is made available or delivered to his parent, or is otherwise given general publicity within any school to which it applies.

3. Any principal may deny a student the right to attend school or take part in any school function for a period of up to 5 school days. The school board may limit the principal's supervision to less than 5 school days and if such is done, the board can require approval of the superintendent.

4. Short term suspension (up to 5 days) may be made after the principal has determined that such suspension is necessary to help any student, to further school purposes or to prevent an interference therewith. However, within 24 hours or such additional time as is reasonably necessary, following a suspension, the principal must send a written statement to the student's parent describing the student's conduct, misconduct or violation of rule or standard and the reasons for the action taken.

5. *Expulsion* of a student is defined as separation from school in excess of 5 days, for the balance of the current semester or year, or receives some other penalty which prevents the student from completing his course of study with the normal time. *Exclusion* is defined as separation from school because of a communicable disease, removal of the student is necessary to restore order or protect persons on school property, or the student is mentally or physically unfit for school purposes.

If a student is disciplined by expulsion or exclusion then the following due process must be followed:

a. A written charge shall be filed by the principal with the superintendent. If the superintendent deems that there are reasonable grounds for investigation or that an investigation is desirable, he shall within one (1) school day after such charge is filed appoint a Hearing Examiner.

b. The Hearing Examiner shall within two (2) school days after he is appointed, or such additional time not to exceed two (2) school days as is reasonably necessary, give a statement to the student and his parent, custodian or guardian that a hearing upon the charges will be scheduled if the student or his parent, custodian or guardian requests in writing delivered to the Hearing Examiner in person or by registered or certified mail within ten (10) calendar days that such a hearing be held. Included within such a statement shall be the following:

A statement that before expulsion or exclusion can be invoked, the student has a right to a hearing, upon request, on the specified charges. The request must be made to the Hearing Examiner in writing and delivered to him in person or by registered or certified mail by the student, his parent, custodian or guardian within ten (10) calendar days after the statement is given. If such hearing is not requested, the punishment in the charge by the principal or his designee shall automatically go into effect upon the fifth (5th) school day, such automatic punishment shall immediately be rescinded, whereupon the authority to make findings of fact, to recommend punishment, if any, and to impose any interim suspension beyond the principal's authority shall be transferred to the Hearing Examiner. If such a hearing is not requested within ten (10) calendar days following this statement, all rights, administratively and judicially, to contest and appeal the punishment requested in the charge by the principal or his designee shall be waived.

The student or his representative shall have the right to examine the records and affidavits provided in subsection (b) 5 above and the statement of any witness in the possession of the school corporation.

c. If a hearing is requested as provided, the Hearing Examiner shall within two (2) school days thereafter or such additional time as is reasonably necessary, not to exceed two (2) days given notice to the student, his parent, custodian, or guardian of the time and place for the hearing.

Such hearing shall be held within a period of five (5) school days after it is requested, but such time shall be changed by the hearing examiner for due cause. No hearing shall be held upon less than two (2) school days notice to the student and to his parent, custodian or guardian of the date and time for such a hearing except with the consent of such student or his parent, custodian or guardian.

d. The student may within thirty (30) calendar days following a hearing appeal the superintendent's determination to the governing body by a written request, such request to be filed with the administrative office of the governing body or with the superintendent. Such an appeal shall be made on the record, except that new evidence may be admitted to avoid a substantial threat of unfairness. After examining the record and taking new evidence, if any, any body to whom an administrative appeal is made in accordance with this chapter may withdraw to deliberate privately upon such record and new evidence and to arrive at its decision; provided, that any such deliberation shall be held in the presence only of members in attendance at the appeals proceeding but may be held in the presence of legal counsel who have not previously advised the principal or his designee as to presentation of the school's position. Should questions arise during such deliberations which require additional evidence, the deliberating body may reopen the hearing to receive such evidence. The governing body may alter the superintendent's disposition of the case if it finds his decision too severe.

The final action of the governing body shall be evidenced by personally delivering or mailing by certified mail a copy of the governing body's decision to the student and his parent. At any time within thirty (30) days therefore, the student may appeal such determination to the circuit or superior court in county where the principal office of the governing body is located. Such appeal shall be initiated by the filing of a complaint which shall be sufficient if it alleges in general terms that the governing body acted arbitrarily, capriciously, without substantial evidence, unreasonably or unlawfully. The trial of the appeal, except as provided herein, shall be tried in the same manner as other civil cases. The defendant shall be the school corporation; and within the time provided for a responsive pleading, it shall file therewith the record.

e. The hearing and determination of a case of student expulsion or exclusion by a Hearing Examiner or hearing committee shall be completed within ten (10) days of the time the student is suspended from school, unless it cannot be reasonably held within such time or unless the student requests a delay of the proceedings.

A student may be suspended pending a hearing on his expulsion or exclusion by the principal for a period not to exceed five (5) school days, or for a period extending to the time of hearing by the Hearing Examiner. In such event the student, his parent or representative shall have the right as soon as reasonably possible after the charge is brought against the student to a preliminary conference with the principal or Hearing Examiner to persuade the principal or Hearing Examiner that there is a compelling reason why the student should not be suspended pending a hearing.

6. Where a student or his parent believes that the student is being improperly denied participation in any educational function of the school corporation, or is being subjected to an illegal rule or standard, if he is unable to work out his problems with members of the administrative staff; is entitled to initiate a hearing by filing a charge with the superintendent in the same manner as a charge is initiated by the principal.[13]

The following set of rights for juveniles summarizes the components of a due process procedure:

1. The right to a hearing.
2. The right to adequate notice.
3. The right to counsel.
4. The right to protection against self-incrimination.
5. The right of confrontation and cross-examination.
6. The right to the reasonable doubt rule of evidence. (A fair and impartial decision based on substantial evidence.)[14]

STUDENT ATTENDANCE AND DISCIPLINE

Because of much concern related to poor school attendance records of students, many schools have adopted specific programs to deal with attendance problems. A traditional method of dealing with those not attending school is to suspend them for a few days (3 to 5) and deduct from their grades. Many schools have found success in reducing attendance problems by giving no credit for a course after missing that class for a certain number of days (such as 10 or 15 times per semester). Additionally, students are expelled from school for the remainder of the semester when they receive no credit in two classes. The success of these programs depends to a great extent, upon the degree to which faculty, students, and the community are involved in the development and implementation of them. Principals are cautioned to have the school lawyer review all state and federal laws relating to the desired attendance procedure to insure compliance with all laws, regulations, and local board policies. The board of education must be fully aware and supportive of such a program. The program should have built into it a procedure which provides for student due process at all levels prior to actual dismissal from a course or expulsion from school. This due process normally is provided for by developing an established procedure which notifies the student and parents of the attendance status of the student and provides a chance for a hearing at various times.

STUDENT DISRUPTION

Secondary school leaders maintain an equilibrium within a dynamic and changing society. They cannot be static in their administration of maintenance of this balance. They must be aware of changing conditions within their school as well as with society in general. Pressure from society has created a demand by students, and in many instances by parents, for a freer atmosphere in the school. Some have termed it as the cause for a more humane school.

The National Association of Secondary School Principals has attempted to provide the principal with guidelines in dealing with these new pressures by publishing *The Reasonable Exercise of Authority II,*[15] *Disruption in Urban Public Secondary Schools*[16] and *How Students Rate Their School and Teachers.*[17]

Bailey, in his study of student disruption, concluded:

1. The size of the student body is a more important variable than the size of the city in which a school is located.
   Larger schools have more problems.
2. Disruption is positively related to integration. All white or all black schools have little disruption.
3. In schools with a higher percentage of black staff in integrated schools, there is little disruption.

This study shows that urban center children, many of them fatherless, live in squalor among junkies and pimps. Black revenge is often dominant—"It's Whitey's turn to take some heat." Bailey believes that students show unrest when they are not involved in developing dress and grooming regulations and policies governing extra-curricular activities. Students oppose limits on athletic and cheerleading participation such as grade requirements, or attendance and tardiness records. Bailey writes:

1. Most principals feel that the mere presence of uniformed police inside a school building is a cause rather than a deterrent of school disruption.
2. Special schools for the unruly is an exemplary practice.
3. Students desire more electives, spontaneous field trips, wider and more varied schedule options.
4. Black administrators and black teachers are needed in black schools.
5. In an integrated school, a good administrator arranges for a black band as well as a white band at a dance.
6. Large city school systems must develop meaningful and publicized ways in which the distance and impersonality of the "down-town board" is dissipated.[18]

The possibility of student disruption necessitates the preparation of locally prepared guidelines for dealing with disorders. Some concepts which should be included in these guidelines follow:

1. A lay advisory committee of parents should meet regularly with the principal and teachers.
2. A student advisory committee to meet with the principal and teachers should be developed.
3. A specific plan of action to deal with disruption should be formulated.
4. The principal and the staff should keep lines of communication open and seek new ways to encourage communication between and among students, faculty and administrators.

CREATING AN ENVIRONMENT WHICH ENCOURAGES APPROPRIATE STUDENT BEHAVIOR

It is imperative that a proper school environment be established when dealing with the underlying causes of discipline problems. Administrators must recognize the fact that the mere establishment of rules and regulations governing student behavior in no way insures that students will comply with the standards set.

Traditionally, rules and regulations have spelled out rather specifically what students were not to do, and emphasis was placed on the consequences of breaking the rules and regulations. It would seem more appropriate to establish general guidelines for acceptable behavior and to work individually with students to achieve these standards. This tends to place the whole matter of discipline in a positive rather than negative light.

The emphasis then should be on developing general guidelines for acceptable behavior rather than on developing measures to be taken if the students would fail to follow the guidelines. This action seems necessary in order that students be treated as individuals, since it is almost impossible to describe totally a set of specific conditions and consequences that would apply to all students. What will guide or change one student's behavior will not necessarily guide or change another's.

The discipline program should consist of (1) the formulation of general guidelines for appropriate behavior, (2) a means of analyzing the underlying causes of inappropriate behavior, (3) actions to remedy those causes, (4) actions to prevent inappropriate behavior, and (5) corrective measures or punishments to control inappropriate behavior when other means fail.

More important than this list of factors is the creation of a school environment conducive to the establishment of acceptable student behavior. The school administrators, faculty, students, parents, and community all help create the school environment.

The curriculum, which in this case is defined as the total experience which students undergo while under the direction of the school, is a reflection of the needs of students as perceived by those who provide input into the development of the curriculum. If an environment is to be created which indeed fosters acceptable behavior on the part of students, then it is extremely important to insure that student needs are being met by the school curriculum.

A PROPOSAL FOR DEVELOPING
AN EFFECTIVE DISCIPLINE PROGRAM

Considering what has been said concerning the establishment of a discipline program, the following would seem appropriate actions to take:

1. Provision should be made for involving the student governing body in the development of procedures to handle discipline matters.

    a. Decisions should be made relating to the extent of student involvement in the development of school guidelines for student behavior.

    b. Decisions must be made relating to the extent of student involvement in the enforcement of behavioral guidelines and in the means of handling those who violate the guidelines.

2. The total faculty and staff must be involved in developing the discipline program, since the principal and administrative staff must rely heavily on the teachers and supporting staff members to assist in carrying out the discipline program.

3. The total program for handling discipline problems should be written down. Caution should be exercised in developing behavioral guidelines to insure enough flexibility to allow students to feel that they are being handled as individuals rather than inanimate objects. Time and money for supplies to develop and print the entire program should be allocated. All students, staff, and faculty should receive a copy of the program.

4. The emphasis of the total program should be on preventing misconduct, therefore, the principal must make an analysis of the cause of the misbehavior.

    a. Consideration must be given to the conditions which led to the misconduct.

        (1) What type of attitude do students have toward their total school experience? Do students feel teachers and administrators are against them?

        (2) What type of home background does the student have?

        (3) Was the misconduct an individual matter or was a group involved?

        (4) Is this first offense or a repeat offense?

        (5) Did the offense occur in a supervised situation such as the classroom or in a relatively unsupervised situation such as the halls or lunch room?

        (6) Was the student reacting to the behavior of another student or a teacher?

    b. Consideration must be given to what the school can do to remedy those conditions which led to the misconduct.

        (1) What facilities and services are available in the school system to provide assistance to the student involved so that he or she may adjust or so that the casual factors of misconduct may be removed? Are counseling services available to assist students in solving personal problems?

        (2) Do conditions exist which would allow the student to achieve success in some way at school? What provisions are available in the curriculum to provide the student with opportunities to engage in activities that are appropriate to personal interests and abilities? Is assistance available to the student to help identify his or her interests and abilities, and placement in appropriate learning situations?

5. Corrective measures or punishments should be used to correct a student's behavior only if other means are not feasible or effective. In administering corrective measures the following factors should be considered:

    a. Is the student who has a behavior problem treated as an individual or is his or her behavior classified and a punishment prescribed only on the basis of the severity of the misdeed?

    b. What effect will the corrective measure have on the student's psychological well-being and future behavior, from a short and long term perspective?

    c. Is the student's behavior so disruptive to the group that it creates an atmosphere where learning cannot take place?

    d. What will be the reaction of other students if the corrective measure is administered?

    e. Is the corrective measure consistent with established board policy and state and federal laws?

    f. Is the corrective measure administered in such a way to be consistent with democratic procedure?

6. An appeal procedure should be established that allows students a fair and equitable hearing concerning their case. The appeal procedure should be written down, specifying such things as: (1) proper channels through which students may file their appeal; (2) conditions under which the appeal may be filed; (3) how the appeal is presented; (4) the students' rights during the appeal process such as their right to counsel. Proper appeal procedures involving the principal, the superintendent, and the board should assist in reducing the need for students to resort to court action.

7. A record keeping system should be developed to allow sufficient documentation of problems each student has faced so that an understanding of the total scope of a current student behavior problem can be secured. However, it would not seem wise to keep extensive records of all infractions committed in order that a case may be built against a student over a period of time. With possible court cases facing principals, there is the temptation to develop files to support the principals' side of the story. An effort should be made to periodically remove materials from records that relate to behavior problems especially if a student has shown that he or she has developed acceptable behavior.

8. An analysis of school attendance records can be helpful in determining students who are facing problems. Perhaps revision of school attendance policies would permit students to realize ways in which they could more effectively make up missed work and more successfully complete the requirements of the class when they missed school. The development of methods of encouraging school attendance may result in higher student morale and thus reduce student behavior problems.

9. A proper school environment is important in preventing discipline problems and in making a discipline program work effectively. A curriculum which meets students' needs can play a vital part in creating that proper school environment. Much consideration should be given to developing a curriculum which supplies students with a variety of interesting and relevant experiences on a day-to-day basis. The following questions assist in determining the extent to which the curriculum fosters an environment conducive to an effective program.

    a. Who is involved in developing the curriculum: administrators, faculty members, students, parents, etc.?

    b. By what method will students' needs be determined and how will they be met in the curriculum?

    c. Will homeroom period be used for discussing problems students have or will it be limited to administrative announcements?

    d. Are learning opportunities available to students in areas such as fine arts, industrial arts, business, and homemaking as well as in traditional academic areas such as history, math, etc.?

    e. Are courses offered which are relevant to the issues of today, such as race relations, ecology, etc.?

    f. Are remedial programs available to students who need help in a particular subject?

    g. How much freedom will the students be given in choosing their curriculum on a day-to-day basis or a week-to-week basis, etc.?

    h. Are teachers committed to providing students with a variety of interesting and relevant experiences in their classes?

    i. Are teachers interested and involved with students and open to students' suggestions?

    j. Are there sufficient extra-curricular activities to meet the needs and interests of all students?

    k. Is there a proper balance between intramural and interscholastic athletic programs?

10. A periodic review of all rules and regulations should be undertaken to determine if the objectives of the discipline program are being met. Some record should probably be kept of the nature of offense and the disposition of the case to facilitate this analysis.

DRUGS

Our society today is drug-oriented. Listening to the radio, watching television, or reading the newspaper provides convincing proof of this statement. Young people see their mothers and fathers taking pep pills to wind them up and sleeping pills to wind them down, yet youths who smoke pot to experience a similar sensation are thrown in jail because doing so is illegal in many states of the nation. Perhaps the overreaction to pot smoking and the resulting unrealistic proclamation of its danger has caused youths to not heed the warnings of other more dangerous and powerful drugs.

What is the best way to combat the ever increasing use of drugs? Should more restrictive laws be instituted? Should an extensive educational program concerning drug use and abuse be developed? What form should an educational approach take?

These questions and others are particularly relevant for today's principal since the focus of attention concerning the drug scene has centered around the schools. Parents and board members expect the principal to be able to deal successfully with these problems.

The principal must decide whether or not to call the police when drug use is suspected. A decision must be made as to how the curriculum should be adapted to deal with the drug problem. Should separate courses be developed to handle instruction on the use of drugs or should drug education be integrated within the present courses?

The answers to these questions can best be sought in each individual community. The principal should emphasize to the faculty, students, and community that the school is only one aspect of the total program to combat drug usage. An environment must be created which encourages open discussion of the problem of drug usage. The law enforcement agencies, the medical profession, the drug dispensing companies, and other community agencies all need to play a role in the total drug education program.

A Proposal for Action When Drug Use is Suspected

It is imperative that a procedure be established to handle the drug problems that arise. Administrators, faculty, parents, students, medical and pharmaceutical personnel, and law enforcement officials should be involved. A general procedure for a principal to follow is:

1. The foremost concern should be with the physical welfare of the student. Judgments as to whether the student is "drugged" or ill from some other cause should be made by someone with training qualified to make that judgment.
2. Determine if the student is taking prescribed medication. The parents or guardians should be called.
3. Psychological help should be made available to the student through a drug crisis center or through a school or community counseling service.
4. Determine if this is the first time the student has been involved with drugs. Have there been other cases involving drugs?
5. If lockers are to be searched, the student probably should be there if physically able.
6. An appeal procedure should be established to handle the cases where students are suspended or expelled from school for the use of drugs.

TORT LIABILITY

It is a general principle of law that the state, as the sovereign, is not liable in damages for injuries resulting from the negligence of its officers, agents, and employees. It appears, however, that the legal principle of "the King can do no wrong" may indeed not withstand the pressure being applied against the concept today. Many states permit boards of education to purchase liability insurance on their employees, which some say implies that the school as an agent is liable.

There is a lack of court case references to the liability of the principal in working with students. It must be assumed that courts will handle principal liability cases much the same as with teachers. Assuming this to be true, principals would be held liable for student injury if:

1. They were proved to be negligent.
2. They directed the student or teacher to perform a harmful act.
3. They were careless in any particular situation, and in such a way that an ordinary prudent person would have acted differently.

Principals have the responsibility to protect the safety of students by seeing that adequate supervision is provided. It is unlikely that principals will sustain liability if they have a policy which provides for careful supervision of the student and his or her activities, and if they provide adequate supervision in the enforcement of this policy.

Some areas of the school have greater potential for tort liability than others. These include such areas as industrial arts, home economics, science laboratories, physical education, and outside of school activities, such as driver education. The principal must be careful in the selection of teachers for these areas to insure that they exercise care and prudence in their instruction. Safety should be emphasized through education of the student, design of the faculty, location of equipment, and the utilization of safety equipment such as goggles, helmets, seatbelts, etc.

NONTEACHING PERSONNEL

The principal holds the same legal status with the nonteaching personnel as with professional teachers. If the school board employs teacher aides, the possible negligence of such employees could not be imputed to the principal so as to hold him or her personally liable. Like any other individuals, of course, the teacher aides would not be immune from personal liability, but conceivably could be personally liable for their negligent conduct which directly caused injuries to pupils.

On the other hand, if the principal rather than the board of education was involved in the selection of teacher aides, it is conceivable that if such personnel were negligent, the principal might be subject to being sued. Such a suit could be filed on grounds that the principal was involved in the selection of incompetent persons, presuming of course that it was established that such individuals were incompetent. In any situation involving the liability of a principal for injury to a pupil, a cause and effect relationship must be established before the court will hold a principal liable. For example, it must be established that an injury of a pupil is caused by an action of the principal.

SUMMARY

From the preceding comments on legal aspects of secondary education and a review of the literature, the authors conclude the following in reference to student conduct:

1. The principal and teachers are expected to insure an orderly atmosphere conducive to study and learning.
2. Students may forfeit their rights to an education by engaging in conduct detrimental to the good order and morale of the school.
3. Students do not surrender their constitutional rights by enrolling in a school.
4. Students have no right to abuse and harass administrators of the school or engage in conduct detrimental to its well being.
5. The principal, teachers, and board of education may adopt and enforce policy for maintenance of reasonable discipline in the school.
6. Teachers and administrators may extend measures to control student behavior to and from school and in extracurricular activities.
7. Although a recent Supreme Court decision has upheld the use of corporal punishment in schools, it's use should be exercised in a judicious and prudent manner.
8. A principal may suspend students from school for a limited time, but the rights of the students in danger of being suspended should be considered.
9. Demonstrations, wearing of arm bands and buttons, dress, and appearance can be regulated by school authorities if such regulation is necessary to maintain discipline in the school.
10. The rights of students to privacy must be respected by school authorities. If regular locker checks are made during the year, this must be known to students. If the search of lockers or other property of students is made to prevent injury to the students or others, the search is proper and legitimate.
11. Teachers and principals must exercise the duty of care expected of a reasonably prudent person performing their duties.

The educational leader must also use sound judgment in the operation of the school to prevent student disruption. The authors suggest the following common sense be applied:

1. When a discipline problem is serious or the student has chronic discipline problems, the parents should be involved.
2. Involve student government in establishing a student conduct code.
3. Develop a local school policy concerning discipline, involving the faculty and students. This policy should be approved by the board of education.
4. Avoid mass assemblies, etc., to admonish students for poor behavior, sloppy dress, etc. If a problem exists, work with student leaders, the student government, or through home rooms.
5. The educational leader must give everybody reason to believe that their school is the best. Careful planning and organizing gives students such an impression.
6. Strive for the best in all student activities—the best football team, the best band, the best dramatics, etc.
7. The building and equipment are important in student conduct, but nothing is more important than good teachers. The educational leader must constantly strive to improve teachers through inservice education, workshops, intervisitation, etc.
8. The esprit de corps of the teachers and administrators does much to determine the conduct of students.

NOTES

1. George H. Gallup, "Eighth Annual Gallup Poll of the Public's Attitudes Toward the Public Schools," *Phi Delta Kappan* 58:2 (1976), p. 188.

2. Carter V. Good, ed., *Dictionary of Education* (New York: McGraw-Hill Book Company, Inc., 1973), pp. 185–186.

3. Helen B. Shaffer, "Discipline in Public Schools" (Washington, D.C.: Editorial Research Reports, 1969), p. 643.

4. Phillippe Aries, *Centuries of Childhood* (New York: Vintage, 1965).

5. Shaffer, "Discipline in Public Schools," p. 644.

6. Herbert Arnold Falk, *Corporal Punishment: A Social Interpretation of Its Theory and Practice in the Schools of the United States,* 1941, p. 644.

7. Shaffer, "Discipline in Public Schools," p. 644.

8. Lawrence E. Vredevoe, "School Discipline—Third Report on a Study of Students and School Discipline in the United States and Other Countries," *Bulletin of the National Association of Secondary School Principals* (March, 1965), pp. 216–217.

9. Peter F. Oliva, *The Secondary School Today* (Scranton, Penn.: Intext Educational Publishers, 1972), p. 417.

10. J. Mark Ackerman, *Operant Conditioning Techniques for the Classroom Teacher* (Glenview, Ill.: Scott, Foresman, and Company, 1972), p. vi.

SUMMARY

11. Ralph O. Blackwood, *Operant Control of Behavior* (Akron, Ohio: Exordian Press, 1971), pp. 2–3.

12. Ackerman, *Operant Conditioning Techniques,* p. 83.

13. Newton Edwards, *The Courts on the Public Schools,* 3rd ed. (Chicago: The University of Chicago Press, 1971), p. 663.

14. Indiana Acts of 1973, Public Law 218, Chapter 5, pp. 1128–1142 and Public Law 223, pp. 1189–1199.

15. W. Richard Brothers, "Procedural Due Process: What Is It?" *National Association of Secondary School Principals Bulletin* 49:367 (1975), pp. 1–8.

16. Robert L. Ackerly and Ivan B. Gluckman, *The Reasonable Exercise of Authority II* (Reston, Va.: The National Association of Secondary School Principals), 1976.

17. Stephen K. Bailey, *Disruption in Urban Public Secondary Schools* (Washington, D.C.: National Association of Secondary School Principals), 1970.

18. Gordon A. Sabine, *How Students Rate Their Schools and Teachers* (Washington, D.C.: The National Association of Secondary School Principals), 1971.

19. Bailey, *Disruption in Urban Public Secondary Schools,* 1970.

11
Guidance and Counseling Services for Students

In order to insure effective guidance and counseling services, the principal must (1) understand the basic principles of guidance, (2) be aware of the scope of guidance services, (3) establish an effective working relationship between and among the counselor, teachers, and students, and (4) be able to evaluate guidance services. This chapter is designed to provide the principal with an overview of each of these aspects.

HISTORIC DEVELOPMENT OF GUIDANCE

Guidance counseling has no definite beginning but seems to have evolved simultaneously in several major cities around 1900.[1] Social change had created some turmoil within the school and vocational education was becoming more widespread. This, coupled with compulsory attendance laws, seemed to create a position for someone interested in the student's welfare and future. This position generally was given to teachers on a part-time basis. They were under direct control of the principal and had no formal training. These people considered themselves teachers first and counselors second.[2]

The advent of educational testing for the schools in the 1920s, along with social change caused by World War I, brought about the need for professional training for counselors and separation of attendance from vocational guidance and training. Still, the counselor remained a teacher first and was directed by the principal.[3]

One of the biggest pushes toward modern guidance counseling has been provided by the federal government with several programs aimed at upgrading guidance and making it a separate function within the school. In conjunction with money provided to the schools, the National Defense Act of 1958 provided money to colleges to conduct counselor training programs. Now almost every state requires some specialized training for counselors.[4] Today the counselor is seen as a specialist more akin to the psychologist or the social worker than to the teacher, but he or she is still treated like a teacher in many instances.

Finally, a most important influence in the development of guidance has been the emergence of nondirective or client-centered therapy as envisioned by Carl Rogers. Older methods of paternalism and authoritarian attitudes characteristic of earlier guidance methods had to be modified. This theory made counselors more aware of the unity of personality and the counseling of people rather than problems. These new developments made counseling more complex than ever. All areas of the personality had to be considered in helping the individual whether the counseling involved vocational guidance, interest testing, or behavior modification.[5]

Thus, we have a picture of the development of guidance counseling. It has been linked with teaching from its inception, and even today the counselor is often considered a teacher and expected to teach classes as well as do guidance work. Despite these handicaps, counseling is emerging as an independent but closely related part of the total school. By 1975, fifty-three out of fifty-five states and territories had recognized counseling as a function separate from teaching with minimum certification requirements.[6]

GUIDANCE AND COUNSELING RELATIONSHIP

Much discussion has centered around trying to specify the distinct and separate functions of guidance and counseling. The following discussion by Glanz provides insights into this relationship:

> Guidance as a part of education focuses on the individual and his use of the facts, knowledge, and concepts he has obtained through education. The goal of guidance is the mature, self-directed person with the skills of critical thinking that permit him to become free and responsible.
>
> *Guidance, guidance personnel, guidance workers, school counselors,* and *pupil personnel workers* are descriptive terms that have arisen as the guidance movement has developed and matured. The semantic confusion of terms, titles, and functions has its roots in the history of guidance and remains a part of the current scene.
>
> Counseling is the basic process or technique of guidance. Yet counseling is not the *all* of a planned program to individualize educational and growth experiences. Counselors are at the center of a guidance program, but guidance requires additional personnel who are involved in activities other than counseling. Pupil personnel services provide many distinct opportunities for students to acquire information and to profit individually from the various resources available. Occupational information, psychological test data, work experience, and job-placement are all

critical within a planned program that can best be summarized in the word *guidance* or, sometimes, a *pupil personnel program*.

Guidance is the single most usable term to describe and circumscribe the varied activities and involvements that provide for the individualization of educational and personal growth experiences. *Counselor* and *counseling* are the keystone concepts within guidance.

As long as professional guidance personnel do not confuse guidance or pupil personnel services with counseling; as long as counselors can be certain that in counseling they must be counselors and not wide-ranging guidance or pupil personnel workers; and as long as words do not interfere with meanings, the semantic confusion can be reduced.

More positively, guidance personnel or pupil personnel workers are responsible for the design and operation of a total program. Counselors are responsible for the one-to-one learning or group counseling experiences of the student in a guidance program. Many guidance and pupil-personnel-service programs are similar. Emphasis upon an overriding concept or quality of experience usually characterizes the use of *guidance* as a term; *pupil-personnel-service programs* frequently stress the varied nature of services or assistance available to students or pupils. Counselors may also be guidance workers, but they must recognize that a counseling experience with students or pupils is a peculiarly unique process, not the same or even similar to other guidance or personnel services. Alternately, guidance personnel or workers may also be counselors and involve themselves in counseling if they recognize the nature of counseling.[7]

BASIC PRINCIPLES OF GUIDANCE

The following discussion lists the basic principles underlying the guidance function. These principles are a compilation of statements of several of the writers in the guidance field.[8]

Principle I. The primary concern of any guidance program is the personal development of the individual. This principle centers on knowledge of self as a key in guidance. Whereas a teacher is primarily centered on intellectual development, the guidance counselor works toward development of self and creation of meaning in a student's life.

Principle II. The primary tools of guidance lie in individual behavioral processes. Personal interviews, test interpretation, counseling relationship, and knowledge of personal records are used to advance a student's understanding of his or her own internal structure.

Principle III. Guidance counseling relies on cooperation and not compulsion. Guidance cannot be forced on a person but must involve mutual consent and cooperation. Students referred to the counselor must be received openly and without condescension. Guidance relies on willingness to change which cannot be achieved in a hostile atmosphere.

Principle IV. Guidance is based on recognizing the dignity and worth of the individual and his or her right to choose. The counselee is respected because he or she is a unique individual with personal worth and dignity. Because of this uniqueness each student must be allowed to select his or her own goals and means to accomplish them. Hopefully the student will develop responsibility and self-restraint through the exercise of freedom within a structured society.

Principle V. Guidance is a continuous, structured process. A united effort and single theme should run through the entire school structure from elementary school to high school with teachers and administrators as well as guidance personnel involved.

Implementation of Guidance Principles

Of course, the key to any guidance program is the individual counselors. Their personal knowledge, skill, and energy determine the success or failure of the program. The following list provided by Jessell shows some key abilities needed by any good counselor.

1. Competency in understanding the processes which characterize individual educational and psychosocial development within the culture.
2. Competency in understanding the basis for and characteristics of the philosophical conflicts which stem from the interaction of pupils, teachers, and administrators within the context of the school.
3. Competency in counseling with students through helping individuals talk effectively about individual concerns and helping them to make decisions.
4. Skills and knowledge to capitalize on group procedures whenever appropriate and possible.
5. Competency in assisting parents to understand the developmental progress of their child and to assist them in other ways which directly or indirectly contribute to the welfare of the child.
6. Competency in consulting with teachers, school administrators, and other school personnel for purposes of contributing to pupil development.
7. Competency in soliciting the support, cooperation, and par-

ticipation of teachers, administrators, other school
personnel, and parents in the guidance program.

8. Competency in interpreting the purposes, and procedures
   of guidance activities to staff members, parents, and the
   community at large.

9. Knowledge of the major theoretical approaches to career
   development and capable of utilizing their implications
   in assisting pupils in their career development.

10. A knowledge of information sources, materials, and activ-
    ities appropriate for providing occupational and edu-
    cational information to pupils involved in the process
    of planning their future.

11. A working knowledge of resources and opportunities for
    help available to pupils with special problems.

12. Understanding the purposes, appropriate uses, and limita-
    tions of standardized tests and instruments used for
    student appraisal.

13. Skills in evaluating and discriminating among standardized
    tests and instruments for use in pupil appraisal.

14. Skills in the techniques of administering, reporting, and
    interpreting test results to pupils, parents, and school
    personnel.

15. Competency in assisting pupils in considering and making
    transitions from school to employment or from one
    level of education to the next higher level.

16. Competency in conducting research at the local level for
    purposes of evaluating and improving the guidance
    and/or the school program.[9]

The following is a statement by the American School Counselor Association which was developed to identify and clarify the role of the secondary
school counselor:

THE ROLE OF THE SECONDARY SCHOOL COUNSELOR*

PROFESSIONAL RATIONALE

As members of the educational team, secondary school counselors believe that each child possesses intrinsic worth and
inherent and inalienable rights and that each child is the focus

---

* Copyright 1974, American Personnel and Guidance Association. Reprinted with permission.

of the educational process. No other country in the world devotes so much attention to the individual student. Schools in all societies are concerned with the transmission of cultural heritages and with the socialization of youth. In the United States there is the additional emphasis on the individual and on his needs and desires. Guidance in schools is an American phenomenon, and is, as one phase of pupil personnel services, a unique and integral part of the total school program.

The counselor believes that most students, given the experience of an accepting, nonevaluating relationship, will make intelligent decisions.

When effective, school counseling functions as a continuous process to assist the student through identifying and meeting his needs in the educational, vocational, and personal-social domains. Although personal counseling is a major function of the guidance staff, other responsibilities and involvements include, but are not limited to, staff consultation, parental assistance, student self-appraisal, educational-vocational information and planning, referral to allied community agencies, and public relations.

Guidance is a function of every member of the educational team, but the responsibility for leadership is one of the primary functions of the school counselor. It assists the student to understand himself by focusing attention on his interests, abilities, and needs in relation to his home, school, and environment. Counseling assists the student in developing decision making competence and in formulating future plans. The school counselor is the person on the staff who has special training for assessing the specific needs of each student and for planning an appropriate guidance program in the educational, vocational, and personal-social domains.

The continual changes in society bring new and different challenges to schools. New knowledge is constantly available. The effective school counselor, through training and retraining, remains informed and approaches each counseling situation realistically.

PROFESSIONAL RELATIONSHIPS

Counseling Relationships

Counseling relationships are based on the following principles:

• The counselor's obligation respects the integrity of the counselee and promotes the welfare of the student with whom he is working.

• Before entering the counseling relationship, the counselee should be informed of the conditions under which he may receive assistance.

• The counselor shall decline to initiate or shall terminate a counseling relationship when he cannot be of professional assistance.

• The counseling relationship and information resulting therefrom must be kept confidential and consistent with the rights of the individual and the obligations of the counselor as a professional person.

• The counselor reserves the right to consult with other professionally competent persons about his counselee.

• In the event that the counselee's condition is such as to endanger the health, welfare, and/or safety of self or others, the counselor is expected to consult the appropriate responsible person. In some instances, referral to a specialist may be desirable.

The Counselor's Relationship with the Student

Through the counseling relationship, the counselor seeks to help each student to understand himself in relation to the world in which he lives. He helps the student to know himself and to recognize his strengths and weaknesses. The counselor helps the students to establish values and to know how to make realistic and positive decisions. To accomplish these goals in the high school environment, the secondary school counselor:

• Sees the student as an individual and acknowledges his right to acceptance as a human being.

• Recognizes that each student's behavior is meaningful and represents his attempt to develop within his environment as he perceives it.

• Is available to all students and works with them in relation to their educational, vocational, and personal-social needs.

• Creates an atmosphere in which mutual confidence, understanding, and respect result in a helping relationship.

The Counselor's Relationship with the Parent or Guardian

The school counselor serves as consultant to parents or guardians regarding the growth, educational and career planning, and development of the counselee. To accomplish this goal, the secondary school counselor:

- Accepts the parent as an individual and acknowledges his right to uniqueness.
- Approaches the conference in a courteous, professional, sincere, nonjudgmental, and respectful manner.
- Respects the basic right and responsibility of parents to assist their children in decision making.
- Conveys a sincere interest in establishing a helpful and cooperative relationship.
- Assures parents of confidentiality of information received.

The Counselor's Relationship with the Teacher

The counselor assists teachers to better understand the plan for the educational, career, and personal-social development of the students. To accomplish this goal, the secondary school counselor:

- Views the teacher as a member of the guidance team.
- Serves as interpreter of the school's guidance program to teachers and familiarizes them with the guidance services available.
- Shares appropriate individual student data with the teacher, with due regard for confidentiality, and assists the teacher in recognizing individual differences in students, as well as their needs in the classroom.
- Assists the teacher in making referrals to other appropriate school personnel, such as the remedial reading teacher, the school nurse, or the school's learning disabilities specialist.
- Supports teachers of vocational and/or cooperative programs offering students on-site work experience.
- Cooperates with efforts of the middle school/junior high school and senior high school teachers to articulate academic course work for the benefit of the student entering the senior high school.
- Maintains an objective and impartial view in teacher-student relationships, endeavoring to understand the problems which may exist and to assist in their solution.
- Assists in the planning of classroom guidance activities and acts as a resource person for obtaining appropriate up-to-date materials and information.
- Makes current information available to the teacher about the myriad of careers and job opportunities during and beyond high school.

- Involves the teacher in conferences with students and parents, promoting a better understanding of the student and his development.
- Develops a teacher consultation program to help teachers with students who show discipline and learning problems in the classroom.

The Counselor's Relationship with the Administration

The work of the school counselor should contribute directly to the purposes of the school. To accomplish this goal, the secondary school counselor:

- Recognizes that the administrator is the major member of the guidance team whose outlook, leadership, and support create the atmosphere for success in his important school services.
- Serves as interpreter of the guidance program to the administration, familiarizing it with the guidance services available.
- Works closely with the administration in planning, implementing, and participating in inservice training and other programs designed to maintain and promote the professional competency of the entire staff in curriculum development, in adapting learning activities to pupil needs, and in effecting positive student behavior.
- Serves as liaison between the guidance staff and the school administration by preparing pertinent information regarding student needs and abilities or other data related to the guidance program and curriculum development.
- Is aware that any statement on role and function of the secondary school counselor does not supersede nor is it in direct conflict with legislation dealing with confidentiality, privileged communications, or contract agreements between counselors and boards of education.

The Counselor's Relationship with Significant Others

The counselor has professional responsibilities to a number of significant others as he makes an effort to utilize all available community resources to assist the student. It is essential that a good working relationship be established and maintained with these community and area resources. To assure ongoing rapport with community and area resources, the secondary school counselor:

• Maintains good communication with the office of the probate judge and with law enforcement agencies.

• Retains a cooperative working relationship with community and social agencies.

• Consults with students' previous counselors in order to utilize valuable knowledge and expertise of former counselors.

• Maintains a close and cooperative relationship with the admission counselors of post-high school institutions.

PROFESSIONAL RESPONSIBILITIES

The Counselor's Responsibility to the Student

In addition to specifying the counselor's professional relationships with the student, it is important to consider his responsibilities to the student. In a counseling relationship, the secondary school counselor:

• Demonstrates respect for the worth, dignity, and quality of the student's human rights.

• Shows concern for and assists in the planning of the student's educational, career, personal, and social development.

• Aids the student in self-evaluation, self-understanding, and self-direction, enabling him to make decisions consistent with his immediate and long-range goals.

• Assists the student in developing healthy habits and positive attitudes and values.

• Encourages the student to participate in appropriate school activities with a view toward increasing his effectiveness in personal and social activities.

• Participates in the planning and designing of research that may result in beneficial effects to the counselee.

• Assists the student in the development of an awareness of the world of work and in the utilization of the school and community resources to that end.

• Helps the student to acquire a better understanding of the world of work through the acquisition of skills and attitudes and/or participation in work-related programs.

• Encourages the student to plan and utilize leisure time activities and to increase his personal satisfaction.

• Clearly indicates the conditions under which counseling is provided with respect to privileged communication.

• Assists in the student's adjustment to senior high school, evaluates his academic progress, and reviews graduation requirements.

• Makes referral to appropriate resources whenever his professional or role limitations limit his assistance.

• Assists the student in understanding his strengths, weaknesses, interests, values, potentialities, and limitations.

The Counselor's Responsibility to the Parent or Guardian

The counselor holds conferences with parents or guardians about the student's growth and development. Through individual or group conferences, the secondary school counselor:

• Provides the parent/guardian with accurate information about school policies and procedures, course offerings, educational and career opportunities, course or program requirements, and resources that will contribute to the continuing development of the counselee.

• Makes discreet and professional use of information shared during conferences.

• Shares with the parent/guardian information and interprets pertinent data about the counselee's academic record and progress.

• Assists the parent/guardian in forming realistic perceptions of the student's aptitudes, abilities, interests, and attitudes as related to educational and career planning, academic achievement, personal-social development, and total school progress.

• Interprets the guidance program of the school to the parent/guardian and familiarizes him with the guidance services available.

• Involves himself and the school's guidance staff with parent/guardian groups.

• Involves the parent/guardian in the guidance activities within the school.

The Counselor's Responsibility to the Staff

In a democratic society, the school's basic purpose is the education and development of all students toward individual fulfillment. To contribute toward this important responsibility, the secondary school counselor:

• Works with all members of the school staff by providing

appropriate information, materials, and consultative assistance in supporting teacher efforts to understand better the individuality of each pupil.

• Contributes to curriculum development and cooperates with administrators and teachers in the refinement of methods for individualized learning.

• Contributes to the development of a flexible curriculum to provide a meaningful education for each student.

• Acts as the coordinator in the school's program of student appraisal by accumulating meaningful information and interpreting this to students, parents, and the professional staff.

• Utilizes modern technology, techniques, and paraprofessional personnel to disseminate educational and career information.

• Assists in research related to pupil needs by conducting studies related to the improvement of educational programs and services.

• Assists students in planning programs of educational and vocational training consistent with their goals.

• Coordinates the use of services available beyond those he can provide by making appropriate referrals and by maintaining a cooperative working relationship with community specialists.

• Serves the school's program of public relations by participating in community groups and by furnishing information regarding the guidance programs to the communication media.

• Acts as a consultant to administrators, to teachers, and to significant others, sharing appropriate individual student data, identifying students with special needs, suggesting materials and procedures for a variety of group guidance experiences, and participating in inservice training programs.

• Implements student articulation between the junior high school and high school and the high school and post-high school experiences.

• Accepts professional obligations related to school policies and programs.

• Participates in the planning, development, and evaluation of the guidance program.

The Counselor's Responsibility Regarding the Community

The secondary school counselor has a professional responsibility to have accurate information about current programs in operation in the community, including knowledge of such services as health clinics, planned parenthood clinics, volunteer programs, cooperative programs, apprenticeship of labor organizations, Chamber of Commerce, and other community agencies.

The Counselor's Responsibility to His Profession

The American School Counselor Association presumes that the professional identity of the school counselor must be derived from his unique training and service. To assure his continued professional growth and contribution to his profession, the secondary school counselor:

• Has an understanding of his own personal characteristics and their effects on counseling relationships and personal-social encounters.

• Is aware of his level of professional competency and presents it accurately to others.

• Continues to develop professional competence and maintains an awareness of contemporary trends inside and outside the school community.

• Fosters the development and improvement of the counseling profession by assisting with appropriate research and participating in professional association activities at the local, state, and national levels.

• Discusses with related professional associates (counselors, teachers, administrators) practices which may be implemented to strengthen and improve standards or conditions of employment.

• Prepares meaningful, objective, and succinct case reports for other professional personnel who are assisting the student.

• Discusses with other professionals situations related to his respective discipline in an effort to share unique understandings and to elicit recommendations to further assist the counselee.

• Enhances the image of counselors and of other related professionals by positive references in communicating with students, parents, and the community.

• Maintains constant effort to adhere to strict confidentiality of information concerning counselees and releases such information only upon the signed release of the counselee and/or parent/guardian.

• Becomes an active member of the American School Counselor Association and state and local counselor associations in order to enhance his professional growth.

The Counselor's Responsibility to Self

Beyond the counselor's responsibility to his profession is a further responsibility to himself. To meet the significant responsibilities to self, the secondary school counselor is expected to:

• Maintain a strict adherence to the concept and practice of confidentiality and recognize the right to share such information only with a signed release.

• Be well informed on current theories, practices, developments, and trends.

• Use time primarily for guidance and counseling and constantly strive to reduce demands of clerical or administrative duties.

• Become a professional individual and, in so doing, develop and maintain a well-rounded educational, social, and professional attitude.[10]

In an updating of guidance services, Carlton Beck sees the following additions to a projected guidance program interested in helping the whole individual:

1. Draft counseling even with an all volunteer army.
2. Understanding of drug problems including reasons for use, available help, and referral procedures.
3. Awareness of special help for racial minorities.
4. Causes of student unrest and new student rights.
5. Understanding of the "new morality."
6. Interpreting of 1–5 to parents.
7. Working toward "humanizing" curriculum, procedures, and personal relationships.[11]

RELATIONSHIP OF PRINCIPAL AND COUNSELOR

The first area which must be given some consideration in this section is whether or not the principal should have any role in guidance. Beginning with Kehas in 1965, some guidance writers have begun to advocate that the role of the guidance counselor be autonomous within the school.[12] The principal's goals include such things as smooth operation of the school, discipline of unruly students, and compliance to rules within the school; while the counselor is concerned solely with the individual. According to these writers this diversity of roles sometimes forces the counselor to act in ways contrary to the principles of guidance because the principal has no special expertise in guidance yet tries to lead guidance efforts.[13]

According to Filbeck, the principal often has the following view of counselors. When there is a conflict between a student and student practice the counselor should:

1. Be supportive of school policy.
2. Reinforce conformity to social standards.
3. Seek acceptance of the status quo.
4. Reduce the likelihood of challenge to school authority.

On the other hand counselors tend to emphasize student decision making based on individual values and factors.[14]

As an alternative to the principal leading guidance activities, some writers such as Humes and Lavitt envision an autonomous guidance department with its own director responsible directly to the superintendent or to a director of guidance services.[15]

The traditional approach is for the principal to direct guidance efforts as part of a total school program. Part of the push for independence has been due to principal misuse of guidance personnel and activities. The following is a list of abuses often cited by guidance personnel:

1. Inadequate programming by emphasizing large group work instead of individual counseling.
2. Justification of guidance work to the public in terms of "our school" over "their school" when guidance is an individual not school activity.
3. Justifying new counselors because of increased need and then assigning them administrative duties.
4. Postponing guidance programs because of disagreements within the field of guidance.
5. Inadequate facilities, budget, and personnel.
6. Seeing guidance as a cure all for school problems and then complaining when it isn't.[16]

If the principal is going to act as leader of the entire school, including guidance, the following is a list of areas where guidance leadership can be expected.

1. Procurement of facilities and supplies.
2. Selection of counselors.
3. Development of a favorable attitude toward guidance among teachers, parents, students, and the community.
4. Definition of functions of self, teacher, and counselor.
5. Distribution of guidance duties among various counselors.

6. Collection and distribution of college and vocational information.[17]

In setting up a guidance program the principal should consult with counselors and use them as resource experts. The principal should consider the following components before designating any guidance program.

1. Size of school.
2. Availability of personnel.
3. Legal requirements.
4. Available funds including federal assistance.
5. Community setting and support.
6. Needs of the students.
7. Attitude of teaching staff.[18]

Along with these areas of guidance leadership, counselors should expect the following from the principal:

1. Challenge and vitality in leadership.
2. Administrative insistence on complete service integrated into the total school system.
3. Use of guidance personnel in planning programs, not programs handed to counselors to implement.
4. Maintenance of an evaluative attitude seeking evidence of achievement.
5. Reduction of clerical burden and administrative duties.[19]

In return, administrators can legitimately expect the following:

1. Championing of the student and care for the individual.
2. Research evidence on achievement, interest, progress, and post-school activities.
3. Help in recognizing problems and needs of students.
4. Responsible, professional actions such as reading current literature, growth within the counseling position, and membership in professional organization.[20]

As suggested in the list of counselor expectations, one function of the principal in the guidance program is evaluation of the program. This aspect of the total school must be evaluated periodically just like every other part.

EVALUATION OF GUIDANCE SERVICES

Ohlsen discusses the Cooperative Self-Study approach to evaluation of guidance services. He recommends the development of an evaluation committee made up of representatives from the teaching and administrative staff and those members of the guidance services who desire to participate. In addition to this approach, Ohlsen also recommends the use of (1) the case study approach which involved the development of specific objectives in behavioral terms for each guidance service and criteria that can be used to appraise the outcomes of that service, and (2) systematic research on outcomes of the guidance services offered.[21]

The rest of this section represents the procedures Ohlsen suggests for evaluating guidance services utilizing the Cooperative Self-Study approach.

The Educational Program*

There is no substitute for good school policies supported by good teaching in a carefully planned educational program. Therefore, the survey committee appointed to evaluate guidance services must be sure to examine certain elements of the educational program, even though they cannot be expected to do a thorough evaluation of the entire program. The following are types of questions for which the committee should seek answers:

1. To what extent do teachers seem to understand the basic needs of their students? What are they doing to help their students satisfy these basic needs?

2. Do school policies take cognizance of students' needs? Are there any school policies that interfere with helping students satisfy their needs? What adjustment problems do these unsound policies create? To what extent do school policies encourage teachers to help students satisfy their basic needs?

3. Do teachers help students develop good work habits and efficient study skills? To what extent do teachers help students develop proficiency in basic skill subjects?

4. What are counselors doing to help teachers improve affective education as well as students' intellectual development? Who is helping teachers recognize, accept, express, and enjoy their own and their students' feelings in daily living together within their classrooms?

5. Describe some examples of parent-teacher cooperative efforts in improving students' school adjustment. How are these efforts improving school achievement? What do they contribute to the students' social and/or emotional development?

---

* From *Guidance Services in the Modern School,* 2nd ed. by Merle M. Ohlsen, copyright © 1955, 1964, 1974 by Harcourt Brace Jovanovich, Inc. Reprinted with permission.

6. What are teachers doing to further (or interfere with) their students' career development? What do counselors do to enhance both parents' and teachers' contribution to this process?
7. What are teachers doing to help students explore post-high school plans for both work and study?
8. What special provisions are made for the identification and education of exceptional children?
9. Which students are best served by the school? Whose needs are most neglected? How may their needs be better met?
10. What are the primary strengths and weaknesses in the education program? What is being done to help students become acquainted with their national heritage and the problems of today? How and by whom are they prepared to meet their responsibilities as citizens?

Counseling

Inasmuch as they tend to be assigned more duties than they can perform adequately, counselors must continue to confront themselves with these questions: Of all the services that I am asked to provide, which are most essential? Which can be provided only by a professional with my preparation (for example, counseling and consulting)? Which of the requests should I ignore or refuse to do because they damage my professional relationships with students, teachers, or parents? Which of the legitimate duties that I may be expected to perform can I train colleagues to do (and thus clear more time to use my unique professional competencies)?

Since monitoring expenditure of time is so important, counselors may keep a log to determine whether they are using their time appropriately. For this purpose they should randomly select a week and keep a detailed record of what they do and how much time they spend on each activity each day, including time spent on professional activities outside the normal working day. Many counselors have found it useful to classify all activities in their logs into these sixteen categories: (1) individual counseling, (2) group counseling, (3) counseling-related activities (for example, studying a client's cumulative folder in preparation for an interview, screening materials such as tests or vocational information for client's use, or soliciting the assistance of teaching colleagues in a case conference), (4) consulting with teachers,

(5) consulting with parents, (6) counseling parents, (7) leading parent-education groups, (8) arranging for referrals, (9) academic advising, (10) planning group-guidance activities, (11) conducting guidance activities, (12) providing placement services, (13) performing clerical duties, (14) doing committee work concerned with school policies or curriculum, (15) performing administrative duties, and (16) doing research and/or other evaluation of guidance services.

One very useful self-study approach is to provide those who participate in the evaluation of the counselors' services with a list of all specific duties that counselors may be expected to fulfill. Then ask them to check every service that they believe their counselors provide. Next, for the services checked, ask them to write: *A* in front of the three on which they believe counselors spend *most* of their time; *E* in front of the three on which they believe counselors spend the *least* of their time; *B* in front of the six items on which they believe counselors spend *next most* of their time; and *D* in front of the six items on which they believe counselors spend *next least* of their time. With the assumption that all the remaining checked items are *C,* values can be assigned to each letter (for example, A = 5, B = 4, C = 3, D = 2, E = 1, unchecked items = 0). It will then be possible to obtain a score for each item and to rank the items as they are perceived by each group of raters. When any one group—students, teachers, or administrators—perceives the ranking of duties very differently than counselors do, that group tends to be most disappointed with the counselors' services.

This approach has been used frequently by consultants to help counselors discover how these other groups perceive a counselor's job priorities. Hearings are then held to solicit from each group their reactions to the evaluation and their suggestions for improving counselors' services. For example, counselors in a particular high school recently reported at such hearings that they wished they had more time for personal counseling, but they felt such a shift in emphasis would be criticized by parents and teachers and be looked on with suspicion by students. During that same two-day period, while separate hearings were being conducted for parents, teachers, and students, the consultant discovered that they wanted counselors to be freed of much of their routine clerical work to enable them to do more personal counseling. Interestingly, most of the counselors already possessed the professional skills to provide individual counseling, and over half of them exhibited interest in developing the new professional skills needed for group counseling.

When this approach is used, questions such as the following may be asked of teachers and students in hearings (or included on a questionnaire):

1. If you were worried or upset about something and really needed to talk to someone whom you could trust (or, for teachers, if a student were worried, and so on), to whom would you turn for help?
2. Who is this person?
   Counselor
   Friend about my age
   Parents
   Pastor or priest or rabbi
   Principal or some other school administrator
   Teacher
   Other _____
3. What kind of assistance should students expect from counselors?
4. How have they helped you?
5. How have they helped your friends?
6. How have they helped your teachers?
7. How have they helped parents?
8. How do you think counselors' services could be improved?

Counselors should be encouraged to answer questions such as:

1. What do students expect from you?
2. How would you like to change these expectations?
3. What do parents, teachers, and administrators expect from you?
4. How would you like to change parents', teachers' and administrators' expectations of you?
5. What duties absorb most of your time? How do you feel about this use of your time? How would you like to reorder these priorities? Why don't you?
6. What are your clients' goals for counseling? How were these goals defined? With which goals have you been most successful in helping clients?
7. What proportion of your clients are self-referrals?
8. Who else refers clients for counseling? For what purposes are they referred? What proportion of these clients genuinely accepts counseling? What proportion accepts it for the purposes for which they were referred?

9. In what specific ways have you helped your clients? Can you cite any evidence that indicates whether or not you have been more successful with self-referred than with other-referred clients?

10. How do you decide whom you counsel and whom you refer?

11. How may you make better use of group techniques to improve services?

12. Who are your best candidates for successful counseling?

13. To whom have you made referrals and for what purposes during this school year?

14. What record do you keep on your counseling sessions? Who is permitted to see your interview notes?

15. What, if anything, interferes with your developing a good working relationship with either students or staff?

16. What changes should be made in your job description in order to improve your effectiveness?

For the other services, the committee charged with responsibility for evaluation of guidance services should obtain answers to the following questions:

Child Study

1. What do teachers feel they need to know about their students in order to teach them effectively?

2. What additional information is needed by those who provide guidance services?

3. To what extent are all the needs of these staff members met by the child-study service?

4. What do teachers contribute to child study?

5. By what means do teachers make their contributions?

6. Who decides what data are included in the cumulative folder, and who maintains the folder?

7. What tests are given? Who selected each? For what purpose was each test given? Who is expected to use and interpret each of them? What steps are taken to insure that those who are expected to use and interpret each test are qualified to do so? To what extent are tests actually used for the purposes for which they were selected?

8. Are appropriate nontest data used to supplement tests? When a test is chosen, what is done to insure that appropriate nontest data can be obtained to supplement the test results?

9. To whom are test scores released and/or interpreted?

10. For whom have tests actually been interpreted? What precautions have been taken to insure adequate interpretation?

11. To what extent has the child-study service increased students' understanding of themselves?

12. How does the child-study service contribute to students' career development?

13. How are child-study data used to help students develop post-high school educational plans?

Information Services

1. For what questions do students want answers concerning themselves and their environment? Which of these questions should be answered by parents? How can the school help parents better meet their responsibility? Which of these questions should be answered in regular classwork? For which should students be encouraged to find answers for themselves by reading? For which should they be encouraged to seek the assistance of a teacher or counselor?

2. What materials are available for students' use? Are the materials appropriate for their use? What additional materials are needed?

3. What proportion of the students actually use the materials?

4. With what success have the materials been used by students? Have students obtained satisfactory and accurate answers to their questions? What testing has been done to assess the accuracy of the information that students obtained by seeking answers to their questions?

5. Are the materials organized for students' most efficient use? How may the materials be better organized?

6. What organized efforts are made to provide students with the information they need outside of the usual classwork (for example, guidance classes)? What are the objectives for these activities? What has been done to evaluate their success? For example, how do the students react to them? What do they think the activities do for them? How do they think that they could be improved?

Orientation

1. To what extent does the orientation program prepare students for their new school experiences?

2. How may students be encouraged to plan and revise the orientation program?

3. Why is orientation in the new setting preferred over orientation prior to the move to the new setting?

Career Development

1. When do most students make their first career choice?

2. What do counselors do to motivate students to accept responsibility for their own career development?

3. What proportion of the students who graduated from high school last year left school with specific vocational and educational plans?

4. What proportion of these students had plans you believe were reasonable and achievable? What percentage of them actually followed through and implemented the plans that they made in high school?

5. Of those who went to work following graduation, what percentage of them succeeded? What percentage were satisfied with their jobs?

6. What percentage entered some type of post-high school education? What percentage succeeded? Were those who had developed well thought-through post-high school plans any more successful than the others?

7. For what others would post-high school education also have been appropriate? Why didn't they plan for further education? What else could the school have done for them?

8. What proportion of the students who entered high school with last year's class failed to graduate with them? Why did they leave school? What are they doing now?

9. What proportion of those who left school last year (both dropouts and graduates) had made a vocational choice? For what proportion was the choice a reasonable one? For what proportion were their educational plans appropriate for their vocational choice? What proportion are either employed in a job related to their goal or preparing for their vocational goal?

10. What provision does the school make for helping former students examine and revise educational and vocational plans?

11. Who has been best served by your cooperative education programs? What other students could profit from them? How may these programs be changed to better serve college-bound students?

12. How could summer and part-time employment be coordinated with cooperative education programs more
effectively to aid in the identification and development
of salable skills for college-bound as well as noncol-
lege-oriented students?

13. What can be done to help students obtain more relevant
part-time and summer employment?

14. To what extent are the school's placement efforts coordinated with the services of local and state employment
offices?

15. What improvements may be made to help students develop
and present their salable occupational skills.

Follow-Up Service

1. What follow-up studies have been completed recently?
What suggestions did you obtain for improving guidance services or for improving the curriculum? How
were these suggestions used?

2. What may be done to obtain responses from a more representative sample of former students?

3. What percentage of the former students who graduated five
years ago implemented their high school vocational
plans?

4. What percentage was satisfied with their employment?
What can the school do to help those who are not
satisfied with their jobs to obtain more suitable
employment?

Administration of Guidance Service

1. Are guidance positions clearly defined, and are compatible
duties assigned to individual workers? Do job descriptions include adequate definition of professional qualifications of workers? Are staff members selected with
care?

2. Are members of the staff encouraged to share ideas, to
grow on the job, and to contribute to the development
of appropriate school policies?

3. To what extent have individuals assumed responsibility for
their own growth? How has the administration encouraged this self-development?

4. What provision has the administration made for inservice
education of the guidance staff? What part has the
staff had in the development of this inservice education program? How do they react to this program?

What specific improved practices have resulted from it?

5. Who has responsibility for supervision of guidance services? What supervision is actually done?

6. To what extent do parents, teachers, and students understand the various guidance services and realize who provides each?

7. Who has the responsibility of speaking for guidance services and for releasing news stories to the public?

8. What kind of working relationship does the guidance department have with referral agencies in the community? What use is made of these referral agencies?[22]

RELATIONSHIP OF TEACHERS AND COUNSELORS

Philosophically, teachers and counselors are often seen as closely related. Counselors are former teachers and often still teach some classes. Teachers and counselors both work closely with individual students, and both groups generally seek the same ends for the students. On the other hand, there are some great differences. Methodology, training, time in individual and large group work, and facilities all vary. Too often, though, teachers are expected to function as counselors, and counselors are expected to teach. In each case, one of the two or more likely both jobs will suffer. Arbuckle has listed several reasons why teachers cannot be effective counselors. These include:

1. The teacher's major responsibility is to society and the class rather than the individual.

2. Teachers are usually the dominant figure in an overt teaching role rather than listeners more atuned to the learning role.

3. Teachers handle problems in public rather than behind closed doors.

4. Teachers are usually friendly to the students while the counselor must maintain a professional relationship because friendship may impair clinical judgment.

5. Teachers are not professionally trained in counseling techniques.[23]

This list indicates reasons why it is difficult for teachers to be effective counselors, but this does not mean that teachers have no place in the guidance function of the school. On the contrary, they play a major role. The following list provided by Shertzer shows some of the areas in which teachers should actively be engaged in the guidance function.

1. Teachers engage in child study and diagnosis and gather information such as background, ability, and needs.
2. Teachers identify and refer pupils who have special needs.
3. Teachers contribute to and make use of guidance records.
4. Teachers help students develop effective study and organizational habits.
5. Teachers contribute to educational and vocational planning, and placement by outlining future subject matter and discussing career opportunities.[24]

Glanz, too, makes a strong case for teacher involvement in counseling, group work, testing, and case study procedures.[25]

Grobman has listed another area, which has yet been largely unexploited, in which teachers and administrators can both aid an important guidance function.[26] Teachers and administrators come from a wide variety of college backgrounds and have visited many schools. Lists of these schools should be compiled and teachers and administrators be used as resource people who will give a much more candid, easy-to-understand evaluation of colleges than catalogues or public relations people will. Panel discussions and personal discussions on colleges can also help foster better teacher-student relations. This is, of course, only one of many ways in which interested teachers can aid the guidance function.

Many of these preceding ways in which teachers are involved in guidance do not involve teacher-counselor function. Often, teachers expect counselors to have immediate answers to classroom problems, a trap which good counselors will hopefully not fall into. What is needed is a mutual understanding that the ultimate goal is helping the individual child. Then a pooling of information and joint plan of action can be worked out. The counselor can help teachers understand why students behave the way that they do and also help teachers interpret standardized test score meanings.[27]

Finally, counselors can be useful in classroom situations where a class and teacher seem to have reached an impasse. Anandam and Williams describe such a situation and how the counselor was able to step in and help achieve a solution.[28] Such measures as behavior contracting, student determination of punishment, a reward system, and other behavior modifying techniques changed students to the point where the teacher could again function effectively. Teachers also learned new teaching techniques which could prevent such a situation from reoccurring.

RELATIONSHIP OF STUDENTS AND COUNSELORS

Throughout this chapter the emphasis has been on guidance and how it can best help the individual student. Adults have one perception of the student, peers have a different perception of the student, and the student has a self-perception which may be completely different than either of the other two. Each of these perceptions affects how the child acts and reacts, and the counselor must be able to see all of these perceptions and act within them to help the child.

Probably the most concise statement concerning the counselor's relationship with and responsibility to students has been developed by the Governing Board of the American School Counselors Association and was presented earlier in this chapter.

Any presentation of counseling technique within the context of one chapter would be an oversimplification and would lead to a somewhat false picture of the counseling process. In the past, a very general description of counseling approaches was envisioned as one ranging from a nondirective, client-centered approach to a very directive approach by a counselor who is working with students as they strive to make a decision. Some counselors considered themselves as eclectic, which means they utilized techniques from both ends of the continuum. It is rare to find counselors at either end of the continuum. Many writers in the guidance and counseling field now have moved away from the continuum approach and talk more about using basic helping skills to assist in behavior change. The act of counseling requires the professional skill of the trained counselor. Cooperation of teachers and administrators can facilitate the counselor's work, but he or she must be the one to really effect the result.

In order to provide adequate time for counseling it is important that a sufficient number of counselors are available. One accrediting agency, the North Central Association, lists the following standard for guidance counselors:

> Member schools shall provide qualified guidance workers at a
> ratio of one counselor for each 450 students with no school
> having less than a half time counselor. Schools are encouraged
> to try a variety of approaches to guidance services including
> individual school ratio adjustments. They may utilize coun-
> selors, supportive personnel, and teachers, and such plans for
> organizational changes may be submitted to the State Commit-
> tee for Approval.[29]

It should be noted that these are minimum requirements of the North Central Association. Because of heavy counseling loads, group counseling is being explored as a way to provide counseling service to more students.

SUMMARY

It is essential that the principal and supervisor of the secondary school work together with the guidance director in providing guidance services for students. Conflicts often occur between guidance personnel and administration since some principals in the past have felt counselors were not as supportive of their efforts to maintain effective behavior of students as they would like. In like manner, principals have often felt that counselors mitigate against their effectiveness in providing effective supervision of teachers. What is often needed is frequent communication with guidance personnel to share viewpoints and to reach agreement upon responsibilities.

A mutually agreed upon job description for the guidance counselor is essential. It is also essential that the principal be aware of the current thinking of the professional organizations of counseling and guidance personnel in order to be more commensurate with their goals and objectives. College credit guidance courses provide another excellent avenue for the principal or supervisor to achieve better understandings of the guidance and counseling functions in a school setting.

Guidance services as a concept in a secondary school received great impetus from the National Defense Education Act passed by Congress shortly after the USSR orbited their first Sputnik. This provided the impetus which later led to state departments and accrediting agencies creating standards that made guidance services mandatory.

The following are suggestions and areas of concern for the educational leader in the counseling and guidance program of the secondary school:

1. The guidance department must have adequate funds and space for operation of an effective counseling program. This would include secretarial help for record keeping and the handling of such routine duties as making appointments, and managing the office.

2. The guidance program is a cooperative effort of all professionals within the building. Counselors cannot go it alone. They must have the help of teachers and other professionals. The teachers also need the help of counselors in their instructional activities.

3. Among the responsibilities of the counselors is the development of an effective testing program, which provides the school with a measure of its successes or failures.

4. The principal must remove any roadblocks thay may prevent effective referral of problems to such outside persons as psychologists, ministers, psychiatrists, social agencies, and juvenile authorities.

5. Guidance services should not be limited to job or college placement although this is an important segment of the guidance operation. Personal counseling is an extremely vital aspect of the total program for guidance services.

6. The entire student population should be involved in the guidance and counseling program. To accomplish this, regular group sessions at regular intervals should be held to discuss such matters as job opportunities, college opportunities, and major problems confronting students.

SUMMARY

7. The role of the guidance counselor in discipline affairs is yet unclear. Some counselors want to be informed of all students who have discipline problems. Others want to avoid the disciplinary actions. The authors have experienced assistant principals for discipline who also provide excellent counseling to their students. Each school is unique with unique personnel, and no set pattern of the counselor's relationship to discipline can be established. But one point is very clear. Counselors cannot wash their hands of all discipline problems if they are to be effective in helping students. It is strongly recommended that the counselors hold frequent conferences with the assistant principal responsible for discipline in mutually assisting each other.

8. An organizational arrangement should be established so that students have frequent opportunities to talk with guidance counselors. One way to accomplish this is through the establishment of advisory groups of students, who would have a choice of a teacher, principal, or guidance counselor as a leader of their group.

9. A regular and systematic evaluation of the guidance program should be made. This can be accomplished by teacher and student opinion surveys, outside consultants, and a school guidance committee.

NOTES

1. Donald G. Ferguson, *Pupil Personnel Services* (Washington, D.C.: Center for Applied Research in Education, 1963), p. 17.

2. Charles W. Humes, "Solution to School Counselor Role: Administrative Change," *Counselor Education and Supervision* 10 (Fall, 1970), p. 88.

3. Bruce Shertzer and Shelley C. Stone, *Fundamentals of Guidance* (Boston: Houghton Mifflin, 1976), pp. 44–47.

4. Ibid., pp. 46–47.

5. Ibid., p. 47.

6. Ibid.

7. Edward C. Glanz, *Guidance: Foundations, Principles and Techniques* (Boston: Allyn and Bacon, Inc., 1974), pp. 40–41.

8. Shertzer and Stone, *Fundamentals of Guidance*, pp. 47–49.

9. Statement developed by Dr. John C. Jessell, Professor of Education, and Director, Division of Guidance and Counseling, Indiana State University, Terre Haute, Indiana.

10. American Personnel and Guidance Association, "The Role of the Secondary School Counselor," *The School Counselor* 21:5 (May, 1974), pp. 380–386.

11. Carlton E. Beck, "Philosophy of Guidance Services in the Secondary Schools," *High School Journal* 54 (January, 1971), p. 240.

12. Chris Kehas, "Administrative Structure and Guidance Theory," *Counselor Education and Supervision* 4 (Fall, 1965), p. 148.

13. Edward Landy, "Who Does What in the Guidance Program?" *The School Counselor* 10 (March, 1963), p. 115.

14. Robert Filbeck, "Perceptions of Appropriateness of Counselor Behavior: A Comparison of Counselors and Principals," *Personnel and Guidance Journal* 43 (May, 1965), p. 895.

15. Charles H. Humes and Jerry A. Lavitt, "Counselor Attitude Toward Administrative Practices," *Counselor Supply and Supervision* 10 (Winter, 1971), pp. 153–157.

16. Shertzer and Stone, *Fundamentals of Guidance*, p. 394.

17. P. W. Huton, "Education of the Guidance Team," *Counselor Education and Supervision* 9 (Summer, 1970), p. 234.

18. Dale Baughman et al., *Administration and Supervision of the Modern Secondary School* (West Nyack, N.Y.: Parker, 1969), p. 171.

19. Shertzer and Stone, *Fundamentals of Guidance*, p. 395.

20. Ibid., p. 396.

21. Merle M. Ohlsen, *Guidance Services in the Modern School* (New York: Harcourt Brace Jovanovich, Inc., 1974).

22. Ibid., pp. 402–412.

23. Dugald Arbuckle, *Pupil Personnel Services in American School* (Boston: Allyn and Bacon, 1962), p. 108.

24. Shertzer and Stone, *Fundamentals of Guidance*, pp. 377–378.

25. Glanz, *Guidance: Foundations, Principles and Techniques*, pp. 360–368.

26. Neil Grobman, "A Common-Sense, Personal Approach to Advising Students About College," *The School Counselor* 18 (November, 1970), pp. 135–138.

27. Shertzer and Stone, *Fundamentals of Guidance*, p. 370.

28. Kamala Anandam and Robert L. Williams, "A Model for Consultation with Classroom Teachers on Behavior Management," *The School Counselor* 18 (March, 1971), p. 254.

29. North Central Association of Colleges and Schools, Commission on Schools, *Policies and Criteria for the Approval of Secondary Schools* (1976–77), p. 28.

12
Effective Scheduling: A Key to the Efficient Operation of the Secondary School

The schedule provides a vehicle for representing the purposes of the secondary school as well as freeing the students and teachers for optimum achievement. Without a schedule which provides for reasonable utilization of the teachers' and students' time, the school is likely to sink into a sea of mud, without purpose and without contributing to the achievement of students. The secondary school leader who desires the most from the students, teachers, building, and facilities will spend many hours planning, experimenting, and designing a relevant and purposeful schedule. This schedule should be dynamic and flexible to meet the needs of a reliable faculty and vigorous student body.

New challenges in schedule making have been brought about by the many variations in which the school day may be divided. It is estimated that close to one-third of the secondary schools have modified their traditional lock-step scheduling procedures with some form of flexibility during the past ten years. The basic purpose has been to reach toward greater individualization of instruction characterized quite recently by self-scheduling procedures (arena or college-type[1]) where the student is allowed a choice of classes and teachers.

A recent thrust in schedule making, in addition to dividing the school day differently, has been to divide the school year into varying patterns of grading periods. For example, many schools are using two nine-week periods per semester, three-week phase-elective programs, and even shorter periods for minicourses. Looming on the horizon are the year-round school plans which have three basic purposes according to McCloskey, who conducted a recent study. He suggested the intent is to (a) diversify and enrich instruction, (b) accelerate completion of normal school requirements and (c) accommodate more students and adults in existing facilities by increasing the number of days per year and the hours per day school buildings are being used.[2]

MEETING REQUIREMENTS IN THE
SECONDARY SCHOOL SCHEDULE

The public secondary school schedule must meet minimum state regulations. Local boards may impose additional standards and, if accredited by a regional association, that body's policies and standards must receive attention in the development of the school schedule. To illustrate, the following has been taken from the Administrative Handbook of the State Department of Public Instruction in Indiana:

1. The minimum length of the school year shall be 175 instructional days, i.e., days of actual school attendance.

2. The minimum length of the normal school day shall be six hours in grades seven to twelve.

3. A minimum of two hundred (200) minutes of supervised instruction in a subject shall comprise the class time for a week in a secondary school. A school may organize its daily and weekly schedule on a pattern that is appropriate for its educational program, provided that at least two hundred (200) minutes per week are scheduled for non-laboratory courses. At least two hundred and seventy-five (275) minutes per week shall be scheduled for courses requiring laboratory experiences.[3]

Each state may vary somewhat in their criteria for schedule construction so it is imperative that principals be familiar with the standards in their particular state. There is also a tendency for state departments of public instruction to allow for flexibility in interpreting the traditional measures of school course credits. In Indiana, for example, the state has provided two options to secure credit for minicourses which are offered by the schools.

In terms of what local school districts may do above and beyond the minimum standards set forth by the state, the couse offerings and scheduling opportunities will probably be limited only by the ability to secure appropriate human and material resources which will support them. The principal is encouraged to seek accreditation by a regional agency such as the North Central Association of Colleges and Schools (NCA). Such affiliation gives the schedule maker additional muscle for developing the optimum educational plan. This is true not only because of meeting the quantitative standards set forth in the "Policies and Standards for the Approval of Secondary Schools,"[4] but also because of the influential forces relating to sound educational philosophies and purposes exerted within the consortium of schools. Implications of these forces for the schedule maker relate to the provisions for (1) teacher experimentation, innovation, and research in seeking better teaching-learning situations, (2) flexibility in classroom organization and administration to serve varying groups and situations, and

(3) the master schedule devoted to suitable investments of time, staff, space, and material resources in the student activity program to encourage widespread participation and insure worthwhile involvement.

GENERAL FACTORS IN BUILDING THE SCHEDULE

The creation and implementation of the school schedule provide the points of focus where parents see their child's educational plan in action and teachers firmly understand their work loads. This surfacing information undoubtedly suggests that the principal must exercise an enormous amount of pre-planning in schedule construction.

First and foremost, input from parental, student, teaching and policy-making groups must be sought and their recommendations given high consideration in the ultimate schedule that is developed. In addition, the schedule must be so designed as to provide students and teachers with a sense of confidence and security from the first school day to the last. This is not to indicate in any way that it may not be flexible, but students and teachers must have confidence in the flexibility that is built into the school schedule.

The schedule must communicate to parents the vehicle by which their young people are attaining educational goals, thereby strengthening the student-parent partnership in the educational process. They will also know how each student will be directed into programs meeting his or her individual needs and the effectiveness of these programs.

In the internal environment of the school, the principal must review the board of education policies and the teachers' master contracts before developing the master schedule. Factors to be considered in schedule construction include those that relate to the length of the school day, length of the school year, number of subject area assignments, released time during the day for teachers, and the length and time of faculty conferences and meetings during the scheduled day and school year. All of these and more become input factors for the principal.

As indicated earlier, most secondary schools have developed philosophies of education with stated goals and objectives to attain their overall purposes. The master schedule is an implementation of these purposes or objectives which have been developed in conjunction with community lay people, students, faculty members, and outside consultants. The purposes of the school as developed by these groups should be incorporated into the schedule.

If the philosophy of the school is an individual program for each student, then the master schedule will be quite different than if the philosophy is block grouping of students according to ability. Nongradedness, continuous progress, phasing, etc., would mean entirely different kinds of schedules than the traditional schedule. The authors would favor a schedule that allows for as much individuality as is feasible. In any case, the philosophy behind the concepts of continuous progress and nongradedness should be incorporated in developing the educational plan for the local school in whatever manner possible.

Morale factors of both staff and student groups are important internal environment considerations of schedule constructionists. The best way to help insure high teacher morale (beyond what is indicated in negotiated agreements or master contracts) is to develop an orderly educational program in which the teachers have been involved. The principal involves teachers in formulating a schedule by asking them their preferences and consulting them before making major changes. High teacher morale will be more likely when the principal arranges a schedule which avoids putting teachers and students in conflict situations. The band room being next to the English room, for example, is bound to cause conflict. While the principal involves the faculty in schedule building, he or she reserves the right to make final decisions. Teachers who are convinced the principal honestly considered their desires before putting the finishing touches on the schedule are not likely to be discontent.

In terms of student morale, the master schedule obviously has a great effect as students move through the educational processes of the school. Such factors as ample passing time, breaks in morning and afternoon classes, scheduling of activity classes at the end of the school day, and meaningful homeroom periods are ways of increasing student morale. Students should also be involved in developing a workable schedule, which will not only give them a feeling of being a contributor, but may also result in a much more desirable schedule.

STEPS UTILIZED IN MAKING A SCHEDULE

The school schedule and school calendar involve technical skills of the school principal, and as such, may not command a great amount of interest for the principal who likes to work with people rather than things. Nevertheless, these two activities must not be slighted since a poorly constructed schedule or calendar may ruin the best instructional leadership efforts of the principal.

In essence, the purpose of the master schedule is to fit the human, material, and physical resources together so that optimum learning will take place. In accomplishing this, the principal reviews the goals and objectives of the school several months prior to the opening of the school year. As mentioned before, these goals and objectives have been prepared in consultation with lay community members, the faculty, the students, central office staff, and the school board where appropriate.

While routine details of schedule making can be delegated to secretaries and assistants, delegation of *all* responsibility for schedule making lets the most important opportunity for the principal to provide leadership to slip away. The principal should be involved at least in a supervisory manner, in all the following steps of schedule building:

1. Registration of students.
2. Determining the number of students registering for each course. A computer can be used here.
3. Determining the size of classes—large group instruction, small group discussion.
4. Determining the length of periods and the length of the school day.
5. Determining the opening and closing times, intermission between classes, etc.
6. Preparation of a room availability chart, including the number of pupil stations in a room.
7. Preparation of the conflict sheet.
8. Preparation of teacher qualifications and preferences on subjects and activities.
9. Completion of the final schedule board, assignment of subjects, activities, etc., to teachers.

SPECIFIC FACTORS TO CONSIDER IN SCHEDULE CONSTRUCTION

Before the master schedule is completed there are many specific areas that require a number of decisions to be made. It is therefore important to utilize the general factors and guidelines as discussed in the previous section to form a framework coordinating information regarding the following factors: (1) courses to be offered, (2) nature of subjects, (3) teacher qualifications, (4) room availability, (5) student course requests, and (6) types of schedules available for use.

Courses to be Offered

Shall four years of a language be offered? How many languages? What kind? Shall physical education be required of all students? What shall be the curriculum? These and other questions must be answered by the principal within the framework of the nature of the community, the students, and board of education policy. Additional information must be secured on the nature of the student body, follow-up study data on graduates and dropouts, financial resources, employment availability studies both locally and nationally, and certainly the number of students electing given courses of study such as vocational post-secondary training programs and the like.

Nature of Subjects

The courses offered have a great deal to do with the development of the master schedule. Foreign languages generally are taught best with a forty- to fifty-minute period each day; whereas art and classes of this nature are best conducted in blocks of time up to two hours in length. Some courses are fitted for cooperative teaching, while others are most satisfactorily taught by individual teachers. Different academic courses which require more concentration such as mathematics, English, etc., should be scheduled as early in the day as possible. These and other decisions need broad-based input from the faculty.

Teacher Qualifications

In developing the master schedules, the qualifications of the faculty must be at the fingertips of the principal. Besides asking teachers for their preferences in teaching, the principal must insure that teachers meet regional accreditation and state standards on college education and experience. The teacher qualifications file would include the preferences of teachers as well as a transcript of their college preparation. Department heads can be extremely valuable in securing data in this area. Certainly, master contracts, seniority of staff, and balance in loads are important considerations.

Room Availability

When scheduling, the principal should have a drawing of the available rooms. This drawing would include the number of student stations available and the nature of equipment with the room. Ordinarily, an 80 percent utilization of rooms during each period is optimum usage. A higher percentage of utilization would result in a highly inflexible schedule, one which would enhance conflicts among teachers.

The principal should consider teacher preferences, student preferences, traffic movement, and noise level of classes in making room assignments. Action type classes such as band, art, and industrial arts should be scheduled away from lower noise level areas of instruction.

Student Course Requests

Student registration cards are usually completed in the early spring of the preceding school year. If possible, the student schedule should be completed in consultation with the guidance counselor, who will have a cumulative record of each student. In addition to the conference with a counselor, each student should have parental approval of his or her schedule. A written form signed by the parents is quite useful, but a parent-student-counselor conference is ideal.

One satisfactory method which may be used is the student-prepared, marked sense cards which may be automatically punched into computer cards. These cards fed through a computer, as discussed in more detail later, provide conflict sheets which may be used in building the master schedule. Even without computer assistance a conflict sheet should be developed when hand scheduling is made. This enables the schedule builder to determine which courses may be scheduled during the same period.

The principal can train an office assistant to develop a conflict sheet which determines subjects that may not be placed in the same period. Subjects with several sections need not be plotted for conflicts, since they may be scheduled throughout the school day. A conflict sheet containing single section subjects is illustrated in Figure 12.1.

The office assistant sorts through the registration cards of the students and records the single subject conflicts on the chart. In the conflict sheet shown in Figure 12.1, the principal must schedule advanced biology, calculus, orchestra, band, and German IV at different periods of the day. Journalism should not be scheduled at the same time as band. French III should not be scheduled at the same time as the orchestra. Art and band should be scheduled at different periods.

Figure 12.1
Conflict Sheet

	Advanced Biology	Calculus	Journalism	Orchestra	Band	German IV	French III	Art III
Advanced Biology		7	0	17	8	9	0	0
Calculus			3	12	12	9	0	0
Journalism				5	6	0	10	0
Orchestra					27	6	18	13
Band						19	11	12
German IV							2	0
French III								0
Art III								

A marginal punch card as illustrated in Figure 12.2 may also be used in developing a conflict sheet. A needle-like sorter to select cards is used in determining conflicts. Stacking the marginal cards together and inserting the needle through certain holes on the margin provides the schedule builder with immediate conflicts. It also is possible to determine the number of students in each class, the total number of boys in a class, etc., depending upon what has been punched in the cards. Use of the marginal punch card is a unique way of building the schedule, although the procedure is time consuming.

One of the newer methods of securing course requests from students in the secondary schools is the arena type. Students are permitted to choose both their teachers and time period after they have established which courses they are going to take. Juniors and seniors usually are permitted to exercise their choices first. The process may occur in the gymnasium or large arena where students go to the instructors of their choice to sign up. When a teacher's class is full, students must use their second or third option.

Figure 12.2
Marginal Punch Card Used in Scheduling

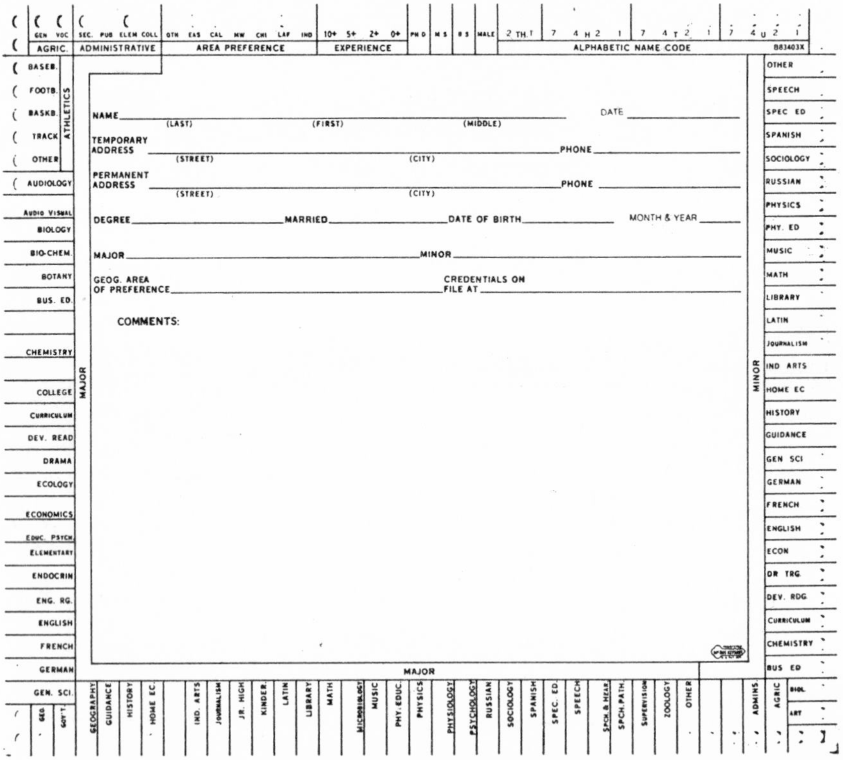

Weaknesses of the method include the risk of teachers being in a popularity contest, students all wanting morning classes, students opting for the easier electives, and the like. Of course the main advantage is the freedom of student choice, which may outweigh a multitude of concerns of lesser significance. In any case, the success of the method has not yet been completely established.

Types of Schedules

In concert with the collection of all of the preceding information and data, a decision must be made on the scheduling pattern that will be employed. Anderson and VanDyke classify schedules into two types—conventional and variable. They describe conventional schedules as "characterized by periods of fixed length, classes meeting at the same hours each day, assigned study halls and similar uniform provision."[5] Variable schedules are described as introducing "a degree of flexibility by means of functional variations in length of periods, hours, and days of class sessions, activity periods and the like."[6]

Variable period schedules include several kinds of flexible schedules such as the modular, the revolving period, the period flexible, the daily demand, and the smorgasbord. Another type which provides simple, effective, and speedy variation in the school day is the rotation schedule.[7]

Conventional or Traditional Schedule

In making a conventional or traditional schedule one may choose from a variety of patterns incorporating different lengths of the school day and each of the periods within that school day. Figure 12.3 shows nine forty-five-minute periods each day with double periods allowed for laboratory classes and with each student being assigned three to four supervised study periods during the day. The big disadvantage of the traditional schedules is that there is a lack of time in many classes for effective supervised and independent study within the classroom. The traditional schedule is losing its popularity as a desirable organizational pattern for a school.

Figure 12.4 illustrates a schedule designed to eliminate or cut down on the number of study halls and provide for supervised study within the regular classroom. Most periods are fifty-five minutes in length, which is quite typical throughout the country. However, the lunch hour in most schools utilizing this pattern is one, two, or three half-hour segments which overlap with the regular class periods. Such a staggered arrangement permits better use of cafeteria facilities.

Variable or Flexible Schedules

Revolving Period Schedule. A revolving period schedule merely moves a certain period (one which is utilized by such activity as the student council or an assembly) around to different times each week, so that no one class will

Figure 12.3
Traditional High School Schedule

Teacher	Period 0 7:15-7:57	Period 1 8:00-8:42	Period 2 8:45-9:27	Period 3 9:30-10:12	Period 4 10:15-10:57	Period 5 11:00-11:42	L 11:45-12:45	Period 6 12:45-1:27	Period 7 1:30-2:12	Period 8 2:15-2:57	Period 9 3:00-3:42
Mr. Smith Dr. Rm. S 10	10 - Dr. Tr. (B)$_B$ / 10 - Dr. Tr. (A)$_B$	Study Hall Cafe.	DRAFTING II - III Dr. Rm.		Study Hall Cafe.	10 - Dr. Tr. (B)$_G$ / 10 - Dr. Tr. (A)$_G$		Drafting I		Prep.	
Mrs. Martin 108 11	Homemaking II		M - 8 - Home Ec. (B) / T - 8 - Home Ec. (A) / W - 8 - Home Ec. (D) / T - 8 - Home Ec. (C) / F - Prep.	Pd. 3 - Study Hall	Homemaking I	(Study Hall)		Homemaking I			
Mrs. Wood Ch.		Business English 209	Clerical Practice C.O.E. 211	Shorthand II & III 211	Typing I 211	C.O.E. Coord.		C.O.E. Coord.	C.O.E. Coord.	C.O.E. Coord.	
Mrs. Jones Cafe. 7		Adv. Typing B.O.E. 211	Office Practice B.O.E. 208	Shorthand I B.O.E. 208	Office Machines B.O.E. 208	B.O.E. Coord.		Shorthand I 208	Office Machines 208	PREP.	
Mr. Bell 211 10	Personal Typing & Notehand	Gen. Bus. 204	Gen. Bus. 207	Treasurer	Book-keeping 110	PREP.		Personal Typing & Notehand 211	Typing I 211		
Mrs. Watt		D. E. Juniors	D. E. Juniors	D. E. Juniors	D. E. Conf.	D. E. Coord.		D. E. Coord.	D. E. Coord.	D. E. Coord.	

Figure 12.4

Modern Long Period Schedule

Teacher	Room	Period 1 8:00-8:57	Period 2 9:00-9:55	Period 3 9:58-10:53	Period 4 10:56-11:51	5 L	Period 6 12:25-1:20	Period 7 1:23-2:18	Period 8 2:21-3:16
Mr. Ankram	35								Band
Miss Beatrice	6	Algebra II	Gen. Math	Conference	Lunch Duty		Algebra I	Algebra I	Algebra I
Mr. Boeman	20	English I	English I	Conference	English I		English I	Prn. S. H.	English I
Mr. Cass	Guid.	Psych.-19	W. Geog.	W. History	Conference		Am. Hist.	Am. Hist.	W. Geog.
Mr. Farling	22	Study Hall							
Mrs. Fikle	9	Gen. Bus.	Pers. T.-8	Book.-21	Typing I-8		Typing I-8	Book.-7	Conference
Miss Fleckman		Art I-7	Art I-7	Art II-7	Conference		Conference		
Mr. Glazier	7	Speech-22	Conference	Speech-20	Speech-22		S.H.-7	S.H.-18	Am. Hist.
Mr. Hall	47	Am. Hist.	Conference	Study Hall	Am. Govt.		Am. Hist. / Comp. 13	Am. Govt.	Am. Govt.
Mr. Hunger	Guid.	Econ.-21							
Mrs. Kinch	41	Latin I	Latin I	Eng. II	S.H.-41		Latin II	Latin II	Conference
Mr. Kolcha	10	M. Dwg. II	Study Hall	Ind. Arts III	Ind. Arts I		Ind. Arts. II	M. Dwg. I	Conference
Mr. Korman	27	Conference	Biology I	Biology I	Biology II		Biology I	Biology I	Biology I
Miss Lancer	24	Eng. III	S.H.-24	Span. II	Study Hall		Span. I	Eng. IV	Conference
Miss Lawrence	1	Home Ec. III	Home Ec. I	Home Ec. OP	Home Ec. I		Home Ec. II	Home Ec. II	Conference
Mrs. Menen	41	Conf.-1 Sem. / S.H.-2nd-13	Eng. III	Conf.-2 Sem. / S.H.-2nd-13	Eng. III		Eng. III	Reading	Reading
Mr. Nelson	28	Chemistry	Aud. Vis.	Physics	S.H.-6		Phys. Sci.	Chemistry	Conference
Mr. Peters	Gym	Boys PE-E / S.H.-0-46	Boys PE-E / S.H.-0-47	Boys PE-O / Boys PE-E	Jr. High		Jr. High	Ref. Math 9 / Dr. Ed.-2nd	Conference
Mr. Pyle	23	English II	English II	English II	English II		English II	Study Hall	
Mrs. Smith	19	Conference	Geometry	Gen. Math	Adv. Math		Study Hall	Gen. Math	Geometry
Mr. Steiner	45	Library	Library	Library	Library		Library	Library	Library
Mr. Turnerman	8	Steno II	Conference	Off. Prac. 9	Steno. I		B. Eng/ Com. Law	Typing II	Typing II
Mrs. Warren	35	Conference	Con. Choir	Girls Che.-0	Jr. High		Elem.	Elem.	Elem.
Mr. Wood	(HR)13	Gen. Sci.-27	G. Sci.-28	S.H. 6	G. Sci.-28		Study Hall	G. Sci.-23	Conference
Mrs. Wood	13	Health-1st / Conf.-2nd	Health-1st / Health-2nd	Health-2nd / Conf.-1st	Jr. High		Jr. High	Girls PE	Girls PE

Notes: —O Classes meet on "odd" dates   (Classes are in teacher's room unless indicated otherwise in
        —E Classes meet on "even" dates   period.)

Assembly Schedule Times: Morning Assembly—   Afternoon Assembly—
8:00-8:05—Home Rooms; 8:08-9:06—Assembly 10:31-11:09—3rd Per.   12:25-1:01—6th Per., 1:04-1:40—7th Per.
9:09-9:47—First Period, 9:50-10:28—2nd Per. 11:12-11:51—4th Per.   1:43-2:19—8th Per., 2:22-3:16—Assembly

suffer any greater loss of time than another. The revolving period may be assigned to period one the first week, period two the second week, etc. Thus, over the period of a school year, this technique balances the amount of time devoted to the various subject areas.

Period Flexible Schedule. From an examination of Figure 12.5, it may be seen how a period flexible schedule is constructed. It is designed to vary the length of periods throughout the week. This type of schedule has the advantage of a thirty-minute period one day for a presentation or a demonstration of some sort by the teacher, and a longer ninety-minute period another day for extended research in the library or other similar type of independent study. The disadvantage of this type of schedule is that every class, whether it be foreign language, physical education, etc., must have the same variability of times during the week.

Modular Scheduling. The modular schedule is usually thought of as a schedule that provides for periods of no longer than thirty minutes. These periods or blocks of time can be arranged so that a class section may meet for one block of time on one day of the week, two blocks on another day, and perhaps three blocks a third day. The advantage of the modular schedule is that the teaching or learning activity can be fitted to the time need. For example, an educational film might fit a 30-minute block of time, whereas an activity, such as art work or physical education, might better fit a ninety-minute block of time. Usually the modular schedule is flexible, and it is often developed by the computer.

A modular schedule consisting of twenty-four fourteen-minute time periods is illustrated in Figure 12.6. The variety of choices in this pattern of scheduling is enormous. There appears to be no one pattern clearly superior to another, but the essential ingredient is to provide for options and alternatives in instructional modes for teachers.

The Daily Demand Schedule. This is a schedule that changes everyday according to the desires of the faculty, and in some instances, the desires of the students. It is a complex arrangement that must have the use of a carefully designed program for the computer or the attention of a person who is allowed full time to coordinate the daily schedule. One of the best known daily demand schedules was developed by Swenson at Brookhurst Junior High in Anaheim, California. Glines writes that:

> . . . through the use of Royal-McBee Keysort cards and four
> staff members, Brookhurst had generated a brand new master
> schedule each day planned three days in advance, which
> allowed for most groups to meet without conflict and which
> provided individualized schedules for most students.[8]

The Daily Smorgasbord Schedule. The campus school at Mankato, Minnesota, through the efforts of Glines, has developed a schedule to

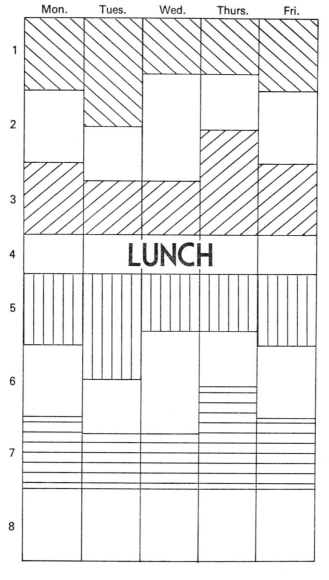

Figure 12.5
Period Flexible Schedule

	Monday	Tuesday	Wednesday	Thursday	Friday	
1	8:25-9:22	8:25-9:52	8:25-9:07	8:25-9:07	8:25-9:22	1
2	9:25-10:20	9:55-10:35	9:10-10:35	9:10-9:50	9:25-10:20	2
3	10:23-11:18	10:38-11:18	10:38-11:18	9:53-11:18	10:23-11:18	3
4	11:18-11:50 everyday—LUNCH					4
5	11:50-12:46	11:50-1:16	11:50-12:31	11:50-12:31	11:50-12:46	5
6	12:49-1:44	1:19-1:59	12:34-1:59	12:34-1:14	12:49-1:44	6
7	1:47-2:42	2:02-2:42	2:02-2:42	1:17-2:42	1:47-2:42	7
8	2:45-3:40 everyday					8

Figure 12.6
Modular Schedule

Teacher	Mod	Mr. Donnely	Mrs. Dowling	Mrs. Firestone	Mr. Foust	Mrs. Fostyk	Mrs. George
7:50-8:04	1	Physics	English I	H. Ec. II	Boys Phys. Ed. H.S. Gym	Spartana	H. Ec. II
8:08-8:22	2		26				107
8:26-8:40	3			111		24	
8:44-8:58	4	307	English I	H. Ec. III	Boys Phys. Ed. H.S. Gym	Prep.	H. Ec. IV
9:02-9:16	5	Prep.	26				
9:20-9:34	6						
9:38-9:52	7	Alg. II	English I	111	Boys Phys. Ed. H.S. Gym	Mass Media 37	107
9:56-10:10	8	112	26	H. Ec.			
10:14-10:28	9						
10:32-10:46	10	Prep.	Prep.		Prep.	Class. Heritage 37	H. Ec. Senior Foods 107
10:50-11:04	11	Lunch			Supvan		
11:08-11:22	12			111	Prep.		
11:26-11:40	13	208 S. Hall	Lunch	Lunch	Lunch	S. Hall 36	Lunch
11:44-11:58	14	Resource	R				
12:02-12:16	15	30 Center	E	Prep.		Lunch	Prep.
12:20-12:34	16	Algebra II	A	H. Ec. II	Boys Phys. Ed. H.S. Gym	Mass Media 31	H. Ec. II
12:38-12:52	17	214	D				
12:56-1:10	18		I				
1:14-1:28	19	Physics	N		Boys		
1:32-1:46	20		G	111	Phys. Ed. H.S. Gym	Resource 17 Center	107
1:50-2:04	21			H. Ec. Sr. Clothing		36 S. Hall	
2:08-2:22	22	307		111	Boys	Poetry	H. Ec. Senior Foods 107
2:26-2:40	23	S. Hall	LAB		Phys. Ed. H.S. Gym	37	
2:44-2:58	24	Cafe. E.			Boys		

improve upon the daily demand schedule. Glines describes this schedule as follows:

> . . . It is built by hand in about one and a half hours for 600 kindergarten through 12 students at no increase in cost except for the quantity of paper devoured, the need for a scheduling clerk, and the manpower of people necessary each day to develop the schedule.[9]

The reader who is interested in learning the mechanics of Glines' daily smorgasbord schedule will want to read *Creating Humane Schools,* which outlines the purposes and mechanics of this schedule. Glines believes that any size school can build daily schedules, but that a 3,000-pupil high school will have problems of logistics not faced by his 600-pupil school. He recommends that the large high school reorganize to the "school within a school" concept if daily smorgasbord scheduling is desired.

FLEXIBLE SCHEDULING PITFALLS

Flexible-modular schedules have much merit, especially if their purpose is to individualize instruction. On the other hand, there are many pitfalls that the wise principal will want to avoid. One of the most common pitfalls of flexible scheduling is inadequate planning. Planning means involving teachers, parents, and students in preparing for such a major change. Two years of careful planning, discussion, and experimentation would be a minimum amount of time needed before initiating across the board flexible scheduling.

A second pitfall in flexible scheduling is the idea that one must go all the way or not at all. If desired, only some areas of a secondary program could be on a flexible schedule. Frank Brown, when he was a principal at Melbourne, Florida, emphasized that one should use the "spin-out" approach. That is, experiment with an idea; and as the idea catches on, more and more teachers will desire to use it.

Third, the responsibility for building a flexible schedule should be retained by the principal. The principal knows more about the overall educational program than anyone else and must keep a very close tab on the development of the schedule, whether it be traditional or flexible. The schedule is the operational plan of the school and is the primary vehicle for implementing instruction. It is difficult to see how the principal can be the instructional leader of the school, if he or she delegates this responsibility to someone else.

A fourth difficulty is the lack of flexible spaces. Since flexible scheduling is designed to utilize the advantages of small, medium, and large group instruction as well as cooperative teaching, one must have spaces for these activities. A comprehensive, flexible schedule, per se, without variable sized rooms is not likely to succeed.

A fifth area of concern may be the failure to provide for students who are unable to study independently or assume the independence of a flexible schedule. Constant attention must be directed toward this concern. School officials have handled this problem in a variety of ways.

Failure to establish a learning resource center is another pitfall to avoid in flexible scheduling. One of the advantages of flexible scheduling is providing greater blocks of time for independent study. Without an extensive learning resource center with study carrels, individual film projectors, record players, etc., the flexible schedule is destined for failure.

A seventh pitfall of flexible scheduling is attempting to keep an accounting of students by the central office at all times. Under flexible scheduling, student accounting must be decentralized. The teacher must assume more responsibility for assuring that students don't cut classes. The teacher makes the decision as to when attendance is such that parents should be notified.

Another difficulty is attempting to grant Carnegie Unit Credit based upon the standard 225 minutes a week (nonlab class) and 275 minutes (lab class). The flexible schedule demands a method of granting credit based upon performance rather than time spent in class.

Failure to provide for varying sizes of groups which include large and small group instruction is to be avoided in the flexible schedule.

Flexible scheduling is not a fad which will fade. It has been estimated that from 15 to 20 percent of the high schools in the United States are on some type of flexible scheduling. No doubt this percentage will increase until all schools have some form of flexible scheduling. The principal's responsibility for fitting the human, material, and physical resources together for most effective learning can be accomplished through flexible scheduling. The importance that the principal places on pre-planning can result in flexible teaching, which research shows is effective. The flexible schedule also gives the teacher greater freedom in evaluating the learning of his or her students.

With all the possibilities which the flexible schedule holds for improving learning of students, it would be a shame for the principal to find that failure to avoid the preceding pitfalls has forced a return to the traditional schedule either because of community pressure or confusion.

DEVELOPING A MASTER SCHEDULE MANUALLY

It is possible to build a master schedule utilizing manual techniques. It is very important to use the results of a conflict matrix to assist in the development of such a schedule. A tag board is extremely helpful in developing a master schedule. The sections of individual subject offerings have tags as does each teacher. The tags are moved around the board until a schedule without conflicts is developed.

THE USE OF THE COMPUTER IN SCHEDULING

The computer may be programmed to aid the principal in constructing a modular, modular-flexible, or traditional secondary school schedule. Heller, Chaffee and Davison[10] describe two computer-based programs which facilitate the assignment of students to classes, and have gained wide acceptance by school administrators. One is called the Class Loading and Student Scheduling program (CLASS) which serves as a vehicle for the sectioning of students once the schools' master schedule has been developed. Thus, many of the details of the scheduling process are accomplished by technocracy. CLASS usuage has the advantage of requiring very little understanding of data processing fundamentals.

Another widely used program is known as the General Academic Simulations Program (GASP), which requires a more comprehensive background of staff members involved in its implementation. The basic reason for this is that the program is more sophisticated since it is designed to construct the entire master schedule. Probably the greatest advantage of the program is realized in schools which have innovated curriculum and organizational patterns. These patterns often suggest an introduction of several new variables in schedule construction which can be more expeditiously handled through the GASP usuage.

Many other groups throughout the nation have developed automated systems to aid school principals in the scheduling of students. An example is one in West Lafayette, Indiana, called Midwest Data Processing[11] (MDP) which prides itself on quick feedback to schools by having a short turn around time. The key elements of the system include a prepunched mark-sense card for students which contain their name, sex, identification number, and grade level. (See Figure 12.7.)

The student fills out the card from a sign-up sheet which lists all the courses offered in the school. The courses are coded in order to be entered on the student card. Ultimately, principals use this information to develop a conflict matrix such as that shown in Figure 12.8. From the information compiled from these sources, a coding form for the master schedule is ultimately developed. An example of a teacher's assignment is presented in Figure 12.9. The schedule builder is in a position to determine which class sections and subject conflicts would occur if the subjects or class sections were scheduled at the same time.

In addition, most computers are programmed to perform several other time-consuming tasks of the teaching and administrative staffs. These

Figure 12.7
Prepunched Student Card

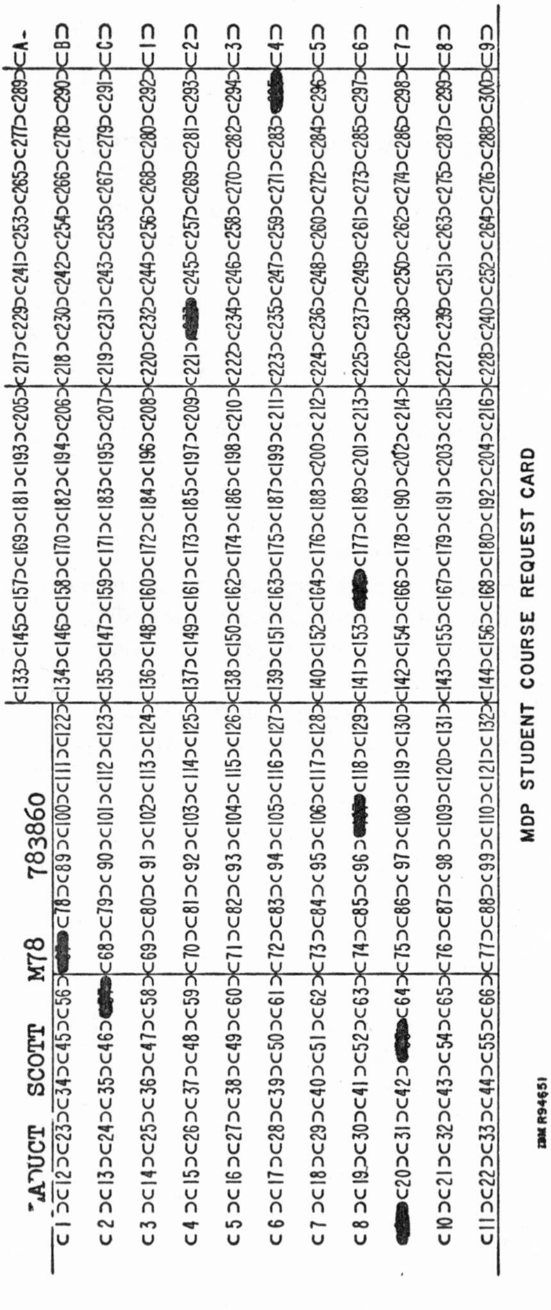

MDP STUDENT COURSE REQUEST CARD

Figure 12.8
Potential Conflict Chart of 1, 2, and 3 Section Courses
(Suggested Number of Sections Included)

	1 ENG 600	3 SST 101	2 SST 201	3 SST 203	2 SST 321	1 SST 421	1 SST 404	1 SST 405	1 SST 406	1 MAT 121	1 MAT 105	3 MAT 201	3 MAT 202	2 MAT 401	2 MAT 402	1 MAT 501	3 SCI 121	2 SCI 203
1 ENG 600	8	0	0	0	0	0	2	2	4	0	0	1	1	2	2	2	0	2
3 SST 101	0	64	2	9	2	0	0	0	0	0	3	6	6	0	0	0	5	1
2 SST 201	0	2	33	2	0	0	0	0	0	0	1	4	4	0	0	0	0	1
3 SST 203	0	9	2	64	0	2	0	1	0	0	0	5	6	1	3	3	3	3
2 SST 321	0	2	0	0	34	0	0	0	0	0	0	0	0	0	0	0	0	0
2 SST 421	0	0	0	2	0	23	0	0	0	0	0	0	0	0	0	0	1	6
1 SST 404	2	0	0	0	0	0	21	3	0	0	0	0	0	3	3	3	0	1
1 SST 405	2	0	0	1	0	0	3	15	0	0	0	0	0	0	0	0	0	0
1 SST 406	4	0	0	0	0	0	0	0	27	0	0	0	0	6	5	2	0	0
1 MAT 121	0	0	0	0	0	0	0	0	0	12	0	0	0	0	0	0	3	0
1 MAT 105	0	3	1	0	0	0	0	0	0	0	20	0	0	0	0	0	0	0
3 MAT 201	1	6	4	5	0	0	0	0	0	0	0	85	65	1	1	0	0	13
3 MAT 202	1	6	4	6	0	0	0	0	0	0	0	85	67	1	0	0	0	14
2 MAT 401	2	0	0	1	0	0	3	0	6	0	0	1	1	37	36	0	0	1
2 MAT 402	2	0	0	3	0	0	3	0	5	0	0	1	0	37	36	0	0	0
1 MAT 501	2	0	0	3	0	0	3	0	2	0	0	0	0	0	0	11	0	0
3 SCI 121	0	5	0	3	0	1	0	0	0	3	0	0	0	0	0	0	32	0
2 SCI 203	2	1	1	3	0	6	1	0	0	0	0	13	14	1	0	0	0	42

Figure 12.9

MIDWEST DATA PROCESSING
Daniel Kinder
West Lafayette, Indiana 47906

Coding Form For Master Schedule

SCHOOL Logansport H.S.
ADDRESS
DATE 4-4-77 PAGE 13 OF 81

Teachers No.	Teachers Name	S	Course Coordination	Period	[illegible]	Days Met (M T W TH F)	Room	Seats Available
13	GORA		65	1	204	X X X X X	5227	
		1		2	79	↑	↑	5
			66	2	80			30
		2		2	81			5
		1		3	79			5
			67	3	80			30
		2		3	81			5
		1		4	79			5
			68	4	80			30
		2		4	81			5
		1		5	79			5
			69	5	80			30
		2		5	81			5
		1		6	79			5
			70	6	80	↓		30
		2		6	81	X X X X X	↓	5
		1	71	7	248	X	7118	35
		2	71	7	248	X	7118	35
1-3		5-6	7-9	11-12	14-16	19-23	24-27	29-31

include the development of class schedules for each student, providing the decision makers with information on the number of students registered for each course, providing homeroom lists, providing class lists for each section, and providing address labels of parents of the students. In addition, class rankings, honor roll lists, failure lists, and grade reports are often produced by these programs. Thus, it can be seen that the principal does indeed have the opportunity to utilize his or her valuable time in such things as professionalizing staff, individualizing instruction, and refining curriculum as opposed to the mundane aspects of schedule construction.

THE SCHOOL CALENDAR

In recent years there have been many plans submitted to reschedule the school year. And each year there are a few school systems which implement a new type of school calendar. Many reasons are given by proponents of year-round schools, including economies in the use of school facilities, differing life styles emerging from agrarian to almost total urban and suburban patterns, and opportunities for staff members to be employed for the full year. Recent efforts to conserve energy in school plant operation have influenced school planners in school calendar arrangements. Nevertheless, we still have a vast majority of schools employing the traditional nine-month school year from September through May or June.

Figure 12.10 is illustrative of the traditional school calendar. This calendar has been developed in cooperation with students, parents, teachers, and central office administrators. The school year usually contains 180 teaching days, with 5 days for preparation and orientation for the school year, and 5 days reserved for faculty professional days and closing of the school year, or a total of 190 duty days. The calendar containing the major events of the year is usually published and made available to students, teachers, and parents.

In contrast to the typical school calendar, Figures 12.11 and 12.12 illustrate two of the many plans suggested for rescheduling the school year.[12]

In Figure 12.11, school is in session for all twelve months of the year and is based on four terms and four sections of the student body, whereby the sections rotate vacations on a quarterly basis.

Figure 12.12 illustrates one of the more discussed continuous learning year plans, the 45–15 calendar. All students are divided into various streams. In essence, all students in a given stream attend school for 45 days exclusive of holidays and weekends and then have 15 days off. Varying patterns of starting a new school year are shown in the illustration. The staggering of vacations with the four 45-day periods, however, still permits the student a total of 180 school days each year, the same as the total number in the traditional schedule.

EFFECTIVE SCHEDULING: A KEY TO EFFICIENT OPERATION

Figure 12.10
Example of a School Calendar

	SEPTEMBER								OCTOBER								NOVEMBER				
S	M	T	W	T	F	S		S	M	T	W	T	F	S		S	M	T	W	T	F	S
					1	2		1	2	3	4	5	6	7					1	2	3	4
3	4	5	6	7	8	9		8	9	10	11	12	13	14		5	6	7	8	9	10	11
10	11	12	13	14	15	16		15	16	17	18	19	20	21		12	13	14	15	16	17	18
17	18	19	20	21	22	23		22	23	24	25	26	27	28		19	20	21	22	23	24	25
24	25	26	27	28	29	30		29	30	31						26	27	28	29	30		

Labor Day — Thanksgiving

	DECEMBER								JANUARY								FEBRUARY				
S	M	T	W	T	F	S		S	M	T	W	T	F	S		S	M	T	W	T	F	S
					1	2			1	2	3	4	5	6					1	2	3
3	4	5	6	7	8	9		7	8	9	10	11	12	13		4	5	6	7	8	9	10
10	11	12	13	14	15	16		14	15	16	17	18	19	20		11	12	13	14	15	16	17
17	18	19	20	21	22	23		21	22	23	24	25	26	27		18	19	20	21	22	23	24
24	25	26	27	28	29	30		28	29	30	31					25	26	27	28	29		
31																					

Christmas — New Years — County Workshop

	MARCH								APRIL								MAY				
S	M	T	W	T	F	S		S	M	T	W	T	F	S		S	M	T	W	T	F	S
					1	2		1	2	3	4	5	6					1	2	3	4
3	4	5	6	7	8	9		7	8	9	10	11	12	13		5	6	7	8	9	10	11
10	11	12	13	14	15	16		14	15	16	17	18	19	20		12	13	14	15	16	17	18
17	18	19	20	21	22	23		21	22	23	24	25	26	27		19	20	21	22	23	24	25
24	25	26	27	28	29	30		28	29	30						26	27	28	29	30	31	
31																					

Easter — Memorial Day

	JUNE					
S	M	T	W	T	F	S
						1
2	3	4	5	6	7	8
9	10	11	12	13	14	15
16	17	18	19	20	21	22
23	24	25				

◇ Teacher days only
○ Vacation days
□ First & last student days

School starts for Teachers—September 5
School starts for Students—September 6
School for Kindergarten—Orientation—Sept. 6, 7, 8
NEOTA—November 3
Thanksgiving—November 23 and 24
Christmas—December 21—January 1 (Inclusive)
End of Semester—January 26—92 Days
County Workshop—February 22—No School
Vacation Day—February 23
Easter Vacation—April 11 through 15
Memorial Day—May 30
Last school day for Students—June 6
Last school day for Teacher—June 7

	Grading Period	Student Days	Report Card
First Semester	Sept. 6 - Oct. 20	33	October 2
	Oct. 23 - Dec. 1	27	December
	Dec. 1 - Jan. 26	32	February
		92 days	
	Jan. 29 - Mar. 8	28	March 14
	Mar. 11 - April 26	32	May 2
	April 29 - June 6	28	June 7
		88 days	
		180 days for students	
		+ 4 days for teachers	

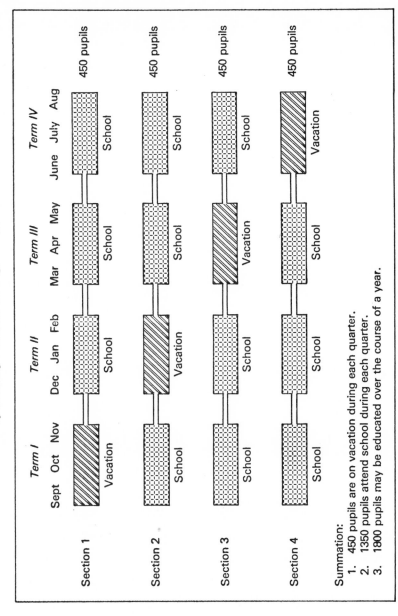

Figure 12.11
The All Year School Based on the Use
of Rotating Vacations on a Quarterly Basis*

Summation:
1. 450 pupils are on vacation during each quarter.
2. 1350 pupils attend school during each quarter.
3. 1800 pupils may be educated over the course of a year.

* George Isaiah Thomas, *Administrator's Guide to the Year-Round School* (West Nyack, N.Y.: Parker Publishing Co., Inc.), 1973, p. 40.

Figure 12.12
Student Vacation Patterns in the Four Stream Continuous Learning Year Program With a Variation of the Forty Five/Fifteen Plan*

CALENDAR	STREAM I M T W Th F	STREAM II M T W Th F	STREAM III M T W Th F	STREAM IV M T W Th F	CALENDAR
July 3	H	H	H	H	July 3
10					10
17					17
24					24
31	Term 1				31
Aug. 7	45 Days				Aug. 7
14		Term 1			14
21		45 Days			21
28					28
Sept. 4	H	H	H	H	Sept. 4
11	VACATION		Term 1		11
18			45 Days		18
25					25
Oct. 2				Term 1	Oct. 2
9	H	H VACATION	H	H	9
16					16
23	H Term 2	H	H	H	23
30	45 Days		VACATION		30
Nov. 6		Term 2			Nov. 6
13		45 Days		VACATION	13
20					20
27	H H	H H	H H	H H	27
Dec. 4			Term 2		Dec. 4
11	VACATION		45 Days		11
18					18
25	H Winter Recess	H Winter Recess	H Winter Recess	H Winter Recess	25
Jan. 1	H	H	H	H	Jan. 1
8		VACATION			8
15				Term 2	15
22	Term 3			45 Days	22
29	45 Days		VACATION		29
Feb. 5		Term 3			Feb. 5
12		45 Days			12
19	H	H	H	H VACATION	19
26					26
Mar. 5			Term 3		Mar. 5
12			45 Days		12
19	VACATION				19
26					26
Apr. 2					Apr. 2
9	Spring Recess H	Spring Recess H	Spring Recess H	Spring Recess H	9
16					16
23		VACATION		Term 3	23
30	Term 4			45 Days	30
May 7	45 Days		VACATION		May 7
14		Term 4			14
21		45 Days			21
28	H	H	H	H VACATION	28
June 4			Term 4		June 4
11	VACATION		45 Days		11
18					18
25					25
July 2	H	H	H	H	July 2
9		VACATION			9
16	START OF A			Term 4	16
23	NEW SCHOOL			45 Days	23
30	YEAR		VACATION		30
Aug. 6		START OF A			Aug. 6
13		NEW SCHOOL		VACATION	13
20		YEAR			20
27			START OF A		27
Sept. 3	H	H	NEW SCHOOL	H	Sept. 3
10	VACATION		YEAR	START OF	10
17				A NEW SCHOOL	17
24		VACATION		YEAR	24
Oct. 1					Oct. 1

H = HOLIDAYS

* George Isaiah Thomas, *Administrator's Guide to the Year-Round School* (West Nyack, N.Y.: Parker Publishing Co., Inc.), 1973, p. 56.

SUMMARY

The secondary school schedule represents the educational plan of the local school. It is imperative that principals be actively involved in the conceptualization of the schedule even though most of the technical aspects will be delegated to their staff.

Principals must be aware of the requirements of the state department of public instruction and those policies and standards of regional accrediting agencies with which their school is associated. They must also constantly be concerned with securing input into the schedule-making process from the community, the students, the teachers, and other groups ultimately affected by the schedule. In terms of output, the schedule must take into consideration philosophies, goals, and objectives of the school and students therein. In this manner it may provide a vehicle of communication to parents regarding their children's pursuit of educational goals.

Many highly specific variables must be considered in the process of schedule development. These include information on student course requests, class size, instructional organization and strategies, length of periods, availability of facilities, and many similar types of variables. A knowledge of conflict-sheet construction is important as is that of the many types of schedules that may be utilized along with the advantages and disadvantages of each. It is also important for principals to know how they may use the computer in scheduling students into the most optimum instructional modes. While traditionally, school is in session for only nine to ten months, it is possible to have year-round scheduling patterns. Wise principals will constantly be seeking better ways of representing and implementing the educational plans of their school as well as those of each student by bringing to bear all the human material and informational resources on the schedule-making process.

NOTES

1. John P. Eichorn, "College Scheduling for the High School," *The Bulletin of the National Association of Secondary School Principals* 60:404 (December, 1976), pp. 93–94.

2. Gordon McCloskey, "Year Round Community Schools: A Framework for Administrative Leadership" (Arlington, Virginia: American Association of School Administrators, 1973).

3. Indiana State Department of Public Instruction. *The Administrative Handbook,* Indianapolis, 1978.

4. "Policies and Standards for the Approval of Secondary Schools" (Chicago: North Central Association of Colleges and Schools, 1977–78).

5. Lester W. Anderson and Lauren A. VanDyke, *Secondary School Administration* (Boston: Houghton-Mifflin Company, 1972), p. 142.

6. Ibid.

7. M. P. Heller, *So Now You're A Principal* (Reston, Va.: National Association of Secondary School Principals, 1975), p. 11.

8. Don E. Glines, *Creating Humane Schools* (Mankato, Minn.: Campus Publishers, 1971), p. 109.

9. Ibid., p. 111.

10. R. W. Heller, L. M. Chaffee and R. G. Davison, "Two Computer-Based School Scheduling Programs Analyzed," *The Bulletin of the National Association of Secondary School Principals* 58:380 (March, 1974), pp. 64–82.

11. From interview with Daniel Kinder of Midwest Data Processing, West Lafayette, Indiana, April 1977.

12. George Isaiah Thomas, *Administrator's Guide to the Year-Round School* (West Nyack, New York: Parker Publishing Co., 1973), pp. 40, 56.

13

The Secondary School Principal and Collective Bargaining

The principals of the sixties were encouraged to become instructional leaders in their school, but the seventies brought concern that the real opportunity for leadership by principals was being eroded with escalation of collective bargaining efforts of teachers.

Collective bargaining, or professional negotiations, is the most recent development of teachers in their attempt to gain the status of true professionals. The development of education as a profession has been very slow. Law and medicine are two examples of professions that have grown at a much swifter pace, with a much greater impact, and with more benefit for their members. Factors which had an effect on the development of education as a profession include: (1) the large number of teachers in the profession who were teaching for a second income, (2) the public service nature of the profession, and (3) the lack of control of entrants into the profession by teachers.

Many administrators look upon the increasing militancy of teachers within the last decade as harmful to education. Many are concerned that their positions may be weakened. Principals are caught between the teachers on one hand, and the superintendents on the other. While their loyalties are with the superintendents (since they are considered part of the administrative team), principals also feel obligated to defend the rights of teachers as professional persons.

Principals have a right to expect to be included in any decision making that concerns their leadership at the building level. When negotiated agreements contain provisions concerning the number of times a faculty may meet during the month, the number of students that teachers may teach each day, or the number of classes that may be taught, principals must make their voices heard.

AFT-NEA RIVALRY

One of the perplexing problems facing the profession of education, especially of urban education, is the rivalry which exists between the American Federation of Teachers and the National Education Association. The NEA claims a membership of 1,600,800 teachers; the AFT claims 400,000 members.[1] Teachers are faced with the problem of deciding which organization to join; some join both. As a result of efforts by both organizations to show their worth to teachers, they have been more militant in their demands for the welfare goals of teachers. Even the most adroit principal in tiptoeing around issues is often caught in the middle between these two organizations.

Some would say that this rivalry is good for the educational profession, especially in the light of the recent salary and other welfare advances made by teachers. Advantages as well as disadvantages have arisen from this rivalry. For example, real progress in some school systems has been hampered by the failure of these two organizations to put together a united front, in their bickering over who will represent the teachers in professional negotiations or collective bargaining. On the other hand, conflict between the two organizations has caused both to compete for higher salaries and better working conditions for their members.

The NEA was founded in 1857. The National Education Association has been more tranquil in its evolution, and until recent years, had deplored the use of the strike in obtaining its demands. Collective bargaining for increased teacher salaries and improved working conditions is used by the NEA. If, through the use of collective bargaining, improved salaries and working conditions were not obtained, the organization might have imposed sanctions against a local school district or state. This meant that members of the NEA, other than presently employed teachers of the district, would not sign contracts with the sanctioned district. In recent years, however, the National Education Association has supported strike action to gain desired goals.

The history of the American Federation of Teachers has been stormy. Opposition to unionism led the Chicago Board of Education to outlaw teachers' unions in 1916. However, with the support of labor, the newly organized American Federation of Teachers union was able to obtain an injunction against enforcement of this resolution. The AFT became a critical issue with the Seattle superintendent of schools in 1930, when he said: "It should be known that I am making the facts public so that people will know that I will not attempt to direct the work of the Seattle public schools if the Federation of Teachers, affiliated with the American Federation of Labor, gains a foothold in the schools."[2] *The American Teacher,* the official organ of the American Federation of Teachers, reported a short time later that Superintendent Cole announced that he would not consider continuing the superintendency in any event and that he had resigned to take another position.[3]

While the merger of AFT-NEA may occur in the future, current controversy between the two organizations focuses upon the following areas:

1. Right to represent teachers in negotiations with the local board of education.
2. Use of the strike by both the NEA and the AFT.
3. Denial of administrator membership in AFT, and increasing denial with local associations.
4. Close affiliation of AFT with labor organizations.

The increased collective action by teachers, which has been encouraged by this rivalry, has intensified the activity of principals' organizations to develop guidelines explaining the principal's role. This increased interest in collective bargaining and collective negotiations has practically nullified the school administrator"s leadership of the teachers' professional organization, and his or her membership is no longer desired by the teachers. Besides the new interpretation of the role of the principal in the teachers' organization, the principal is increasingly being faced with the dilemma of what to do when teachers strike. While it is generally accepted that strikes by public employees against their public employer are illegal, courts are reluctant to render clear-cut decisions. Consequently, teachers do utilize this weapon in enforcing demands.

The AFT and NEA approach to collective bargaining for teachers has resulted in the formation of some teacher groups with less militant stances. One such group is The National Association of Professional Educators (NAPE).

STATUS OF TEACHER COLLECTIVE BARGAINING

All principals should be well informed about existing laws, attorney general opinions, and court cases that relate to teacher negotiations. While it is impossible to present the details of the laws in the various states, Table 13.1 indicates the 1975 legal status of regulations in each state. It can be seen that twenty-eight states required teacher negotiations, ten states permitted teacher negotiations, two states had meet and confer provisions, three states prohibited negotiations, while seven states and the District of Columbia had some other position concerning collective bargaining.

Table 13.2 indicates the number of collective bargaining agreements by state for the years 1966-67, 1968-69, 1970-71, and 1972-73. It can be noted that for 1972-73, 934,794 teachers from 2,556 school systems had collective bargaining agreements. This was a rather large increase from the 389 school systems which had collective bargaining agreements in 1966-67. More and more states are establishing laws which clarify the role of the board of education in negotiating with collective groups of teachers. The National

Education Association as well as the American Federation of Teachers is writing and supporting legislation which allows collective groups of teachers to negotiate with the board of education.

THE PRINCIPAL'S ROLE IN COLLECTIVE BARGAINING

It is clear that principals are in limbo concerning their role in collective bargaining. Their leadership is being threatened as more and more bargained agreements for teachers reduce their alternatives for decision making.

It has been suggested that principals help in preparing the agenda for the negotiation meetings of the teacher's association and the superintendent. Others have suggested that principals are really teachers and should serve on the side of the teachers' group in the negotiating process. Some fear that principals will be considered part of management as in the labor-management concept of private industry. This, it is said, will harm the close relationship which principals now have with teachers. Some also say that teaching does not relate to labor and that the labor-management concept does not apply to the educational profession.

Table 13.1
Legal Status of Teacher
Negotiations by State*

A. *Negotiations Required by Statute*

Alaska	Montana
Connecticut	Nevada
Delaware	New Hampshire
Florida	New Jersey
Hawaii	New York
Idaho	North Dakota
Indiana	Oklahoma
Iowa	Oregon
Kansas	Pennsylvania
Maine	Rhode Island
Maryland	South Dakota
Massachusetts	Vermont
Michigan	Washington
Minnesota	Wisconsin

* U.S. Department of Labor, Management Services Administration. Division of Public Employee Labor Relations. Summary of State Policy Regulations for Public Sector Labor Relations: Statutes, Attorney General's Opinions, and Selected Court Decisions (1975).

THE PRINCIPAL ROLE IN COLLECTIVE BARGAINING

Table 13.1 *cont'd.*

B. *Negotiations Permitted***

Arizona	—CL
Arkansas	—CL, AGO
Georgia	—AGO
Illinois	—CL
Kentucky	—AGO
Louisiana	—CL, AGO
New Mexico	—CL, AGO
Utah	—AGO
Virginia	—AGO

West Virginia—CL, AGO (May negotiate and sign written agreeements, but final decision is subject to and may be unilaterally changed by employer.)

C. *Meet and Confer*

California—Statute (Requires meet and confer)
Nebraska —Statute (Board approval required before meet and confer)

D. *Negotiations Prohibited*

Missouri —AGO (Right is granted to present proposals)

Texas —State Statute

Tennessee—CL (Counties and municipalities do not have authority to enter CBA)***

E. *Other*

Alabama	—State Statute (Consultation with superintendent)
Colorado	—AGO (Meet and confer permitted, CL (Public employees have no authority to enter into C.B.A.)
District of Columbia—(History of defacto collective bargaining)	
Mississippi	—(No legislative or policy guidelines for public sector labor relations)
North Carolina	—Statute (Any contract between a public employer and a labor organization is against public policy and of no effect)
Ohio	—No definitive statement of law
South Carolina	—(No provision—prohibited as a matter of state policy)
Wyoming	—No clear legal position

** AGO—Attorney General Opinion
    CL —Case Law
*** CBA—Collective Bargained Agreement

Table 13.2

Distribution of Teacher Collective Bargaining Agreements, By State: 1966-67, 1968-69, 1970-71, and 1972-73.*

	Number of school systems				Number of teachers			
State	1966-67	1968-69	1970-71	1972-73	1966-67	1968-69	1970-71	1972-73
1	2	3	4	5	6	7	8	9
Alaska (1970)**	…	…	2	5	…	…	1,750	2,656
Arizona	…	2	7	16	…	2,352	5,499	9,424
Arkansas	…	1	1	3	…	1,129	1,129	1,873
California (1965)	…	1	13	28	…	4,692	11,447	19,827
Colorado	1	4	11	16	724	9,575	12,554	16,648
Connecticut (1965)	42	71	88	89	15,964	26,344	29,655	31,527
Delaware (1969)	…	…	12	17	…	…	4,100	5,122
District of Columbia	…	1	1	1	…	8,000	8,000	7,250
Florida	…	…	2	5	…	…	4,240	12,781
Georgia	…	…	…	1	…	…	…	1,698
Hawaii (1970)	…	…	…	1	…	…	…	9,769
Idaho (1971)	…	…	2	5	…	…	334	1,755
Illinois	10	33	92	142	22,764	35,566	48,917	58,301
Indiana (1973)	…	8	20	27	…	5,765	15,179	17,132
Iowa	…	…	…	2	…	…	…	1,290
Kansas (1970)	…	1	1	15	…	3,358	3,358	5,515
Kentucky	…	…	2	4	…	…	4,300	7,112
Maine (1969)	…	…	40	44	…	…	5,580	5,846
Maryland (1968)	…	2	21	21	…	9,160	43,128	44,810
Massachusetts (1965)	55	135	167	181	15,677	39,527	47,717	55,126
Michigan (1965)	237	332	354	383	63,072	81,406	83,938	89,809

Minnesota (1967)	1	1	1	58	146	146	146	20,664
Missouri	⋯	1	1	3	⋯	850	850	4,039
Montana (1971)	⋯	2	2	6	⋯	568	568	1,337
Nebraska	⋯	1	6	9	⋯	72	4,657	6,044
Nevada (1969)	⋯	⋯	2	3	⋯	⋯	4,150	4,518
New Hampshire	⋯	⋯	6	13	⋯	⋯	1,436	3,387
New Jersey (1968)	1	6	228	278	3,650	6,357	51,193	68,084
New Mexico	⋯	⋯	1	1	⋯	⋯	2,400	3,200
New York (1967)	8	319	435	476	62,314	148,403	172,068	181,938
North Dakota (1967)	⋯	⋯	3	7	⋯	⋯	653	1,422
Ohio	1	13	63	114	271	15,821	34,098	46,521
Oklahoma (1971)	⋯	⋯	1	1	⋯	⋯	2,830	2,410
Oregon (1965)	⋯	⋯	3	25	⋯	⋯	4,837	10,227
Pennsylvania (1970)	1	5	33	281	11,000	14,477	22,374	74,555
Rhode Island (1966)	9	22	24	26	2,460	7,794	8,098	8,637
South Dakota (1969)	⋯	⋯	2	3	⋯	⋯	986	1,572
Tennessee	⋯	⋯	⋯	1	⋯	⋯	⋯	4,200
Texas	⋯	⋯	1	4	⋯	⋯	766	11,546
Utah	⋯	4	7	8	⋯	4,007	4,982	5,450
Vermont (1969)	⋯	⋯	3	9	⋯	⋯	749	1,573
Virginia	⋯	2	2	4	⋯	2,396	2,396	10,770
Washington (1965)	1	3	22	47	380	2,396	13,667	19,363
Wisconsin (1959)	22	56	141	169	10,011	19,062	31,213	36,367
Wyoming	⋯	1	2	4	⋯	650	1,382	1,699
Total	389	1,027	1,825	2,556	208,433	448,142	697,324	934,794

* *Negotiation Research Digest*, 7:5 (January, 1974), p. 16. Reprinted by permission. © National Education Association.

** Year of passage of P.N. law.

While principals have vested interest in the welfare of their teachers, salaries and sick leave can be negotiated without their direct involvement, although they should be represented in the negotiations session. Principals must have a direct role in the following types of negotiations if they are to maintain their necessary leadership role.

1. Matters related to curriculum.
2. Matters related to the welfare of students.
3. Attendance of the faculty to small-group or large-group professional improvement conferences both inside and outside the building.
4. Matters related to management of the building, which include:
    a. Scheduling
    b. Opening and closing time
    c. Lunch hours
    d. Organization of the school calendar
    e. Hiring, evaluating, releasing, assignment, and transfer of teachers
    f. Assignment of substitutes
    g. Promotion policy
    h. Student discipline policy
    i. Personnel policy
5. Matters concerning parent-school relations.
6. Grievance procedures.

Principals must remember that they will in all probability be the persons charged with implementing the contract. They must insist upon being involved in the negotiation process by either (1) serving as a chief negotiator, (2) serving as an observer, or (3) serving as consultant to the negotiating team representing the board of education.

Weldy suggests that principals should develop their own proposals to prepare for bargaining with teachers and would do well to spend time performing the following:*

1. Review the current contract to identify clauses that have caused problems in its administration, including:
    a. Ambiguous clauses that have been the source of conflicting interpretations requiring grievance action to clarify.
    b. Inconsistencies in the contract, frequently the result of "zero hour" bargaining when last-ditch efforts to wrap up an agreement are made. (Example: confusing and

---

* From Gilbert R. Weldy, "Administering a Negotiated Contract," *The National Association of Secondary School Principals* (Reston, Va.: 1973), pp. 8, 9. Used by permission.

inconsistent language like "normal teaching schedule," "overall teaching schedule," "teacher's normal load," and "classroom teaching.")

   c. Loose or time-consuming procedures for carrying out contractual rights.

   d. Any clauses that would effectively block changes in school reorganization or program innovation that are anticipated by the administration. Such change may not have been contemplated when the contract was negotiated and may not have presented problems. (Example: unanticipated need to reduce staff as a result of dropping enrollment or budget cutbacks or a desire to use differentiated staffing.)

   e. Any clause that interferes with the principal's normal prerogatives. (Example: not being able to change any "working condition" or "customary duty" without the agreement of the teachers' bargaining agent.)

   f. Any gaps in the contract that raise issues over where authority lies.

   g. Any clause that tends to favor certain teachers or certain groups of teachers. (Example: union members favored over non-union members.)

   h. Any clause that does not recognize the administrator's right to evaluate and assign teachers according to their qualifications and abilities. (Example: most seniority provisions.)

2. Review the contract for clauses that have not interfered with the administration of the school and at the same time have been fair and equitable for teachers. These should be included for "no charge."

3. Initiate proposals that administrators need for proper authority and control and for meaningful and efficient decision making on education issues. For example:

   a. Proposals to set up educational decision-making councils with parents, students and teachers.

   b. Proposals to provide school or departmental autonomy.

   c. Proposals to simplify curriculum development procedures.

   d. Proposals to clarify teachers' responsibilities for extra-class activities, supervision, non-teaching duties, definition of the school day.

   e. Proposals to improve teacher evaluation procedures.[4]

Weldy further states:

> . . . that a board position should be developed for each pro-
> posal after the proposals have been divided into economic and
> non-economic issues in the following general categories:
>
> accept without conditions
>
> accept with modifications
>
> accept with a "bargain"—look for a tradeoff
>
> hold and resist to late stages of negotiations for a "hard
> bargain"
>
> resist to the end—a strike issue
>
> non-negotiable—not appropriate for bargaining.
>
> . . . It is imperative that all teacher proposals be analyzed for
> their cost, their effect on the educational program of the dis-
> trict, and if they benefit students.[5]

Principals should further insure that they be involved in setting up the
grievance procedure since they normally will be the first level persons to deal
with grievances. They must understand all provisions of the negotiated contract and how the provisions are to be implemented if they are to avoid
spending a great amount of time dealing with grievances. An analysis of all
grievances filed should be made so that an attempt can be made to prevent a
reoccurrence of similar grievances.

IMPASSE PROCEDURES

Principals should be familiar with procedures utilized to overcome an
impasse or deadlock during negotiations. Three different techniques,
(1) mediation, (2) fact finding, and (3) arbitration, are used to resolve conflicts which bring the negotiation process to a standstill.

Mediation involves the use of a third party who seeks to determine the
causes of differences of opinion by holding separate meetings with the
parties involved. The mediator will then seek to assist the two parties to
reach a compromise on the issues which brought about the conflict, and thus
resume the bargaining process. Mediation is voluntary and the resulting
recommendations are advisory and nonbinding.

If mediation fails, fact finding would normally follow. During fact
finding a single fact finder or a panel of three investigate the causes of the
impasse, prepare a written report, and issue recommendations for settling
the dispute. The recommendations developed as a result of fact finding are
almost always advisory and nonbinding.

Arbitration is a process which utilizes a third party to make a decision
as to how the impasse should be resolved. The results of arbitration are

normally binding unless state laws prevent binding arbitration. Arbitration could also be utilized during the grievance procedure if other steps in the grievance process fail.

THE ROLE OF A PRINCIPAL IN A TEACHER STRIKE

Most often, the attitude of the board of education and administration is to attempt to keep the schools open during a teacher strike. Normally, building level principals are expected to keep the building in operation despite reduced staff numbers.

Bernard Hatch, a superintendent of schools of a K–12 district of 13,000 students described how his district remained in operation during a five-day strike. Hatch is a strong advocate of developing a plan before a strike occurs which describes how to deal with a strike. He indicates that one should follow these steps in devising such a plan:

1. With the board attorney, review pertinent legislation and other legal incumbencies that apply to your situation.
2. Review all pertinent board policies and modify those that are too vague or too rigid.
3. Line up replacement teachers and have them briefed and ready to go.
4. Plan a public information center—its whereabouts, its staff, and its equipment.
5. Plan an internal communications center—its whereabouts, its staff, and its equipment.
6. Have a comprehensive security plan in place well in advance of the anticipated strike date.[6]

Building level principals are probably key persons to assist in determining if a strike is imminent. Some signs principals may observe are (1) teachers performing only duties specifically required of them; (2) teachers boycotting teacher meetings, school related activities, and school board meetings; and (3) enlistment of student support of the teachers' point of view.

DECIDING WHETHER PRINCIPALS SHOULD BARGAIN FOR THEMSELVES

Since principals are part of the administrative team, they face pressure to withdraw from membership in an organization which represents teachers and work toward the establishment of a strong organization composed of members of their own profession. Teacher organizations are no longer interested in offering membership in their units to representatives of management.

The "team management" concept is not accepted by all principals since many feel superintendents only want to restrain principals from expressing their own desires. Principals are concerned that once they align themselves with the management team they will be forced to refrain from voicing their own concerns so that a united front may be presented while negotiating with teachers.

Principals must explore and determine the most feasible way to develop a position of strength in the negotiation process. This will mean that principals can no longer remain members of a teachers' organization. Principals may have to develop a strong organization on a regional or state basis.

Many principals are currently trying to decide if, as a group of principals, they should negotiate with central office personnel and/or the school board to secure benefits of their own. The team management concept has caused frustration among some principals because they feel it may be a scheme to make them feel they have a voice in the operation of the school system so they will not organize and bargain collectively. Some principals have already organized and are bargaining collectively. Some have formed groups which simply present a set of recommendations concerning their desires, but do not bargain in a formal way. Principals normally show a concern about the following items: salaries and fringe benefits, job security (contracts longer than one year and a due process dismissal procedure), job descriptions, and a definitive rational, evaluation procedure.[7]

SUMMARY

In summary, the authors recommend the following approach and attitude by principals in professional negotiations:

1. Negotiation can be a positive force in education and need not destroy the professional relationship of principals with their staff.
2. Perceptive principals can adjust to negotiations and make the best of their working relationship.
3. The positive aspect of professional negotiation includes utilization of greater human resource to advance the educational system and improve the democratic atmosphere of the school.
4. Principals must insist that they be involved in the negotiations process and, if necessary, do so collectively.
5. Principals must protect their right to be the professional leader of their school.

6. Mutual respect, shared decision making, and cooperation should always be promoted by principals.

7. Principals have the right of support by their superintendent, their board, and their teachers. They need to know what their responsibilities are. Therefore, the authors suggest that a general job description of each principal's position should be made.

NOTES

1. Encyclopedia of Associations, Volume 1: National Organizations of the U. S. (Detroit, Michigan: Gale Research Co., 1976), pp. 440, 1105.

2. *The American Teacher* 14:7 (March, 1930), p. 15.

3. *The American Teacher* 14:8 (April, 1930), p. 12.

4. Gilbert R. Weldy, "Administering a Negotiated Contract," *The National Association of Secondary School Principals* (Reston, Va.: 1973), pp. 8, 9.

5. Ibid., p. 10.

6. A. Bernard Hatch, "How to Keep Your Schools Open During a Teacher Strike," *The American School Board Journal* 163:3 (March, 1976) pp. 23–27.

7. Benjamin Epstein, "Principals: An Organized Force for Leadership," *The National Association of Secondary School Principals* (Reston, Va.: 1974).

CHAPTER
14
The Principal and the Management of Supporting School Services

The central office can develop policy and general regulations relating to the operation of the supporting school services; however, building level principals must insure their actual functioning. As such, principals must be aware of guidelines which will permit them to evaluate the effectiveness of the supporting school services in their building. This chapter provides these guidelines.

OFFICE MANAGEMENT

Communication with parents, completing state and local reports, receiving visitors, ordering supplies, and the multitude of tasks involved in keeping the secondary school running efficiently, require that educational leaders provide an effective organizational plan. The first essential is the delegation of office management to a pleasant and well-organized person employed in the school office. In a small school of less than 400 students, it is possible that one full-time secretary with student assistants can handle the position. In larger schools, it may be necessary to assign a full-time secretary to each assistant principal.

Good secretarial help allows the educational leaders and their assistants to use their professional talents in improving the educational program. Principals who must type their own letters and maintain their own records are most likely accomplishing these tasks at the expense of more important ones (and probably less efficiently than a secretary). Professional matters such as assisting teachers and working with students in improving the learning environment are certainly more important considerations for principals.

The secondary school administrative office as the center of educational and extra-class activities portrays to the visitor the nature of the school. It is important, therefore, that it be a warm and friendly place as well as a place that emits efficiency and alertness. Inactivity, unkempt appearance, and other such unattractive aspects of the office reflect the same image for the school program. One of the first priorities of principals should be to develop the office aesthetically, giving the visitor or student the impression that it is an inviting place to visit. Art work and other samples of students' work impress the visitor that the school is a warm and active environment for learning.

While educational leaders spend a minimum amount of time in office organizational matters, they do have an obligation to be available for students, parents, salespersons, and teachers who wish to see them. Some might advocate that principals should have no office so that they are forced to be involved in the educational program. The authors, however, recommend that principals maintain a private office in which conferences may be held in quiet and attractive surroundings.

Anderson and Van Dyke list the following managerial and secretarial tasks that are usually performed by principals and their office staff:*

1. *Communicating*—Exchanging information by such means as intercom systems, bulletins, telephone correspondence, and face-to-face conferences.

2. *Processing materials*—typing, duplicating, etc.

3. *Handling correspondence and mail*—preparing and filing letters for professional staff and processing staff mail.

4. *Procuring supplies and equipment*—for both the professional and non-professional staffs.

5. *Administering attendance*—checking, recording, and clearing student attendance.

6. *Directing the daily program*—control and necessary adjustments in the daily schedule and movement of students.

7. *Administering records*—maintaining, storing, summarizing, and supplying information.

8. *Preparing reports*—the principal's annual report, reports to the state, reports to accrediting agencies, financial summaries, and the like.

9. *Serving as control center for the operation of the physical plant*—making certain that heat, ventilation, lights, cleaning, and other services are functioning.

10. *Implementing relations with the public*—conducting business with lay visitors and providing information.

---

* From *Secondary School Administration,* 2nd ed. by Anderson and Van Dyke. Copyright © 1972 by Houghton Mifflin Company. Used by permission of the publisher.

11. *Troubleshooting*—meeting emergency situations that call
for on-the-spot-action.[1]

Principals supervise these functions of their office, but delegate such
tasks as answering the telephone, processing materials, administering attendance, and keeping records. However, the work of communicating, directing the daily program, preparing reports, and implementing relations with
the public often must be personally assumed by principals.

The following are considerations in the office management of the
secondary school:

1. The overall management of office affairs such as duplicating,
answering the telephone, receiving visitors, and typing should be delegated
to the principal's secretary.

2. The principal should develop effective human relations with his or
her office staff so that they will feel that their work is essential and important. These human relations efforts should also be extended through the
office staff to parents, students, and visitors. It is of prime importance that
the principal promote good feeling within the office and the school.

3. The school office, the principal's office, and the offices of his or
her assistants should be easily accessible to the public and the professional
staff. Usually it is located near the main entrance of the building.

4. In addition to its accessibility, the principal's office must have privacy. This is clearly described in the following educational specification for
the principal's office:

The principal's office must be designed to allow accessibility as
well as privacy. It must be located so that one door opens
directly into or near the secretarial space so that the visitor,
who will be screened by the secretary, can be conveniently
received. In addition, the office must have another door by
which the principal can enter or leave the administrative suite
without being observed from the waiting area.

The office must be sound-isolated from the secretarial space as
well as other offices in the administrative suite. Its character
should be uninstitutional, with consideration given to the use of
wall-to-wall carpeting, wood paneling, and draperies.[2]

5. The central secondary school office should contain a waiting area
and ample space for completion of the function as listed earlier.

6. Typewriters, dictaphones, filing cabinets, copying machines, etc.,
should be in ample supply to complete efficiently the work of the office.

7. An orderly arrangement should be made for the storage of records
and supplies.

Guidelines for Filing, Storage, and Use of Office Records

The filing and storage of office materials and records, if completed under a systematic plan, can result in a neat and efficient office area. It must be a system that is easily understood by all office workers and one in which materials and records accumulate into great masses over the years. Therefore, it is important that only that which is necessary and convenient be kept. Unnecessary materials should be weeded out.

The Family Educational Rights and Privacy Act of 1974 provides the federal government with the right to deny federal funds to any school district that does not permit parents access to their children's files. Specific procedures for granting access to a student's file must be developed. Thus, it becomes most important to make sure that only relevant material is retained in a student's file.

The following guidelines are presented to assist principals in developing procedures for the storage and use of records:

1. Storage facilities should be fireproof and be kept in a vault or other locked quarters.
2. Storage facilities should be located where their security can be insured but still be accessible to teachers when needed. This will probably mean storage close to but not in the principal's private office.
3. Separate file drawers and/or cabinets should be developed for each variety of records kept, such as financial, student activities, cumulative folders for students, information concerning teachers, annual reports prepared by the principal, and curricular information for inservice training.
4. A system of color coding of records and record storage assists in return of records to the proper place after use.
5. Counselors probably should have a separate set of the needed student records for their use located in their office.
6. Forms should be developed to grant permission for those who need to use records and to record names of those using records. These should conform to the intent of such laws or regulations as the Family Educational Rights and Privacy Act of 1974.
7. A periodic review of all information contained in office files should be made to eliminate unnecessary material.
8. The principal should be the certified person responsible for the record keeping system; however, a trained secretary should be delegated the responsibility for the day-to-day storage and use of records. It is helpful in maintaining the order of records to have one secretary designated to secure and file records after use. However, the filing system should be understood by all who need to use them.

9. The record keeping system should be compatible among and between all grade levels and all schools within the corporation.

10. Records should be such that easy duplication can be accomplished in cases where copies of records are to be sent in the mail.

11. When feasible, records should be transferred to a storage area that utilizes automated data processing. This will decrease the amount of storage space needed and increase the ability to retrieve the needed information.

12. Check to see if the state department of public instruction has developed model record keeping instruments and systems. Professional associations also often develop model guidelines for such information.

13. Establish a set of guidelines for data gathering which includes an explanation as to why the data is needed.

14. Periodic inservice training sessions on the use of student records should be conducted.

Improving the Office and Office Staff

Secondary school leaders cannot neglect the office area or their secretarial staff. If first impressions are lasting impressions, as they often are, wise principals will create an office atmosphere that is pleasing to all concerned. They can set the standards by being courteous, friendly, and neat. In addition, inservice training of secretarial help can be established in such areas as telephone courtesy, meeting the public, being courteous and friendly with students, and maintaining good relations with teachers.

The central school office can be an excellent place for students to supplement their regular classroom instruction in learning to become secretaries. They can also be a great help in accomplishing the work of the office. Principals must be careful to insure that the students are not taken advantage of and that they receive a wide variety of secretarial experiences.

The inservice training would involve the development of job descriptions cooperatively between the secretarial staff and the principal. Policies, procedures, and suggestions for accomplishing the work of the office could be detailed in an office manual for new help.

Encouraging them to be active in their professional organization and their attendance at workshops would also enhance the work of the office staff. Involving secretaries in faculty social events would also provide for better relationship between the faculty and office personnel. Secretaries may also be involved in curriculum change and improvement so that they will feel part of the educational program.

The areas of improving the office staff would include:

1. Skills in typing and shorthand.

2. Skills in greeting visitors and answering the telephone.

3. Improving the filing system.
4. Improving and simplifying record keeping.
5. Bookkeeping skills.
6. Human relations skills with students and teachers.
7. Personal appearance.
8. Office housekeeping.

Principals may not have a polished secretary or office staff, but through a good inservice program refinement can be developed. The goal for which principals should be striving is a reduction in the amount of time which they spend in their office so that the time saved can be used in instructional improvement. Without an improvement plan, and with poor organization, it will be necessary for principals to spend too large a portion of their time on office affairs while the instructional program suffers. Principals spending more than one-fourth of their time on noninstructional activities need to review their office organizational structure and their secretarial improvement plan.

Data Processing Procedures

Much of the time consumed in grade reporting, financial accounting, attendance keeping, and class scheduling can be reduced through proper use of electric and electronic data processing machines. Through proper programming, data processing machines can accomplish individual student scheduling, provide printouts of a list of students in each class, maintain data on a magnetic disc which can store information for later retrieval for grade reporting, or other statistical needs. Educational leaders need to be aware of the possible uses of data processing so that they may intelligently utilize these as time and space-saving devices.

Principals have a choice of utilizing local or district data processing equipment, or using various commercial sources outside the school for the processing of data. Some commercial companies provide a full line of data processing services such as school scheduling, progress reporting, attendance accounting, and research and census tabulation. The costs of these services per student are normally well within the range of the average district school budget.

The two principal advantages of automatic data processing are: (1) speed, with the accompanying saving of time, and (2) great reduction in the need for storage space. This is dramatically illustrated by Van Uxem as follows:

Let me give you an idea of the tremendous compactness of magnetic tape for data storage. A standard 2,400 foot reel of tape could easily contain all the data from a card file of 164,000 punched cards. Those cards would fill eighty-two boxes, and those boxes stacked in two equal piles would touch a twelve foot ceiling. That is a lot of data. That reel of tape measures only ten inches in diameter and five eighths of an inch in thickness.

Besides the advantage of compact storage, magnetic tape offers us the advantage of high input speed. We are able to enter data into our processor at much higher speeds than we can with punched cards. This ability allows us to make more efficient use of our processing unit. It does not have to wait idly for data after it completes processing for one record. If we could speed up a card reader to a rate of 5,400 cards a minute, we could match the speed of the slowest tapes. If we could speed up the card reader to 255,000 cards a minute, we could match the fastest tapes.[3]

A wide variety of applications of data processing are possible for the secondary school. These include business accounting; keeping records of instructional materials; personnel records such as applicant interviews; special qualifications of teachers; pupil records containing such information as birth dates, parent employment, attendance, and home address; scheduling of students into classes; class lists and homeroom lists for students; progress reporting with a statistical analysis of grading teachers; and immediate recall of students' records for transcripts to colleges and other purposes.

Student accounting with all its ramifications of scheduling, transcript reporting, etc., provides the most fruitful area for gaining advantage in the use of data processing. Through the use of a telephone line and a terminal (usually a typewriter connected to the computer), much of the communication that is needed to provide useful information to and from the computer can be made.

In the registration process, in which the computer is utilized to complete the master schedule, all information necessary for attendance accounting can be stored in a magnetic tape. This disc storage file can be updated when necessary through a locally installed terminal system.

Data can be provided for the computer which will permit printouts of mailable grade reports for parents; analysis of grades for teachers, counselors, principals, and central office staff; and reports necessary for permanent records. Included with the grade reports can be a student attendance summary.

The authors recommend the following considerations for educational leaders in data processing:

1. A basic course in the processing of data electrically and electronically is essential for those preparing for administrative and supervisory positions. Educational leaders need to understand the possible applications of the computer and automated data processing so that they may take advantage of its possibilities.

2. Educational leaders need to know they can communicate with the computer either through their own understanding of programming or through a skilled programmer. Programming enables the input to be provided to the various machines and the computer so that it will complete the desired outcomes.

3. Educational leaders should have a basic understanding of the economics of the use of data processing. This would include costs of installations and avoiding expensive installation of equipment that would soon be obsolete because of newer developments.

BUSINESS MANAGEMENT

One occasionally reads of school officials receiving bad publicity because of their shabby handling of financial affairs of a secondary school. The financing of student activities and the handling of secondary school financial records can be big business and are a responsibility which must not be slighted by principals. However, managing the financial affairs of the secondary school can waste much of the principals' time, which should be reserved for other educational activities.

The authors recommend that principals understand the bookkeeping system of their activities fund and other financial affairs of the secondary school. With the complete understanding of the financial bookkeeping and reporting system, educational leaders can train a competent bookkeeper-typist in the proper keeping of records. This bookkeeper-typist can be bonded, then held responsible for the financial records, with the principal providing a periodic check to insure that the records are properly kept.

Student Activity Accounting

Figure 14.1 indicates a suggested procedure to follow in effective financial record keeping for student activity funds. Many states have prescribed forms and accounting procedures for use in extra-curricular accounting.

The state legislature of Ohio, after several instances of improper accounting procedures for the student activities programs, has made it obligatory for boards of education (through their appointed school officers) to follow legally prescribed accounting procedures for the activities program. The following procedures have been adopted:

1. *Accounts.* All student activity funds and accounts must be approved and established by the board of education. All monies received into student activity accounts shall be used solely for the purpose of the proper activity program. The transfer of money between funds must be approved by the board of education. The transfer of money between accounts within a fund must be approved by the building principal.

Figure 14.1
Student Activity Fund:
Flow Chart of Purchases and Expenditures

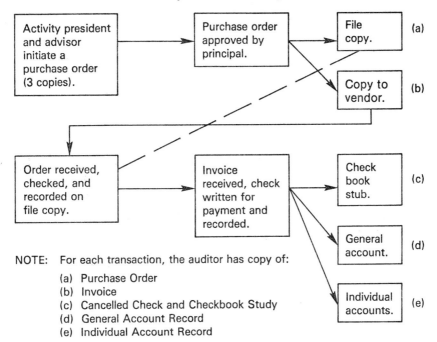

NOTE: For each transaction, the auditor has copy of:

    (a) Purchase Order
    (b) Invoice
    (c) Cancelled Check and Checkbook Study
    (d) General Account Record
    (e) Individual Account Record

2. *Clerk-Custodian.* The board of education shall appoint a clerk-custodian of each school. The clerk-custodian serves at the pleasure of the board of education. The clerk-custodian must execute a bond, in an amount and with surety approved by the board; or, the clerk-custodian must be covered by a blanket bond approved by the board.

3. *Administrative Officer.* The building principal is the authorized accountable administrative officer of each school and must approve all expenditures from the activity funds.

4. *Expenditures.* The clerk-custodian is authorized to certify on the activity requisition and pay-out voucher the amount and, if the account balance is sufficient to meet the expenditure, the certification shall constitute the authorization to purchase the materials and/or services. Such certification must be made prior to the creation of the obligation.

5. *Investment.* Monies declared inactive by board resolution may be invested in certificates of deposit or treasure bills and/or notes. Savings accounts are not permitted. The reso-

lution authorizing such investments must specifically state the total amount to be invested, the type of investment to be procured, and the source of the monies by activity program. Interest earned on such investments shall be prorated to the proper fund or activity account based upon the percentage of investment of such fund to the overall investment. The clerk-custodian shall prepare a pay-in order for all interest earnings when received allocating the proper amount to each activity program. Investments are not expensed from the cash control balance. A check is issued for the amount of the investment but is not posted either to the cash control ledger or to the cash fund ledger. Only the amount received over and above the cost price is picked up on a pay-in order as current income.

6. *Financial Statements.* The clerk-custodian of the activity funds is required to furnish a monthly statement of fund balances and a reconciliation with the depository bank to the board of education with a copy to the faculty sponsor of each activity program. An annual report is also required to be filed with the board of education.

7. *System of Accounting.* The accounting system of student activity program funds consists of the following basic records:

1. Pay-in order
2. Activity requisition and pay-out order
3. Cash control-activity account
4. Cash fund ledger

8. *Pay-In Order Form.* (1) The original shall be retained by the clerk-custodian and used as a source of entry to the cash control and the cash fund ledger sheets, and will be retained, in consecutive numerical sequence, in a permanent file following such posting for audit purposes. (2) The second copy shall be retained by the clerk-custodian and placed in a permanent file by activity program, in numerical sequence for audit purposes. (3) The third copy will serve as a receipt and shall be given to the payee at the time the pay-in voucher is completed by the clerk-custodian.

9. *Activity Requisition and Pay-Out Order Voucher.* Approval for an expenditure must be secured and the availability of funds certified by the clerk-custodian prior to the creation of a liability against any activity account. Upon receipt of the supplies and/or services, the advisor is required to submit the invoice to the clerk-custodian for payment. If payment is for supplies and/or services for which no invoice will be received, a memorandum bill may be prepared on a form designated to meet this requirement.

10. *Distribution of Pay-Out Order Voucher.* (1) The original shall be filed by the clerk-custodian in voucher number sequence and used as a source of entry to the cash control ledger and the cash fund ledger sheets. The voucher number must correspond with the check number. (2) The second copy shall be placed by the clerk-custodian in a permanent file by activity program in numerical sequence for audit purposes. (3) The third copy shall be recorded to the advisor of the activity program preparing same for record purposes.

11. *Cash Control-Activity Account.* The cash control is a record of accounts correlating all receipts and expenditures to available depository balances and other assets. The cash balance per the cash control ledger must reconcile with the depository balance at the end of each month. Contra-postings of each entry on the cash control will be made to the cash fund ledger sheets established for each activity program under the control of the board of education.

The source of entry for posting to the cash control is the pay-in order or the voucher. When posting to the cash control, the date on the pay-in order is used. The number assigned to the activity program is posted in the "account number" column and the receipt number shown on the pay-in order is posted in the "receipt number" column. The amount of the receipt is posted in the "receipts" column which increases the "balance" column. When posting an expenditure to the cash control, the voucher date is used. The number assigned to the activity program is posted in the "account number" column and the check number is posted in the "check number" column which decreases the "balance" column. Postings to the cash control are required to be in numerical sequence.

At the close of each month, all "receipts" and "expenditure" columns must be ruled and the totals for the month entered in ink. Totals for the year to date, that is the accumulation of monthly totals, must be entered on the next line and ruled. The monthly receipts and expenditures should be added or subtracted from the preceding month's balance and the new balance entered in the proper column. The balance on the cash control plus outstanding warrants must agree with the total of the depository balance, investments and undeposited funds in the hands of the clerk-custodian or in transit to the depository.

12. *Cash Fund Ledger Sheet.* Contra-postings to the cash control will be made on the respective cash fund ledger sheets. Each sheet shall be identified by the account number as well as the name of the activity fund. The source of entry for each

account will be the pay-in order of the voucher. The date entered will be the same as that entered on the cash control. In the "items" column, enter the name of the payee when recording payments or the source of income when recording receipts. The entry in the "folio" column will be the page number on which the contra-posting was made in the cash control. When posting an expenditure, the amount will be entered in the "expenditure" column and the "balance" column will be reduced by the amount of the entry. When posting a receipt, the amount of the pay-in will be entered in the "receipt" column and the "balance" column will be increased by the amount of the entry.

At the close of each month, all "debit" and "credit" columns should be ruled and the totals for the month entered in ink. The totals for the year to date, that is the accumulation of monthly totals, should be entered on the next line and the columns again ruled. There is no authority for any fund balance to show a deficit.

The total of all fund balances must reconcile with the balance per the cash control ledger; the total of all fund receipts must reconcile with the total cash receipts; and the total of all fund expenditures must reconcile with the expenditures per the cash control ledger.

13. *Voucher.* The voucher is a part of the activity requisition and pay-out order and provides a jacket cover for the supporting documents. The voucher is used when posting expenditures to the cash control and the cash fund ledger. Vouchers are required to be filed in numerical identification of the corresponding check.

14. *Checks.* All checks must carry two authorized signatures. These may include the principal, an assistant principal, the clerk-custodian, or the clerk-treasurer of the school district.[4]

Instructional Program Budgeting

With the increased cost of financing, modern education school districts are being compelled to evaluate their existing school programs and their effectiveness as viewed by the school community, students, citizens, and legislators.

As school costs and taxes continue to rise, there has been a corresponding increase in having school districts be more accountable. Legislators, who serve as catalysts or suppressants to state and federal enthusiasm and involvement in supporting schools, have developed a keen interest in knowing what will be accomplished with the funds they allocate. The same is true of school board members and local taxpayers when they review school requests.

Still another reason society is generating more thrust into the accountability movement is that educators have recently introduced many new concepts, techniques, and teaching devices into the educational program. Governmental and private sources have channeled millions of dollars into school districts for the establishment of a great variety of experimental and pilot programs in addition to the ongoing regular programs. Society is presently demanding proof of the effectiveness of these programs. There is a growing interest in what works best and what does not.

Against this background of educational change and sharply rising cost, the focus of educational planning is shifting to results. School districts are now attempting to be more responsive and accountable to students and citizens in the delivery of educational services by providing coherent educational programs which allow equal consideration to both the instructional plan and the school budget. Thus, the next section deals with the traditional type of budgeting process. It is followed by a section devoted to greater consideration of instructional programs in constructing budgets to support those programs.

Traditional Budgeting Process

In many school districts, the budget-making process evolved from a relatively simple process with a board clerk or secretary setting forth a series of expenditures to be made according to the state's budget forms. In other school systems, the board entrusted the primary responsibility for budget preparation to the business manager. These procedures tended to keep the budgetary decision-making process primarily in the hands of the school board of trustees. A consequence of this tended to be a budget listing expenses such as salaries, instructional supplies, equipment, and the like, without regard to some of the basic functions of the school.

Over time, traditional budget-making procedures have gone from the specific object categories to categories utilizing a broader function approach. Yet this method was basically structured as a device to facilitate fiscal accounting. Regardless of whether the object or function approach is used in budget determinations, the process typically is accomplished through the following steps:

1. Teachers are asked to submit a list of items needed for the next school year on a prescribed form.
2. The principal reviews these lists for duplication and questions teachers if necessary for clarification.
3. The principal submits a budget to the superintendent based upon teacher requests plus his or her own requests.

4. The superintendent consolidates all requests and submits a budget to the board of education. These budgets tend to be rather detailed and involved.

In traditional budget-making processes, principals do not tend to be involved to the extent many authorities think educational leaders should assume. Research indicates their *real* involvement is on the increase in recent years, but is not at an optimum level and probably will not be until newer approaches are implemented more fully.

Planning Programming Budgeting Evaluating System (PPBES)

The planning programming budgeting evaluating system is a comprehensive planning process that includes a program budget as its major component. The process produces a continuous flow of ideas and information which leads to responsible and accountable decisions.

A major difference between the traditional line-item budget and PPBES resides in the justification for the amounts to be budgeted. Often the traditional budget merely extends last year's budget into the present, modifying it somewhat to take account of inflationary factors, new salary schedules, and the like. It seldom accurately portrays the thinking, planning, and objectives which have gone into the instructional program.

On the other hand, the program budget attempts to organize the categories more reflective of the true outputs of the instructional program and also highlight the educational services needed. It also attempts to evaluate the efforts which have been achieved through the use of fiscal resources.

In the *Educational Administration Quarterly* is a study conducted by Scurrah and Shani.[5] They suggested that available studies have not clarified many of the conflicting claims regarding the results of the implementation of systems like PPBES. Thus, the implications for organizations remain subject to a considerable amount of controversy and speculation.

Even so, PPBES, according to Scurrah and Shani does require a greater amount of information gathering, reporting, and analysis than does the conventional process of budget construction. Hence, a greater sharing of views is likely to accrue which provides greater possibilities for joint and more broadly based decision making. It was also found that PPBES tends to raise aspirations of people in terms of budget expectations. An important conclusion of the study was that, although other experimental research needs to be conducted to confirm or request the findings, it appeared that budgets prepared using the planned program budgeting system were superior to those using the traditional approach.[6]

Regardless of the type of budget principals might become involved with, they would do well to make careful needs assessment involving the staff prior to the formulation of any budget. Their roles are increasingly becoming more significant, and they should be well prepared to respond to the hard question: "What are your budget needs for the coming year?"

Inventory

Inventorying of supplies purchased through the district budget and the activities budget must be completed periodically in the secondary school. This is often one responsibility of the principal that is delegated to others within the building. The inventory may be continuous (equipment and supplies are recorded when they arrive and erased when they are consumed or declared unusable) or at the end of the fiscal year. The inventory serves the following purposes:

1. Enables the principal to know at a glance what equipment and supplies are in the school.
2. Aids in the development of both the student activities and district budget.
3. Assists in establishing values in case of fire.
4. Helps avoid theft or loss from other causes.

Guidelines for Conduct of Business Affairs

The authors suggest the following considerations for educational leaders in the administration of the business affairs of the secondary school:

1. Principals should understand thoroughly the system of accounting which is in use in their school, since they ultimately will be held responsible in case of careless procedures being used.
2. A system of financial accounting should be developed which meets state legal requirements, uniform accounting procedures, and/or the United States Office of Education Uniform Accounting Procedures. This not only is prudent, but assists the auditor when auditing the books.
3. Secondary school leaders should be aware of the legal aspects of activity fund accounting.
4. Much of the business affairs of the secondary school should be delegated to secretaries and other personnel so that principals may devote the major amount of their time to educational matters.
5. The bonded secretary-bookkeeper receives all money for the student activity fund and issues a receipt to the advisor or student. One copy of the receipts is retained in the files.
6. Cash should be banked daily. Only a small amount of money should be kept in the school building.
7. All payments of bills should be made by checks issued by the bonded bookkeeper-secretary after the invoice has been approved by the advisor and the principal.
8. Checks for the activity fund should be signed by the bonded book-

keeper-typist based upon a voucher signed by the principal. The principal should not sign checks.

9. The activity advisor or other responsible adult should be with students selling tickets or handling money.
10. Monthly financial reports should be made to teachers, student treasurers, and the board of education.
11. The activity fund should be audited each year.

SCHOOL PLANT MANAGEMENT

The management of secondary school plants must not be ignored by secondary school leaders. While many of the day-to-day operations such as cleaning, heating, and maintenance can and should be delegated, the professional aspects of spaces for administration and learning must be handled by professionals. Even though school principals are not always involved in designing new school facilities, an understanding of the steps involved and the characteristics of a good school facility are helpful in the management of existing facilities. Whether the facilities are new, renovated, or old, the educational program should decide their use. The building should not be the determiner of the educational program. For example, if the educational program demands a building with large spaces, it may be necessary to remove walls to acquire such a space.

The North Central Association lists the following general characteristics of appropriate physical school facilities:*

1. The school and its facilities are so located as to provide ready access for the students, parents and community served by the educational program.
2. Adequate facilities are provided to meet the goals and objectives of the physical and recreational activities.
3. The physical environment enhances the creation of a feeling of pride and well being of students, teachers and parents.
4. Adequate provisions for parking and safe entry into the building are emphasized.
5. The physical facility contributes to the achievement of the school's purposes and objectives, including the following specific ways:
   a. It allows for variable and flexible teaching and learning arrangements consistent with the successful implementation of the instructional program.

* From *The NCA Guide for School Evaluation, A Workbook for the Self-Study and the Team Visit,* 3rd ed., 1976, pp. 71-72. Used by permission of the Commission on Schools, North Central Association, Boulder, Colorado.

WHILE YOU WERE OUT

To _____

Date _____ Time _____ ☐ AM ☐ PM

M _____

of _____

Phone (_____) _____
   Area Code   Number   Extension

TELEPHONED		PLEASE CALL	
CALLED TO SEE YOU		WILL CALL AGAIN	
WANTS TO SEE YOU		URGENT	
RETURNED YOUR CALL			

Message _____
_____
_____
_____
_____
_____

Operator _____

AMPAD
EFFICIENCY®

REORDER
#23-009

    b. It can accommodate modifications of the educational program.

    c. Provisions are made for the use of media equipment and other educational technology resources.

    d. The full potential of the facility is utilized by teachers, students and administrators and facilities can be adopted to effect varied teaching/learning situations.

6. The school facility provides the student population with opportunities to pursue independent study in relative privacy, and such opportunities are complimented by the services of the learning materials center.

7. Informal gathering areas for students and teachers exist in the school facility.

8. Adequate facilities are provided in order to accomplish the goals and objectives in the areas of science, industrial arts, home economics, music, art and other programs which may require particular space or resource allocations.

9. Regardless of the age of the school facility, proper lighting, ventilation, heating/air conditioning, and safety and health requirements are attended to in order to provide an environment that does not detract from the educational program.[7]

This guide also contains a quick survey worksheet of health and safety features of the school facilities as well as a summary profile of school physical facilities. These provide a valuable reference to secondary school leaders in their management of the school facilities.

Knowing the characteristics of good school facilities, principals are in a position to discover deficiencies in their own building in order to recommend changes. In some instances, while principals may find that they have a great deal of autonomy in the utilization of their building and in recommending changes, they have little autonomy in the management of the building, with the major decisions made at the downtown central office. The ideal situation would be one in which principals play a major role in building change to improve instruction, but a minor role in day-by-day maintenance and cleaning functions.

The Principal's Role in School Maintenance and Cleaning Services

Building rapport between the faculty, the administration, and the custodial staff must be developed and maintained by secondary school leaders. Inviting custodians to attend pre-school orientation meetings, Christmas parties, etc., will help to build a congenial relationship.

While principals should avoid letting the supervision of maintenance and cleaning services become a major part of their workday, it is important that custodians not be besieged with direct complaints and requests from teachers. Rather, these complaints and requests should be directed to principals.

Principals should walk through the building with the head custodian periodically to discuss needed maintenance and problems arising from cleaning services. They should find time during the school day to talk with the custodial staff so that they may be aware of problems as they arise.

If job descriptions have not been established by the central office, principals should arrange for the completion of job descriptions for each member of the custodial staff. The job description should include:

1. Responsibility for cleaning and maintenance of the school building.
2. Time schedule for completing cleaning and maintenance of the school building.
3. Responsibility for furniture care and maintenance.
4. Boiler room responsibilities.
5. Providing for security of the school plant.
6. Protecting the school from fire.
7. Care of lighting, heating, and ventilation.
8. Care of outside areas and landscaping.
9. Responsibility for cleaning chalkboards.

Since the custodial staff plays an important role in the success of the instructional program, they should be kept informed of the nature and purpose of the educational program. Instructional changes which necessitate changes in their work schedule and additional burdens should provide for their involvement and understanding.

Improving the Work of the Custodial Staff

Principals can provide for the improvement of cleaning and maintenance of the school building just as they can provide for the improvement of instruction. Custodial training sessions of three to five days are now held in most states. The custodial staff should be encouraged to attend these schools to update their knowledge and skills as custodians. Improved techniques and new equipment are being introduced periodically which can enhance their work.

Encouraging custodians to hold county-wide or area meetings for the enhancement of improved services could be very useful. These and exchange visits of the school custodial staff with other schools should also be very helpful. Use of these methods and inservice education provide the custodial staff with inspiration and a feeling of importance.

Safety

Such factors as fire hazards, chemical explosions, dust inhalation, injury from machines, and slipping or falling must be considered in providing for a safe and healthy school plant.

The Federal Williams-Steiger *Occupational Safety and Health Act* (OSHA) of 1970 caused most schools to review their safety standards to determine if they met the OSHA guidelines. Principals will be well advised to be aware of the OSHA and state standards even though a central office staff member may head school plant maintenance. General recommendations concerning safety are presented in the following two paragraphs.

The following are recommendations for educational leaders in preventing accidents from fire:

1. Use fire resistant materials whenever possible in school facilities and equipment.
2. Conduct regular fire drills that are carefully planned and led so that if a real fire occurs, the chances for panic will be lessened.
3. Insist that the local fire code as well as the state fire laws are enforced. The authors have observed many instances of fire doors being chained. Workable fire extinguishers in handy locations are essential to prevent fires from spreading.
4. Conduct periodic inspections of the building to check potential fire hazards, such as rags in closets, flammables carelessly used and stored, and thoughtless arrangement of rooms.
5. Bring to the attention of the superintendent or the board of education any potentially dangerous fire hazards that may need remodeling for correction, or cannot be handled within the local school.

The following are considerations for educational leaders in preventing accidents in their school.

1. Make a periodic inspection of the building for potential safety hazards such as slippery stairs or hallways, unsafe machines, and unsafe air pollution caused by sawdust and other byproducts of the educational program.
2. Spend at least one faculty meeting discussing the importance of preventing accidents and promoting safe utilization of school facilities and equipment.
3. Provide for effective supervision of all areas of the school building and the school site so that horseplay and unsafe activities do not occur. One area that must have effective supervision is the bus loading area and the parking lot.
4. Correct unsafe conditions either with local building action or through requisition. This can be accomplished by roughing slippery stairs or halls and providing safety devices such as guards and goggles around chemicals and potentially dangerous machines.

5. Inform the superintendent or central administrative office of potentially dangerous situations which require remodeling or other actions.

PLANNING SCHOOL FACILITIES

The great spurt of school building after World War II brought on by a rapidly increasing population and the lack of construction during the war, resulted in innovative school design. Caudill, who was one of the leading architects in designing schools, considered the planning of school facilities in three ways; (1) education, (2) economy, and (3) environment.[8] His classic book led the way toward designing schools that considered the emotional and physical needs of the school child. Caudill described the physical needs as "those which are taken care of by safe structures, proper sanitation, sound-conditioning, good lighting, adequate heating, proper ventilation and of course, sufficient sheltered space for him to carry on his work and plan."[9] The emotional needs of the school child include homelike conditions, color and texture, comfort and security and a good atmosphere.[10] Figure 14.2 is a flow chart in planning the secondary school plant.

A report by the Educational Facilities Laboratories recommends that a high school with an enrollment of 2,000 students be divided into four 500-student houses to give each student and faculty member a sense of community and identity.[11] Each contains a house commons area with flexible walls

Figure 14.2
Flow Chart: Planning the Secondary School Plant

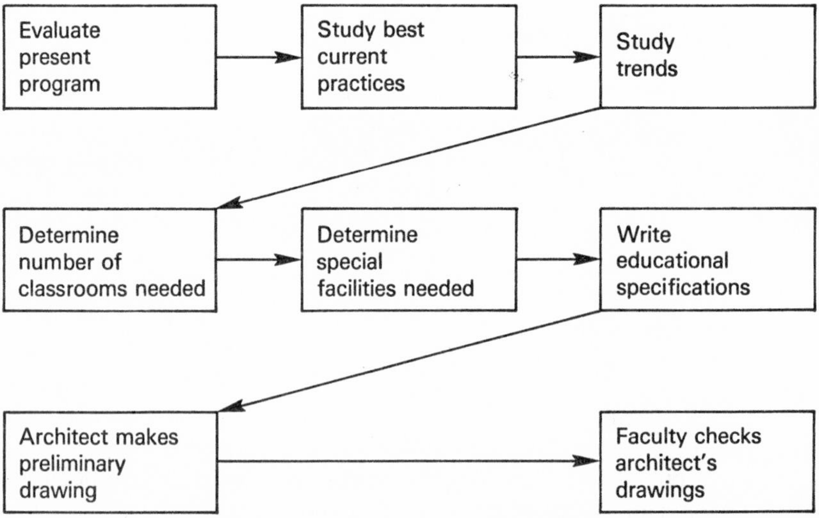

which may be removed so that all five hundred students enrolled in the house may be seated. This circular room may also be divided into five separate rooms or varying sized rooms to allow flexibility in grouping of students. The secondary school of the future must have this kind of flexibility if it is to meet the commonly accepted belief that education occurs best in many kinds of grouping arrangements.

Included also is an administration and guidance facility, a social studies suite, a foreign language suite, and an English suite. It is expected that students will attend a central area for such subjects as sciences and mathematics. The report of the Educational Facilities Laboratory describes this idea as follows:

> English, foreign languages, and social studies are taught within each house. In these subjects which require a minimum of special equipment, the house is largely autonomous and self-sufficient, with its own faculty as well as its own administrative and counseling staff. But there need be nothing rigid about this arrangement. Outstanding teachers or highly trained specialists move freely from house to house as needed, or interested students are brought together from various houses for live or televised instruction in seminar spaces provided in the library. A house might as time goes by, acquire a particular academic flavor of its own—specializing perhaps in English or in advanced work in foreign languages or in history.[12]

The authors expect the secondary school building of the future to reflect these kinds of characteristics:

1. The structure should be built so that changes such as additions and reductions can be made easily.
2. The building should reflect the trend toward individualized instruction, with built-in flexibility and easy adaptability to changing technology.
3. The school should meet the emotional and physical needs of the students, and be attractive and blend into the surrounding environment.
4. The school should have built-in adaptability to meet changing energy needs. Heating and cooling systems should be designed so that advantage can be taken of energy conservation measures and changing energy sources.

Educational Specifications

Educational specifications describe the learning activities which will take place and the needed space and equipment required to conduct these activities. Requirements for offices and special service areas are also described.

The chances that a new building will serve the educational program will be greatly increased if professional educators develop educational specifications for the architect. Ordinarily, such development of educational specifications is accomplished by the principal and the faculty who will occupy the new building. The preparing of these specifications cannot be accomplished in a short time, but requires a series of conferences and meetings with the faculty, architect, and school building consultants.

The Council of Educational Facility Planners, International indicate that educational specifications should include information related to the following matters: (1) project rationale, (2) the community, (3) the educational plans, (4) description of activity areas, (5) general building considerations, (6) summary of spatial relationships, and (7) summary of spatial requirements. [13]

The development of educational specifications in large school districts is often the responsibility of a central office person, who coordinates the planning with supervisors of various subject areas. However, it is essential that local building principals and their faculty play the major role in planning the new facility. The authors suggest that the person assigned to the development of the educational specifications, whether it be the local school principal or a central office person, carefully review educational specifications developed in other school districts. It is also suggested that the faculty and principal involved in the planning visit other schools so that they will have a better idea of possible classroom facilities. It is advisable that an outside consultant who is knowledgeable of good secondary education programming be employed to assist in planning for new facilities. It is important that the building represent a wide spectrum of thinking since it represents a large long-term investment. It is imperative that the architect design a building with spaces which best meet the educational program as defined in the educational specifications. A review of the architect's preliminary drawings should be matched with the educational specifications before final drawings are completed.

HEALTH SERVICES

The concept that health services belong in the private sector and are not a function of education has resulted in limited health service for students attending secondary schools. Traditionally, health care for students attending secondary schools has been limited to screening for impairments, making referrals upon the recommendation of a teacher or a part-time nurse, and the keeping of limited health records. Increased health services for secondary school students may be provided in the future as the actuality of Medicare ultimately filters down to those of earlier ages, including those in elementary and secondary schools.

Health care for students is not an unmerited consideration since total health care is already provided for college students at many universities. In some universities, the total health care includes such departures from tradition as supplying care of dependents of the student as well. The limited health care that students are now receiving in most secondary schools is an important part of the total school program and should not be ignored by educational leaders. The following are characteristics of health services found in some secondary schools under the supervision of a school physician or other governmental health agent:

1. emergency and sick room
2. nurse to provide records and diagnose illness
3. limited physicals for those participating in athletics
4. first aid services
5. voluntary dental inspections for referrals
6. mass innoculation for disease during epidemics.

Emergency and Sick Room

If the school is fortunate enough to have the services of a nurse, the management of the emergency or sick room can be assumed by the nurse. A cot is necessary in the emergency room so that students may rest before being taken to the hospital or home. It is important that this bed, as well as the emergency room itself, be maintained in a clean and sanitary condition.

The School Nurse

In addition to the management of the emergency and sick room, the school nurse provides diagnostic and emergency service to students. Equipment must include first aid supplies to deal with serious accidents or illness of students. The nurse should be well versed in diagnosing various types of drug poisoning as well as understanding the problem of drug usage among adolescents. The school nurse could be assigned the responsibility for administration of the drug education program of the school, stressing the use and dangers of various kinds of drug usage.

The school nurse also insures that in case of a school accident, a report is made which includes the name of the student, parent's name, and accident details. The accident report decreases the possibility of legal action against the principal or a teacher because of negligence, and helps insure that safety procedures will be taken to prevent future accidents. Included in health education which the school nurse provides, is training students in the administering of first aid.

TRANSPORTATION SERVICES

Secondary school principals usually have limited responsibility in the transportation of students. In urban areas, students often find their own way to the secondary school. In the suburbs and rural areas, transportation services for students are an important part of the services the school provides for the student. In most medium-sized rural and suburban school districts, overall administration of transportation of students to and from school is assumed by a full-time person. Obviously, principals cannot assume the responsibility for a large busing operation.

However, most principals are involved in such transportation problems as overseeing parking facilities for students and teachers, controlling students' use of cars, and arranging transportation for such special events as athletic contests and field trips. Principals must also arrange a schedule which meets the needs of bus transportation services. They may also be involved in providing such information as student addresses to the bus transportation supervisor. Another facet of principals dealing with transportation problems is the possibility of being called upon to assist the bus driver in the event of a discipline problem on the bus.

The following are suggestions for administration of the transportation program.

1. Students should be oriented early in the year as to their responsibilities in the parking and driving of cars. This orientation should include the rules of parking, under what conditions students may drive their cars, and emphasis on driver safety.

2. The principal must promote safety in the bus transportation program. While the state school code often specifies standards of safety for buses and drivers, the educational leader needs to provide additional safeguards whenever possible.

3. The student should spend a minimum of time riding the school bus.

4. One potential danger spot in the transportation of students is loading and unloading. The principal must insure that the loading and unloading of students from buses is supervised.

5. The principal should promote safety of students waiting for buses near their home by cautioning them to stay away from the road.

6. It should be a standard rule that no student should be put off the bus for misbehavior. Ejection has the potential danger of injury to the student, and must not be allowed. Bus drivers should be instructed to report misbehaviors to the bus supervisor or to the principal.

7. The principal should promote cleanliness of the buses.

SCHOOL LUNCH PROGRAM

The role of secondary school leaders in the school lunch program may entail complete responsibility including hiring of cooks and food handlers, purchasing food, and management of cold storage facilities. In large school districts, these are normally assigned to central office personnel. But in most instances, school leaders will have major responsibility for such food service activities as arranging the schedule for lunches and supervising the school cafeteria. While they may not have responsibility for all management aspects of the school cafeteria, principals must have concern for the attractiveness, sanitation, and tastiness of the food served to their students.

Lack of total administrative responsibility does not, however, take away the principal's responsibility of improving the overall program whenever possible. The authors make the following suggestions for the school lunch program:

1. The overall responsibility of hiring and dismissal of cooks and food handlers, purchasing food, and management of the preparation and service of food should be assigned to a competent school food services manager. In small school districts, this responsibility may be assigned to a head cook.

2. A wide variety of food should be served and whenever possible, more than one menu should be offered each day.

3. Sanitation and cleanliness is essential to the successful school lunch program.

4. Since cooks and food handlers are often inexperienced, a regular inservice program must be maintained with periodic conferences with regional and state school lunch officials.

5. Many cafeterias have an institutional atmosphere with long rows of tables and chairs. Individual tables of four to six persons with a center piece, in divided areas of the cafeteria will help to break away from the institutional atmosphere. Benches as chairs should be avoided.

6. A separate faculty dining room should be provided. At the same time, teachers should be encouraged to eat occasionally with their students.

7. The school lunch schedule should be arranged so that students may be served promptly.

8. The bookkeeping, collecting money, etc., should be assigned to a secretary-bookkeeper. Guidance for the correct operation of the books is provided by the state school lunch director. The bookkeeper must work closely with the school food services manager.

9. The school food services manager should be encouraged to keep abreast of current state and federal regulations concerning distribu-

tion of government food commodities, reimbursement, etc. Without knowledge of the advantages of this program, the food service program can be very expensive.

10. Great savings can be made in quantity and seasonal purchase of food. The food services manager should attend meetings to keep up-to-date of these possible economies.

11. The school cafeteria can be an instructional area in which students are taught healthful attitudes and sound nutritional practices which carry into the home and later life.

SUMMARY

Principals must realize that efficient management of their office complex is a most important task that can serve as a model for others in the building. A pleasant, efficient office staff can assist in presenting a warm greeting for parents and others who enter the building. It is imperative that the office staff members receive inservice training so that they can understand and become skilled in performing their jobs.

Careful attention must be given to the storage and use of office records so that their security is protected, yet they are accessible to those who need to use them. It is imperative that state and federal laws concerning the maintenance, storage, and use of records be complied with. Where feasible, data processing equipment should be utilized to permit efficient storage and use of records.

Principals must be aware of the state requirements of accounting for funds that are their responsibility. Students and sponsors must be kept informed as to the status of accounts with which they deal. It is extremely important that the bonded treasurer be skilled in appropriate business procedures needed for the operation of the office affairs.

While management of such supporting services as the school plant, custodial health, transportation, and school lunch is the responsibility of secondary school leaders, they must not let this responsibility negate their major role as the instructional leader of the school. These are services which must be accomplished, but most often they are accomplished and managed by others without the principal's direct involvement.

Such aspects as attractiveness of the site and building, expansibility, educational technology, and spaces for a teaching resources center, learning resources center, and a student lounge must be considered in the management and design of the secondary school. The educational specifications for the new secondary school are developed by the professional staff and contain the proposed educational program, purposes and objectives, and space requirements for each of the areas taught. The educational specifications are developed after visits to recently completed secondary schools and after the professional staff has carefully listed its needs and desires.

SUMMARY

Building maintenance is a vital function performed by the custodial staff. Good working relationships must be established between the teaching staff and the custodial staff to insure a smooth functioning building.

Traditionally, health care for students attending secondary schools has been limited to screening for impairments or making referrals for medical care. It is expected that increased health services for students may be provided in the future as Medicare ultimately filters down to those attending secondary schools. The typical health services found in secondary schools include a school nurse, emergency and sick rooms, and health education.

The role of the principal as it relates to transportation depends upon the size and location of the school district. The larger districts which have many buses may have a director of transportation to handle some of this responsibility.

Proper management of the school lunch program can result in higher morale among students and give students an opportunity to develop positive attitudes and practices concerning proper nutrition.

NOTES

1. Lester W. Anderson and Lauren A. Van Dyke, *Secondary School Administration* (Boston: Houghton-Mifflin Company, 1972), p. 447.

2. *Educational Specifications, Central-Hower High School* (Akron, Ohio: Akron Public Schools, February, 1972).

3. John P. Van Uxem, "A Brief Survey of Types of Data Processing Equipment and Their Uses." In Richard A. Kaiman and Robert W. Marker (eds.) *Educational Data Process: New Dimensions and Prospects* (Boston: Houghton-Mifflin Company, 1967), p. 22.

4. Thomas E. Ferguson, "A System of Accounting for the Use of Student Activity Programs in Ohio" (Columbus: 1975).

5. Martin J. Scurrah and Moshe Shani, "PPBES Versus Conventional Budgeting in a Simulated Educational Organization," *Educational Administration Quarterly* 10: 3 (Autumn, 1974), pp. 63–79.

6. Ibid., p. 76.

7. *The NCA Guide for School Evaluation, A Workbook for the Self-Study and the Team Visit*, 3rd ed. 1976, pp. 71–72.

8. William W. Caudill, *Toward Better School Design* (New York: F. W. Dodge Corporation, 1954), p. 20.

9. Ibid., p. 3.

10. Ibid., pp. 9–10.

11. *Educational Change and Architectural Consequences* (New York: Educational Facilities Laboratories, 1968), p. 69.

12. Ibid., p. 72.

13. "Guide For Planning Educational Facilities," (Columbus, Ohio: Council of Educational Facility Planners, International, 1976), p. E-4.

Index